The Seven Sins of Innovation

A Strategic Model for Entrepreneurship

The Seven Sins of Innovation

Dave Richards

to Andy
a great friend and
entrepreneur – with best
wishes for innovation success
in your business, including
your books – which I look
forward to reading!

Dave

palgrave
macmillan

First published 2014 by
PALGRAVE MACMILLAN

Palgrave Macmillan in the UK is an imprint of Macmillan Publishers Limited, registered in England, company number 785998, of Houndmills, Basingstoke, Hampshire RG21 6XS.

Palgrave Macmillan in the US is a division of St Martin's Press LLC, 175 Fifth Avenue, New York, NY 10010.

Palgrave Macmillan is the global academic imprint of the above companies and has companies and representatives throughout the world.

Palgrave® and Macmillan® are registered trademarks in the United States, the United Kingdom, Europe and other countries.

ISBN: 978–1–137–43251–3 hardback

This book is printed on paper suitable for recycling and made from fully managed and sustained forest sources. Logging, pulping and manufacturing processes are expected to conform to the environmental regulations of the country of origin.

A catalogue record for this book is available from the British Library.

A catalog record for this book is available from the Library of Congress.

Typeset by Aardvark Editorial Limited, Metfield, Suffolk.

For my children, Alec, Nick, Tasha, Luke and Bryn, my grandson James, and my wife Ginny – seven fabulous entrepreneurs who add value and give my life meaning, every minute of every day

Contents

List of Figures and Tables

Figures

Tables

Foreword

Writing about innovation is fraught with difficulty because what seems simple and formulaic in theory is hard and disappointing in practice.

I have known Dave Richards over twenty years. I have observed close-hand his outstanding command of the material. Both theoretical material and more importantly the practicalities of innovation. His new book shows the power of his perspective, brilliantly.

Part I links entrepreneurship with innovation. Part II identifies the (classic) seven sins of innovation, while Part III identifies practical solutions to these challenges for both large and small enterprises.

The Seven Sins of Innovation elevates the thinking on this crucial subject to the highest level. It sets Dave's book alongside the best writing on this subject anywhere.

Roger H.D. Lacey
Former chief strategy officer and senior vice president 3M

Preface

This book reflects my efforts to understand what determines enterprise success, particularly in the realm of innovation and entrepreneurship. Throughout my career, I've struggled to make sense of the successes and failures I witnessed or participated in. I often felt I was at the cutting, bleeding edge of innovation, at Bell-Northern Research (BNR), Nortel Networks, and Oracle, as an adviser to various clients, and as a serial entrepreneur. In spite of all the learning experiences – with the scars to prove it – I could see myself and others repeating similar mistakes. We'd go down familiar blind alleys, rocked by similar bumps along the road, and slam into brick walls that all started to look and feel the same after a while.

In parallel with these experiences, I've been privileged to attend seminars, courses, and talks by some of the greatest thinkers, strategists, entrepreneurs, and business leaders of our times. Their words and writings further shaped my thoughts on what enables effective, successful leaders, strategies, and business models.

My early professional focus was on understanding the concept of value. Working in high technology, I could see that the prevalent approach to innovation was what I termed "technology push." Clever "solutions" seeking problems and customers. Through the 1980s, my research on the value of "datacom" applications, based on benefits such as improved productivity, time savings, and effectiveness, reflected a new approach to innovation, complementing and balancing technology push. I authored Nortel's first user-driven design specification for a small digital phone system called Norstar, which became one of the most profitable and globally successful telecom product lines in history. The core values that emerged from our research, for the integration of applications and convergence of delivery mechanisms, became the central message in Nortel's vision for an open world, driving the proliferation of the global multimedia network we now know as the Internet (see Tyson, 2014).

In the early 1990s, as Nortel's bosses drove cultural change, embracing the key themes of entrepreneurship, excellence, globalization, and leadership, I was identified as a "high potential key resource" – someone with potential to serve at the top of Nortel's leadership structure. I was selected as one of Nortel's intrapreneurs, appointed business line manager (BLM) for Global Public Networks Data. In theory, I had global P&L responsibility and authority to run the business as my own, but in practice, Nortel had many layers of bosses, with many tricks for disempowerment. Being incentivized as a global GM and BLM for Data sounded grand, but as a business it was a massive money loser. We lost about $100 every time we shipped a data line card, my R&D budget exceeded global sales, and my business strategy for accelerating data investment was adopted but not officially approved. For a time, I received monthly admonishments from the executive office, the very office in which my strategic business plan awaited approval, threatening me with punitive action if I continued "noncompliant" R&D and operational expenditures.

With my very capable team, I transformed the Data business into a highly profitable and strategically essential line of business, before going on to various roles involving breaking into various key markets and customers, delivering many billions of dollars in profits and shareholder value. But we also had some spectacular failures along the way, such as alliances, joint ventures and acquisitions that failed to deliver, and battleground markets such as China where we, and competitors, lost a lot of blood and IP. Following Nortel, I enjoyed and learned from a couple of my own startup ventures I fondly refer to as "dot.bomb" learning experiences, before joining Oracle to champion its ThinkQuest acquisition, which, for a time, was the flagship social enterprise offering of the Oracle Education Foundation.

Now living in the UK and working independently, I enjoy delivering workshops, presentations (keynotes or talks), and some one-to-one mentoring on the topics and ideas reflected in this book, helping leaders, organizations, and teams develop entrepreneurial cultures, strategies, plans of action, and high impact innovation results.

Getting around to writing this book and getting it done both took much longer than I expected. I've long intended to write a book, but until Palgrave Macmillan approached me, and I signed a contract to produce this specific one, writing was just an idea, on the back burner, prioritized below "real" work. Had I known how difficult the writing process would be, I might have declined. Although the writing flowed, the challenge was enormous. This isn't a story, but rather an attempt to understand the psychology that underlies the success or failure of entrepreneurs, efforts to innovate, and business strategies.

The psychological determinants of success and failure include the "human factors" you may expect – creativity, leadership, intelligence, communications, motivations, attitudes, and expertise. However, you may be surprised, as I have been, to come to understand how these and other factors interact. The process of writing about these factors and trying to describe how they interrelate has been a journey of learning and discovery.

The underlying model or framework was something I had a general notion of from the beginning, but my understanding of it kept evolving as the writing emerged. It was a bit like trying to solve a Rubik's cube, which in my view is a nasty invention. No sooner would I get one part of the model in order, when I'd have to revise another part. The "problem" is that the psychological determinants interact in complex ways within the model and in reality, which the model is an effort to describe.

I've explicitly avoided writing an academic, theoretical text, instead seeking to provide an engaging, practical guide and hopefully stimulating personal insights into ways you can improve efforts to innovate and drive success. Thus, the main challenge in writing this is to provide overarching insights while staying "true" to the underlying model, which kept evolving through the writing process.

Some further ideas that have guided my thoughts came from some sources outside mainstream business or psychology:

- the concept of vital human energy, for example Chi or Qi in Chinese
- the notion of "flow," particularly in understanding sport and performance psychology
- the Ayurvedic concept of chakras, energy centers, that enable or block energy flow

- the idea that there are two sides to every coin, yin and yang, including positive and negative aspects of just about everything, energies, energy centers, and all things human
- the human genome, DNA, and the double helix structure of chromosomes, and the notions of an innovator's DNA and organizational DNA
- the latest thinking on left- and right-brain functionality and how they may link
- the idea that perception and reality are connected, that the human mind exists in relationship to the reality it dreams, and the observed reality exists in and through, and is affected by, the observer
- the resulting fact that our mindset is a key determinant of success, not because of any so-called "secret" law of attraction, but because psychological factors are directly related to the central elements of strategy, such that they either undermine or support the efforts of leaders and organizations to survive or thrive.

All the foregoing sources, experiences, ideas, and inspirations have combined in the form of a new model for entrepreneurial innovation, which is all about bridging between "soft stuff" such as psychology and culture and "hard stuff" such as strategy, performance, and bottom line results. I hope you enjoy learning about these relationships or bridges, and that you will derive specific insights that you can apply to benefit yourself, those you work with, organizations you engage with, and the world.

Acknowledgments

There are so many people who have influenced my thoughts on innovation that I won't name them all individually. Key influencers include a range of thought and practice leaders, past managers, colleagues and clients past and present, family, and friends. However, some individuals clearly deserve special mention:

Eric von Hippel, with whom I cofounded the MIT Innovation Lab over 20 years ago, plus Roger Lacey, with 3M, and Jim Euchner, with NYNEX Corporation at the time – both members of the lab from its inception – all frequently and profoundly influenced my thinking about the nature, antecedents, and precedents of innovation.

My favorite bosses at Nortel, Paul Brant, Steve Jones, and Lorne Hinz, and members of my various teams, most especially Stephen Hampshire, William Wallace, and Matt Thomson, who empowered and enabled me to lead.

Some bosses at Nortel who gave me what felt, at the time, like a really "rough ride," who contributed to who I am.

Former colleagues at BNR, especially Alec Lumsden, Charles Whaley, Don Chadwick, Peter Martin, Mark Dallas, Arnold Campbell, Paul Guild, Jock Ferguson, Roger Bushnell, and John Tyson, who shaped my early journey into user needs and evaluation research.

Former Oracle colleagues and partners I met and in many cases actively keep in touch with, including Agnes Vajda, Peter Waker, Harry Tetteh, Jimi Ballard, Nicole Melander, David Pywell, and Bernie Trilling.

Richard Moss, Dusty Staub, Pamela Marshburn, and James Sale, who mentored me.

Professor Norman Slamecka, my PhD supervisor at the University of Toronto, who taught me a degree of writing proficiency.

Professors William Petrusic and Richard Dillon, my undergraduate supervisors at Carleton University, who encouraged me to a career in psychology.

My brothers and best friends from early days to present – Doug and Rob Richards, Tom Dale, and Deepak Sahasrabudhe – and also all my wonderful grandparents, uncles, aunts and cousins – who contributed to my sense of personal potential.

My parents, Bert Richards, formerly of Bell Canada, and Lorna Richards, who continue to influence and motivate me.

My current wider circle of friends, many of whom are business colleagues, clients and supporters, most especially David Jarvis, Mike Johnson, Steven Neal, Harvey West, Monica McGlynn, Dee Watson, Anthony Woodhouse, and Philip Warr, who provided various valuable suggestions and feedback on various ideas and words contained herein.

My children, Bryn, Luke, Tasha, Nick, and Alec, and my grandson James (by Tasha), who inspire me.

My lovely wife Ginny, who's been with me every step of the way, and whose questions and comments have prompted additional insights throughout the writing process, a journey of learning and discovery.

List of Abbreviations

B2B	business-to-business
BHAG	big hairy audacious goal
BNR	Bell-Northern Research
BS	balanced scorecard
CEO	chief executive officer
CRM	customer relationship management
CSR	corporate social responsibility
DNA	deoxyribonucleic acid
IP	intellectual property
LGBT	lesbian, gay, bisexual or transgender
MIT	Massachusetts Institute of Technology
NCOs	Non-commissioned officers
NGO	nongovernmental organization
NPS	Net Promoter Score
OECD	Organisation for Economic Co-operation and Development
OEM	original equipment manufacturer
P&L	profit and loss
PESTEL	political, economic, social, technological, environmental, and legal (considerations)
R&D	research and development
ROI	return on investment
SME	small and medium-sized enterprise
SRM	stakeholder relationship management
SWOT	strengths, weaknesses, opportunities, threats (analyses)
USP	unique selling proposition
WTF	working through fear

part I

Definitions

"Everything is vague to a degree you do not realize till you have tried to make it precise."

Bertrand Russell (*c.* 1915)

There is, in my view, a general lack of clarity regarding what we mean by innovation and entrepreneurship. It's easy to find websites for major innovation initiatives, by governments, universities, and commercial entities that don't even bother defining the term – as though there might be a universally or widely accepted definition. Instead, as you'll soon see, there are many inconsistent definitions of innovation. Similarly, there are many definitions of entrepreneurship, and widely diverging views on what it might mean to be an entrepreneur. The beginning chapters of this book will point out the confusion in greater detail, and attempt to provide much needed clarity. The following definitions will be developed, and are offered here in summary form, for easy reference:

Entrepreneur: Anyone trying to innovate.

Successful entrepreneur: Someone succeeding at it.

Innovation: The creation of new net value.

Measuring innovation success or failure: Return on investment (ROI)

ROI = (value created – value invested)/value invested

Value: A psychological experience of fulfillment of needs, wants, motivations or aspirations that may or may not be reflected by what someone will pay for it.

Entrepreneurial psyche: The spirit of entrepreneurship, shaped by individual psychology.

Entrepreneurial flow: The psychological state of actualization and fulfillment of the essential purpose of entrepreneurship.

Innovation strategy: Planning, implementing, monitoring, and journeying toward success.

Innovation zoning: Maximizing value creation and innovation success through a phenomenon I call "bridging" – optimizing all the relationships that matter.

Bridging: Maximizing the flow, delivery, and experience of value in any relationship.

chapter 1

The Need for a New Approach

"Success or failure depends more upon attitude than upon capacity."

William James (1890)

Reality bites

Success rates across all types of human enterprise are low, and failing to improve:

- Innovation success rates are generally below 10%, and even when venture capitalists are carefully monitoring their investments, less than a third of innovations succeed. The vast majority (96%) of innovation efforts fail to beat their ROI targets (Doblin Group, 2005, 2012).
- The majority of enterprises report dissatisfaction with innovation performance (Arthur D. Little, 2013).
- Three-quarters of the CEOs of multinationals view external collaborative innovation as vitally important, but only half do it, and they only rate themselves as doing it "moderately well" (IBM, 2006).
- Eight out of ten new enterprises fail within 18 months (Wagner, 2013).
- Two-thirds of organizational "change" efforts fail (Kotter, 2008).
- Most marketing investments don't deliver desired results – "95 percent of what we're doing doesn't work" (Pritchard, 2011).

- Only a minority of innovative ideas ever see the light of day and successful commercialization, even within leading innovators such as 3M and Google.
- Most enterprises don't achieve sustainable competitive differentiation and advantage.
- Mature businesses often struggle to maintain "the love," growth, and relevance.
- The public sector isn't making enough progress in efforts to do more with less, even with input from highly successful private sector entrepreneurs and change agents.
- We're facing a global crisis in youth unemployment, potentially creating a generation that's economically left behind – a lack of job creation that is arguably a failure of entrepreneurship.
- In fact, mediocre results plague all sectors of human enterprise.

What can be done?

The root cause: human nature

In this book, I will put forward the case that the root cause of enterprise mediocrity is human psychology. Seven specific aspects of human nature conspire to undermine efforts to succeed in enterprises of all kinds. These factors are the key determinants of success and failure. The determinants interact multiplicatively, such that if someone is theoretically perfect (100%) on six factors, but weak (say 10%) on the seventh, the overall result would be poor:

$$100\% \times 100\% \times 100\% \times 100\% \times 100\% \times 100\% \times 10\% = 10\%$$

Of course, overall enterprise results are based on much more complex interactions of individual psychologies, but the overall phenomenon is the same – a drift toward mediocrity based on the weakest links, the poor performers and other deficiencies that drag the whole enterprise down.

Depressed? You should be. But my message isn't one of doom and gloom.

A new model: strategic bridging

This book delivers a double breakthrough in understanding:

1 How to drive, manifest, and nurture entrepreneurship in organizations based on understanding entrepreneurial psychology.

2 How to maximize innovation success by making it the heart of strategy, based on a powerfully improved framework for bridging the "soft stuff" of psychology and culture with the "hard stuff" of peak performance and bottom line results (Figure 1.1).

Unlike existing prescriptions for strategy, innovation, creativity, entrepreneurship, and success, this book provides fresh new perspectives and rich insights based on explicitly focusing strategy on innovation, and tackling the vital problem of how to engage the core aspects of human psychology to maximize personal and organizational entrepreneurial potential and results. For organizations, the key is to create entrepreneurial cultures focused on implementing strategic innovation agendas. The purpose of this book is to show you how to increase success rates for your efforts to innovate, create sustainable advantage and potential for value creation, and therefore achieve a more valuable entity than one in which a single entrepreneur or a small entrepreneurial group is the core driver.

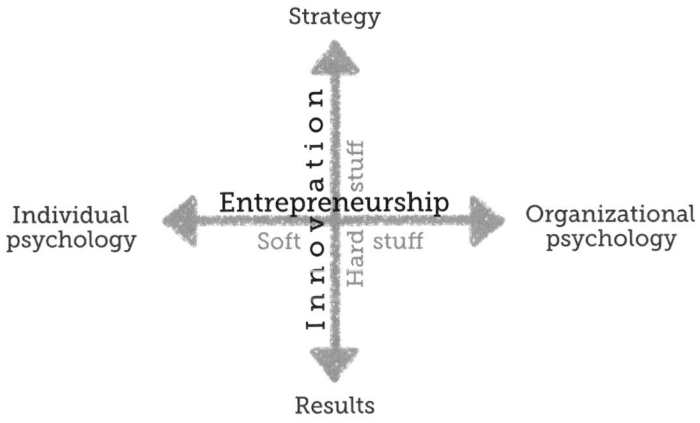

FIGURE 1.1 Bridging overview

Specific insights related to aspects of psychology

The model provides specific insights and recommendations in seven areas:

1 How individual and group psychology must be managed effectively to create entrepreneurial cultures capable of peak performance and powerful innovation.

2. How to maximize creativity, and develop ideas from concept to reality, driving transformational enterprise improvements.
3. How to lead the innovation process, making the right investments of resources and empowering them to achieve sustainable innovation leadership and advantage.
4. How to engage stakeholders in win–win collaborative partnerships, to create powerful business models delivering and manifesting shared value.
5. How to formulate powerful communications, marketing, and sales strategies, feeding enterprise intelligence and driving competitive success and growth.
6. How to formulate a strategic vision based on intelligence and insights, achieving the right balance between audacious dreams and evolving realities.
7. How to engage entrepreneurial spirit and passions toward the fulfillment of strategic purpose, the highest calling that may be applicable for any organization or individual.

What follows

Now that we've discussed why a strategic model for entrepreneurship and innovation is needed, the rest of the chapters in Part I define the various relationships or bridges that require attention, and offer much needed clarity and definitions of the key concepts of innovation, value, and entrepreneurship. The core aspects of the human psyche and entrepreneurial spirit are defined, and related to the critical elements of organizational strategy – the critical success factors for leading innovation.

The "seven sins" of innovation (described in Part II) relate to dysfunctional "psyche centers" – in effect, getting each of the psychological factors terribly wrong, either as an individual entrepreneur, or as an organization trying to innovate. Arguably, when one gets a factor terribly right, it's a virtue. When an individual or organization becomes a paragon of virtue in relation to all seven factors, the result is "entrepreneurial flow" and "innovation zoning." Leaders who invest in creating flow and getting their teams "into the zone" will be astounded at the results. Doing this requires a lot of bridging – building, balancing, and tuning relationships among stakeholders, between individual and organizational psyches, between the critical path elements of strategy and functions within organizations – to name just a few.

Part III offers specific prescriptions for using the model to create success. A range of organizations and challenges are considered. Considering each of these prescriptions will benefit any leader, manager, or organization attempting to start, improve, or grow a venture of any kind. For example, Chapter 17 offers insights on family enterprises that will benefit anyone, whether or not you work with family members. Through each of the prescriptions, leaders will be guided on how to apply the strategic model to effectively engage your own psyche and other people to successfully drive entrepreneurial innovation.

How you will benefit

The key benefit you will derive from this book is an understanding of the need to, and how to, strategically and holistically address all the key aspects of entrepreneurial psychology in order to successfully innovate. You'll see how to formulate and apply strategy to drive entrepreneurial innovation, and become an innovation leader with unbeatable competitive advantage.

Various books and consulting frameworks provide valuable insights and prescriptions for key aspects of the problem, such as stimulating creativity, inspiring change, or managing continuous improvement. But in my opinion, these models and frameworks only *touch* the elephant, without really seeing that it *is* an elephant. The "elephant in the room" is that entrepreneurial innovation remains an elusive goal for most enterprises. The fundamental problem is human psychology, and the solution is a new understanding of how to manage the key psychological elements that normally interact to undermine entrepreneurial innovation efforts.

The specific benefits leaders will derive from engaging the strategic bridging model include:

- Higher business valuations based on sustainable, systemic organizational capacity and capability to collaboratively create and deliver value through innovation.
- More powerful strategy – both planning and implementation – focused around an innovation agenda that builds strategic advantage, a winning culture, and unbeatable teams.

- Improved workforce engagement, morale, spirit, and wellbeing achieved through healthy psychological balance, creativity, motivation, responsible empowerment, and mindset.
- Profitable growth through more innovative communications, marketing, selling, delivery, and service focused on maximizing win–win customer relationships and value experience.
- Greater or renewed passion for your enterprise, and specific ways to spread the love, infecting partners, employees, customers, and other stakeholders with your enthusiasm.
- Higher success rates, improved results, and greater ROI for your innovation or change initiatives, through using a more coherent framework for formulating and implementing strategy, based on entrepreneurial innovation.
- Specific, actionable ideas and insights you will implement within your business activities.

Bridging

Fundamentally, the new strategic model is about "bridging," and the most important bridge may be between the vital hard stuff of strategy and bottom line results and the soft stuff – psychology, mindset, motivations, and beliefs – and the organizational "soup" we call "culture."

The case for focusing on soft stuff has already been made by some of the leading business thinkers of our times. Drucker (1967) eloquently made the case that personal effectiveness has a massive impact on the success of organizations. Drucker's prescriptions for effectiveness are as follows:

- Put "first things first," concentrating on key priorities.
- Manage time carefully, recording (versus trying to remember) how it's spent, and consolidating discretionary time to enable focus on priorities.
- Focus on contributing value in all key relationships (with internal and external customers), through effective communications and conduct of meetings.
- Build productive strengths in organizations through recruiting and developing people, and appropriate succession planning.

- Make and take action on effective decisions by gathering intelligence, engaging creative conflict, and seeking the best outcomes (versus satisficing).

Stephen Covey made a career out of repackaging Drucker's points, also offering specific suggestions on how leaders should engage their principles, values, and beliefs to create more focus on what really matters. He initially suggested seven habits (Covey, 1989) – proactivity, beginning with the end in mind, first things first, think win–win, seek to understand to be understood, synergize, and "sharpen the saw" (work to improve the foregoing), to which he later added an eighth habit – finding your voice and helping others to find theirs (Covey, 2004).

Jim Collins' (2001) research on the differences between great and merely good enterprises offers further support for the point that soft stuff determines success. Great companies tend to be led by people with great humanity – humility, empathy, and concern for people. Further, Patel (2005) points out that good strategies require good strategists, such that personal power, purpose, and principles are at their heart.

Another of my favorite thought leaders on soft stuff is Pat Lencioni (2009). His prescription for team effectiveness is to build trust, enabling vulnerability and creative conflict, leading to shared commitment, and holding each other accountable for achieving agreed results.

Another aspect of soft stuff worth mentioning is the research on emotional and social intelligence (Goleman, 1996, 2006; Albrecht, 2005), suggesting that our human ability to empathize with others is a crucial determinant of success in business and in life.

The McKinsey 7S model is based on recognition that hard stuff (strategy, systems, structures) and soft stuff (superordinate goals or shared values, style or culture, staff or people, and their skills) need to be aligned for organizations to succeed (Figure 1.2). Beyond telling us this is so, offering armies of consultants to help, and reporting numerous case studies of business improvement resulting from working on hard–soft alignment, the model does little to show the way other than a high level call to action and a brilliant visual representation that clearly makes the point that the hard and soft elements are highly interdependent and equally important – although one is positioned as central.

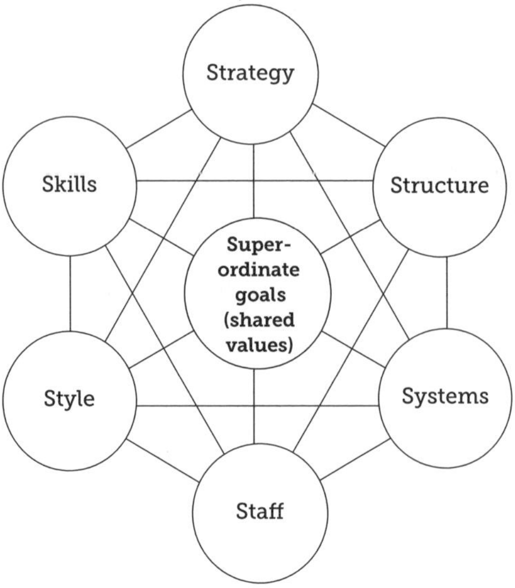

FIGURE 1.2 McKinsey "7S" model
Source: Wikimedia creative commons; user: Pkor43, 2007

The key point of all this is that the successful functioning of enterprises and the individuals that comprise them is hugely dependent on the ability to engage the soft stuff. However, reflecting on the opening points of this chapter, people clearly don't know how to do this very well. We've been helped by Drucker, Covey, Lencioni, Goleman, and others to understand *what* we need to do to be more effective, but evidently we're missing some vital points on *how* to do it.

Of course, various highly successful entrepreneurs and leaders have shared their recipes for success, or at least their personal stories of how they did it. Some of my personal favorites are the biography of Steve Jobs (Isaacson, 2011), and texts by Welch and Welch (2005) and Gates and Hemingway (1999). Lou Gerstner (2002), the former chairman and CEO of IBM, summarized the importance of soft stuff, describing how he pulled IBM back from the brink of extinction:

> My bias coming in was toward strategy, analysis and measurement. In comparison, changing the attitude and behaviors of hundreds of

> thousands of people is very, very hard. I came to see in my time at IBM that culture isn't just one aspect of the game – it is the game.

Or as Jack Welch said: "The soft stuff is the hard stuff."

Even with all these great insights on the need to engage soft stuff when changing organizations, driving strategies, or innovating, what's still missing is a coherent model that more clearly relates soft and hard stuff. To do so requires much greater clarity of definitions – understanding the elements of individual and group psychology and, in particular, entrepreneurship – and how they relate to the elements of strategy. What's needed is a framework for developing and implementing strategy, especially in relation to innovation. We need a model that shows how to bridge between soft and hard stuff, between entrepreneurship and innovation.

Bridging requires being "on the edge," ready, willing, and able to engage in the task of building a bridge from "your edge" to "the other." When done well, collaboration, creative conflict, open innovation, creative partnering, commercialization of technologies, change management, strategic planning, successful strategy implementation, and other realizations of human potential can all be seen as examples of successful bridging. But the most important bridge of all is a systematic, strategic, and systemic approach to bridging the vital hard stuff and soft stuff – a new and valuable tool for enterprise leaders to help achieve entrepreneurial innovation and strategic success.

chapter 2

Innovation and Unnovation

"Our wretched species is so made that those who walk on the well-trodden path always throw stones at those who are showing a new road."

Voltaire (1764)

Defining innovation

What is innovation? There is much confusion. Consider the following:

- Oxford International: (1) the action or process of innovating – crucial to the continuing success of any organization, or (2) a new method, idea, product, and so on.
- Wikipedia: something original, new, and important in whatever field that breaks in to, or obtains a foothold in a market or society.
- Free Dictionary: (1) the act of introducing something new, or (2) something newly introduced.
- Merriam-Webster: (1) the introduction of something new, or (2) a new idea, method, or device.
- Dictionary.com: (1) something newly introduced, such as a new method or device, or (2) the act of innovating.
- BusinessDictionary.com: the process of translating an idea or invention into a good or service that creates value or for which customers will pay.

Clearly, the word "innovation" can refer either to the act or process of innovating, and also to the result. But should we really accept anything "new" as innovation? What about a new strain of flu, accidentally unleashed by a company trying to create a vaccine? What about the Edsel, a new car design introduced by Ford in 1958, which was a spectacular market flop? And what about RentMyChest.com, or InmatesForYou.com? Come on now. We can all think of spectacularly stupid new products, websites, and other offerings that should have never been thought of, let alone brought to market. Clearly, just because something is new doesn't mean it's innovative or an innovation. And therefore we can also soundly reject the idea that innovation includes the act of bringing something unneeded, unwanted, and completely useless into the world. That's "unnovation."

Wikipedia gets closer to an acceptable definition of innovation, by adding that the "new" something must be important and gain a foothold, or break into a market or society. This distinguishes between the invention of something new, and innovation, with the further requirement of importance and adoption. But who says what's important? Are widely adopted fads innovations? How about spray-painting graffiti? One might consider it important, in that it costs governments and businesses considerable amounts of money to clean up. But vandalism is best thought of as unnovation.

Here are a few further examples of widespread and arguably important business trends that I consider unnovations, rather than innovations:

- Spamming: widespread use of email to peddle unwanted rubbish.
- Pfishing: even more malicious communication designed to dupe people into providing personal information, for criminal abuse.
- Inbound call handling: implemented to save money by reducing the underpaid call handlers required, pushing the onus onto their customers to waste their precious time categorizing themselves or providing information such as account numbers that should all be automated based on caller ID, and that, in any event, we are typically asked to repeat when our call is finally answered by a human being.
- Telesales: simply annoying.
- Tweeting: sorry, I simply don't see the point.

BusinessDictionary.com gets closest to an acceptable definition of innovation – as value creation – but restricts the definition to goods and services – product innovation. It's important to note that a product is anything an enterprise produces that is of value, whether a tangible good or an intangible service, and whether the product is commercially paid for by customers or free, such as the products of charities. It's also worth noting that a customer's experience of a product is holistic, and includes elements such as packaging and documentation.

Types of innovation

Beyond product innovation

The introduction of new products or product improvements is arguably what most of us tend to think of as innovation. My iPhone is a great example of a product innovation, as indeed is my Mac, iPad, and iPod, all produced by the same great innovation company. Philips' world-beating MRI scanners introduced in 2002 are another superb example of design-led product innovation (see Brown, 2009 for more examples). On the other hand, PARC (formerly Xerox PARC) is frequently cited (see ICMR, 2005) as an example of product unnovation, based on its spectacularly poor track record of commercializing inventions, which included PCs, the precursor to the Apple Mac, distributed computing, Ethernet, object-oriented programming, ubiquitous computing, and laser printing (which it managed to commercialize).

However, product innovation isn't the only type of innovation. Improvements in the way products are developed, made, marketed, sold, delivered, or serviced can dramatically increase the value experienced by customers, or reduce costs, complexities, risks, delays, and potential quality issues – all of which is of value, whether or not the value is passed on to customers. In continuing to develop a working definition of "innovation," let's consider a few more types of innovation that are widely discussed. Schumpeter (1934) proposed the main types of innovations in his seminal *The Theory of Economic Development*:

- Introduction of new or improved products
- New or improved methods of production
- Developing new markets
- Developing new supply sources
- New ways of organizing enterprises.

Process innovation

Accepting Schumpeter's definition, the OECD (2014) defines process innovation as "a new or significantly improved production or delivery method"; but again, I think we can reject the notion that anything new is innovative, and also question what is meant by "improved." If we aren't careful, the definition becomes tautological: innovation is improvement, and improvement is innovation. The definition only works if additional qualification is added. Creation of value would be an acceptable qualifier, but the additional defining element proposed by the OECD (2005) in the source document for the above definition is "implementation" or "adoption." "According to the Oslo Manual innovation is a market phenomenon. A new good or service, or process, is an innovation only if it is connected to the market" (Gault, 2012). So, by this definition, a firm adopting a new process that changes how it produces or delivers its products to market is considered an innovation.

Marketing innovation

One might argue that marketing innovation includes product and process innovation, as both are key aspects of the marketing mix. However, if we're not careful with our definitions, all innovation becomes marketing innovation, and marketing becomes a concept synonymous with business in the widest sense. I've met marketing people who advocate such a broad definition, but I don't think it's helpful. More to the point, there are other aspects of the marketing mix that can unquestionably enhance customer value experience, such as effective promotions.

For example, a glass of water may have a baseline level of value to a thirsty person, even though the water may be free. But if the consumer is educated regarding the health benefits of the water, the value perceived and experienced by the consumer can increase enormously.

There are arguably two central roles of marketing in any enterprise – influencing customers and potential customers to adopt, enjoy, and advocate the enterprise's products, and shaping product design based on understanding customer requirements and values. More on this later.

A great example of marketing innovation is Cadbury's famous 2007 gorilla advert. Produced by Fallon London and featuring Garon Michaels in a Stan

Winston Studios gorilla suit (an innovative product) mimicking Phil Collins playing the drums, it produced a massive ROI in terms of brand perception and profits, achieving the design brief: "to get the love back!"

On the other hand, a great example of marketing unnovation is that at the height of the tech bubble in 1999, dot.coms spent $1.09 on marketing for every $1 of revenue. Quite possibly the worst single example of marketing unnovation was a startup spending *all* its $4m initial investment round on a single 30-second Super Bowl ad. Ourbeginning.com (online wedding invitations) apparently ignored the fact that an immeasurably tiny percentage of its target market might watch football.

It's interesting to note that Roberts (2002) distinguished between product, process, and market innovations, the three types considered so far. However, various additional types of innovation have been identified, and will now be considered.

Business model innovation

Let's consider business model innovation next, positioned by many (see Davila et al., 2006; IBM, 2006) as the most important kind of innovation, a supposedly higher order than other forms. But what is a business model? Isn't it simply a strategic definition of the marketing mix? After all, a business model defines how a business creates and delivers value, and so does a proper treatment of the marketing mix, starting with the product.

The most fundamental, indeed central aspect of any business model – or marketing mix – is arguably the product. Let's be clear, a product is simply something that's produced; in fact, it's *whatever* an enterprise produces. The inherent assumption, which may or may not be true, is that the product has value to someone, in particular, a customer. A product can be tangible or intangible, a good or a service, delivering rational or emotional benefits, defined qualitatively or quantitatively, experienced in a wide variety of ways by the magnificent beings we call customers, consumers, choosers and/or users. As a product is simply what's produced, it is the heart of the business model. There's not much else to business models, other than the processes used to produce the product (which may involve activities such as development, manufacturing, and supply chains), and the activities employed to get the product into the "hot little hands" of customers (sales, marketing, distribution, and service). A business model therefore boils down to three basic elements:

Production – Product – Delivery

Given this, there can only be three basic kinds of innovation in any business: product, production, and delivery related. So-called "business model innovation" is simply a term to refer to cases where more than one of the three basic kinds of innovation happen.

A simpler term for "business model" is "value model," defining how (end to end) an enterprise creates, develops, produces, markets, sells, delivers, and services the value experienced by customers. The term "value model" is applicable to all kinds of enterprises, not just commercial businesses. An excellent example of value model innovation is IBM's transformation into a business services company, under Lou Gerstner's leadership (see Gerstner, 2002), saving the company from extinction. On the other hand, an example of value model unnovation might be loan sharks, including online offerings of payday loans at extortionate interest rates. For example, Haque (2009) cites Wonga.com as the worst business model ever: "a morally, strategically, and economically bankrupt misallocation of capital to it's [sic] least productive – and most destructive use."

Production innovation

Let's consider quick examples of production innovation and unnovation. Motorola's Six Sigma program is estimated to have saved it over $20 billion internally. Motorola also productized Six Sigma, probably earning at least that much again licensing it to others. An example of production unnovation is the massive ongoing investments in healthcare improvements (barcoding patients and so on) failing to produce the needed step change in patient safety (Nance, 2008).

Delivery innovation

Delivery innovation refers to getting products to customers, influencing them to purchase and adopt products, and helping them use and enjoy the maximum benefits possible. These processes are supported by organizational functions such as marketing, sales, after-sales service, education, training, and user support.

Apple retail stores are a perfect example of delivery innovation, providing unique environments to browse products, seek expert advice, and connect with the Apple brand and products.

In contrast, self-service checkouts at grocery stores seem to be becoming more common, but in my personal experience are examples of delivery unnovation, getting customers to do the work for no added value. In theory, we can get out of the store quicker, but so far that hasn't worked for me.

Service innovation

Various authors have discussed and offered definitions of service innovation, both for cases where the product is a service, and where service is a process in relation to product delivery, including supporting use of the product. In fact, service is always a process. In cases where service is the product offering, the processes of producing and delivering the service product might be thought of as inseparable from the product itself. For example, a musician providing a performance is simultaneously producing and delivering the musical performance, which is the product "consumed" by the audience. The same could be said of a lawyer's performance in court, a surgeon's performance in an operating theatre, an accountant's provision of an audit, or a pilot's flight.

However, is it true that the elements of a service business model are inseparable? Consider the musician. The production process is a physical act, arguably best when the musician is in a state of performance flow – at one with the instrument and the music. This is typically achieved only through a great deal of practice, including development of the required technical skills, expertise, performance capability, and mindset, motivations, and beliefs. So, production in the moment is supported by and is, in fact, a culmination of a developmental process in the past.

Exactly the same point can be made of the lawyer, surgeon, accountant, or pilot. They are only able to perform in the moment with the required skills, expertise, knowledge, and any other relevant aspects of their ability to perform, based on past preparation. There is typically an extensive history including education, practice, experience, and preparation. Present production depends on past development.

Let's consider delivery, and how it might be separate from production. A pianist might play a piece flawlessly in a room with poor acoustics. The issue is one of delivery, not production. But for the audience, the "product" – the performance – is flawed. A lawyer may have prepared the killer arguments to win a client's case – an aspect of production – but then feel ill, and do a poor job of delivery in court, losing the client's case (a poor product). So, although the service product is always, in a sense, a kind of performance in a time and place, there's often considerable preparation that's gone into production, and there can be a range of delivery issues. Therefore, I argue that the basic value delivery model consisting of production-product-delivery also applies to enterprises where the product and the service are one. However, given that service is a special case, we might say (tongue in cheek) that there are "three and a half" kinds of innovation.

Alternatively, we could say there are only two kinds of innovation – product and process – given that production and delivery are both processes. However, the distinction between them is useful, as we'll see later when discussing the challenges of innovating in various types of enterprises. Let's consider a few more types of innovation before summing up, and moving on.

Technology innovation

Another example of a type of innovation that doesn't require a rethink of our core definition is technological or technology innovation. Technology innovation is either an example of product innovation (if technology is the product), or it may relate to production or delivery processes (see Roberts, 1991). There's no question that technology can be a major catalyst for change and innovation. Implementing new technologies can and often does result in new value creation through growth, cost reductions, or other organizational changes.

Organizational innovation

According to the OECD (2014), organizational innovation refers to new methods in business practices, workplace organization, and external relations. Again, these are important phenomena, but they're simply examples of more basic production, delivery, or business model innovations. A more interesting distinction is between structures and functions. There are structural and functional elements of production and delivery models, and indeed of business models, technologies, and even products. In fact, we might more usefully use the term "structural innovation" instead of "organizational innovation," in that it refers to how we structure or organize the elements of enterprise or innovation. Similarly, we might use the term "functional innovation" rather than "process innovation" to more clearly differentiate between structure and function when talking about aspects of enterprises and innovations.

Developmental and educational innovation

There's an important and growing literature on innovation in education (for example Trilling and Fadel, 2009; Evans, 2009; Leadbeater and Staropoli, 2012; Hannon et al., 2013). We might view the provision of education as a service, in which case educational innovation is service innovation. But there's also a case to distinguish the development of skills, expertise, knowledge, and other aspects of *ability* to produce, from the actual *act* of production. Thus, innovation in development and/or education is arguably a special aspect of production innovation – a production *enabler*, as well as an important type of service innovation, where educational or developmental service is the product.

Supply chain innovation

Innovations in logistics, just-in-time inventory management, and delivery are types of innovation worth mentioning, but again, they are simply examples of other, more basic types of innovation. Further, it's worth noting that in some instances, for example containerization, assembly lines, and package delivery tracking, innovations in the supply chain affect or become integral aspects of the product (see Gilmore, 2010).

Collaborative innovation

The vast majority of innovation involves a degree of collaboration. Innovation within firms is rarely an activity engaged in by individuals working in isolation, and more generally involves extensive teamwork.

Further, as cited above, IBM (2006) reported that external collaboration is widely viewed as highly valuable and engaged in by about half of the multinationals it surveyed. Further research shows that customers, and in particular product users, are a preferred external collaborator by many firms and that firms value customer inputs to derisk product development and production processes (Ogawa and Piller, 2006).

There's no question that collaboration is a highly useful act contributing to innovation, but it doesn't seem necessary or appropriate to consider it a type of innovation, as such.

User-driven innovation

Users are a valued source of ideas for innovation (von Hippel, 1988), even when not directly engaged in collaboration, often providing input through specially designed processes (such as surveys or user forums) and operational engagement (typically with sales and service personnel). User-driven innovation is generally a form of product or delivery innovation, or both, related to aspects of enterprise business models that directly affect customer experience.

User innovation

User innovation refers to user modification of products or aspects of delivery (such as customer service). For example, Flowers et al. (2010) found that 8% of UK consumers changed or created products to better meet their needs, and it seems that around a quarter of this innovation is spread to (adopted by) other users or to the product providers (von Hippel et al., 2010).

Open and network innovation

Keeley et al. (2013) define network innovation as creating value through innovative ways of connecting with others. They include collaborative innovation, but also specific ways of creating value through innovative relationships within the enterprise's network such as risk- or resource-sharing alliances, and open innovation. The older concept of "open innovation" (see Chesbrough, 2003) advocates a mindset of looking outside the enterprise for innovation opportunities. This includes user and customer engagement, alliances, product platforming, crowdsourcing, competitions, and engaging networks for ideas. Using social media to engage networks in ways that add value to an enterprise's offerings, which Google, for one, is brilliant at, is becoming increasingly prevalent as organizations wake up to the power and potential of the Internet, as predicted by *The Cluetrain Manifesto* (Levine et al., 1999).

Incremental versus breakthrough innovation

Most innovation efforts focus on improving production, product and/or delivery. Such efforts are often characterized as continuous improvement, in that the effort to improve is never ending, and incremental, in that the improvements are typically small in nature and impact. However, even small changes can add up to big savings and profits, as many firms well know, for example Motorola's Six Sigma program.

On the other hand, the Holy Grail for many innovators is breakthrough (or discontinuous) innovation – paradigm-changing, game-changing, world-changing revolutions, rather than the evolutionary changes of incremental innovation.

Incremental versus breakthrough innovation refer to the intentions and approach of would-be innovators and the results, and may apply to any other type of innovation, including the core three. Therefore, these terms do not refer to types of innovation, as such.

Sustaining versus disruptive innovation

Sustaining innovations refer to improvements within existing value delivery models, markets or industries, whereas disruptive innovations refer to the creation of entirely new value delivery models, markets, or industries (see Christensen and Raynor, 2003). These concepts are also applicable to any types of innovation. They are perhaps best thought of as innovation phenomena rather than additional types of innovation in their own right.

Summary of types of innovation

In summary, as illustrated in Figure 2.1, there are only three basic types of innovation; all the other types are arguably examples or hybrid combinations of the basic types, which reflect the three central elements of value (or "business") models: production, product, and delivery. While Figure 2.1 may show some of the most important connections, arguably all the types of innovation are potentially interrelated.

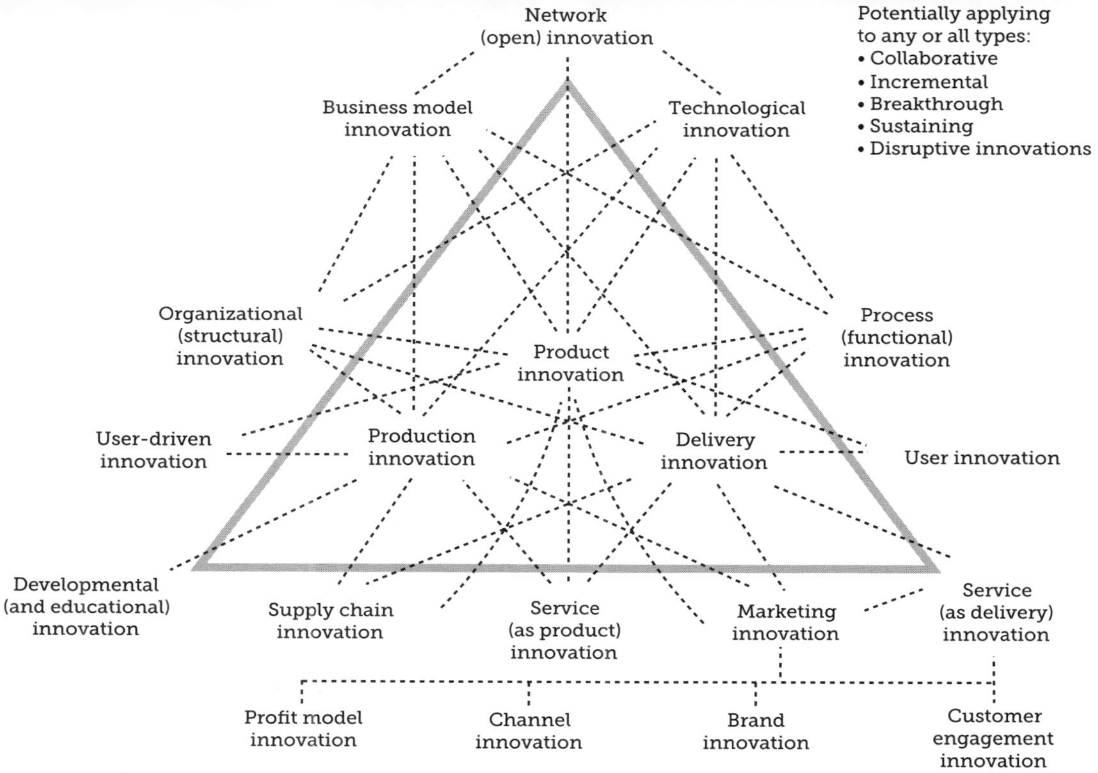

FIGURE 2.1 Types of innovation

Keeley et al. (2013) offer a framework identifying ten types of innovation, and it might be useful to relate their framework to the above. They suggest four types of innovation related to the configuration of the innovating enterprise, two related to the enterprise's offerings, and a final four types related to customer experience. Their ten types of innovation relate to the three basic types and the framework in Figure 2.1, as follows:

1. Profit model: This is defined as innovative ways of pricing, financing, or structuring the enterprise's commercial offerings, and is a key aspect of the marketing mix, and therefore an example of marketing innovation, and more generally innovative delivery.
2. Network: As discussed above, relationship and collaborative innovation in the broadest sense can apply to all other types of innovation, while more specific forms such as open innovation would clearly relate to one or more of the basic types – production, product, or delivery.
3. Structure: Covered – organizational (structural) innovation.
4. Process: Covered.
5. Product performance: Product in action (for example, being used).
6. Product system: Developmental (as in product development platforms).
7. Service: Covered.
8. Channel: A subtype of marketing innovation, related to delivery.
9. Brand: Arguably the most important value-building function of marketing.
10. Customer engagement: An aspect of marketing as well as customer service, which in some instances might extend to direct user engagement in design and innovation.

The most important point to be made about Keeley's framework is that the suggested three basic categories of innovation relate to the three types of innovation suggested here. How an enterprise is configured to produce value is the realm of production innovation. The enterprise's offering is the realm of product innovation. Finally, customer experience is the realm of delivery innovation. It's also worth highlighting the key point offered by Keeley et al. (2013) – the most interesting innovations often occur when enterprises consciously work to combine different types of innovation, often having to ignore organizational boundaries and conventional ways of thinking.

Successful innovation

Now that we've considered various types of innovation, let's return to the task of defining innovation. How do we know when we've done it? What is successful innovation?

Commercialization

Consider the following authors and sources, defining innovation in terms of creating value, wealth, and commercial success:

- "Innovation is the specific instrument of entrepreneurship. It is the act that endows resources with a new capacity to create wealth" (Drucker, 1985).
- "The starting point for innovation is the generation of creative ideas. Innovation is the process of taking those ideas to market or to usefulness" (Ijuri and Kuhn, 1988).
- "Innovation = Invention + Exploitation" (Roberts, 1987).
- "Note the difference between invention and innovation: invention is the creation of a new idea or concept – innovation is taking that idea, reducing it to practice, and making it a commercial success" (THECIS, 2014).
- "Innovation is the conversion of knowledge and ideas into a benefit, which may be for commercial use or for the public good. The benefit may be new or improved products, processes or services" (Smallwood, cited in Waschke, 2011).
- "According to the Oslo Manual innovation is a market phenomenon. A new good or service, or process, is an innovation only if it is connected to the market" (Gault, 2012, referring to OECD, 2005).
- "New products, business processes, and organic changes that create wealth or social welfare" (OECD, cited in Vaitheeswaran, 2007).
- "Fresh thinking that creates value" (Richard Lyons of Goldman Sachs, cited in Vaitheeswaran, 2007).
- "New ideas – plus action and implementation – which result in an improvement, a gain or a profit" (3M's definition, cited in Kelley with Littman, 2008).
- "Innovation is new stuff that is made useful" (McKeown, 2008).
- "Innovation is the creation of a viable new offering" (Keeley et al., 2013).

A sense that innovation is the successful commercialization of ideas emerges from the above definitions. But what is commercialization? One implication is that this must be about making money. But is that true? Does innovation have to result in greater revenues or profits? What if innovation clearly and measurably increases customer benefits and experience of value, but the company providing it chooses not to increase prices? You may then expect their market share to increase, but what if supply is limited? You would certainly expect customer loyalty to increase, and that too might translate into more money, eventually. In my view, commercial success may be a *result* of innovation, but we can't use commercialization as the *definition* of innovation.

Utility, adoption, and wellbeing

Several of the foregoing attempts to define innovation extend beyond commercialization and wealth creation to include concepts such as utility (Ijuri and Kuhn, 1988; McKeown, 2008), market adoption (OECD, 2005), and wellbeing (OECD – Vaitheeswaran, 2007).

But do we require so much complexity to define innovation? Isn't there a single concept that embraces commercialization, commercial success, wealth, utility, adoption, and wellbeing? The concept of "value" does just that, but in a way that doesn't unduly limit our definition or thinking about what constitutes innovation.

For example, McKeown's definition is nice and simple, and we'll see that usefulness and value are related when we get into the all-important definition of value in Chapter 3, but we'll also see that value is a more comprehensive psychological construct than utility. Humans can value, appreciate, and love things that aren't useful.

Value creation

Therefore, we might be inclined to agree with Kelley's pick of the Innovation Network's definition of innovation as the best: "People creating value through the implementation of ideas" (Kelley with Littman, 2008). This definition might be considered best for four reasons:

1. The recognition that innovation is value creation
2. All innovation starts with ideas
3. Successful innovation is all about implementation
4. People make it happen.

However, I still feel this definition is incorrect. Simply defining innovation as creating value from ideas implies that any provision of a good or service resulting from an idea might be innovative. Let's consider a few examples that I don't consider innovations:

- A store clerk has an idea – to ask a customer if they need help. The customer does need help, to find a particular product, which is then purchased. The customer values the product, and the store gains value from the sale, so, arguably, value is created. But is this innovation?
- An ice cream stand owner has an idea – to heap a little more ice cream on a cone for a cute child. The child values the ice cream, and although the owner's cost is slightly higher, there may be a benefit from a happy, loyal customer. So value has been created, at least for the child, but is this innovation?
- A police officer has an idea – to check out a dark area behind a school where a crime is in progress. The crime is stopped, which is considered of great value to the potential victim and the wider community, but is this innovation?
- An auditor has an idea – to look at a particular set of files and numbers in greater detail, and finding some errors that would otherwise cost the client a lot of money. Arguably, avoiding costs is a form a value creation, but is this an example of innovation?
- An executive has an idea – to work over the weekend in order to put together a winning pitch for new business. The pitch is successful, arguably because of the extra time and work, and is hugely valuable to the business, but is this innovation?

Simply delivering value as a result of an idea is not a form of innovation, particularly when the idea might be considered as expected in the normal course of business. Let's consider and reject one more definition of innovation.

"Official" definition

The "official" definition of innovation used by governments to measure and monitor levels of innovation is provided by the OECD (2005), in the *Oslo Manual.* According to this definition, innovation doesn't even need to be useful or commercially successful. It only needs to be brought to market – not to "succeed" there (Gault, 2012).

By this definition, user innovation isn't recognized as innovation unless a firm is the user modifying products (including services) used in its production or delivery processes, which therefore connect to markets. When consumers as users modify products or processes for receiving and enjoying those products, the OECD does not consider this a valid case of innovation, even when many other users adopt their modifications. To me, this is ridiculous. Consumers and users *are* the market, and therefore anything they do is connected with the market. Further, when other users adopt a user's innovations, the innovation might be thought of as popular and therefore successful.

The idea that we should accept as innovation or innovative anything that is brought to or connects to a market, whether or not it's of any value, is absurd.

Interestingly, the more recent OECD definition (cited by Vaitheeswaran, 2007) of innovation as wealth or welfare creation contradicts the *Oslo Manual* definition. Wealth implies successful commercialization or profit, which we've rejected as a basis for defining innovation, but both social welfare and wealth can be considered forms of value.

Innovation and unnovation defined

The best definition of innovation cited above is arguably that given by Lyons (Vaitheeswaran, 2007) – value creation through "fresh thinking." However, the term "fresh" might be considered a little vague. So, let's focus on the Innovation Network's definition, and propose two specific improvements:

1. Innovation is about creating *new* value through implementing ideas *for improvement*, not just normal value through business as usual.
2. The new value created must be new *net* value; in other words, even if new value is created through idea implementation, there must be a *net* increase relative to the value that had to be invested in the creation process for innovation to have occurred.

We'll get into the all-important definition of value in Chapter 3, but for now let me end by providing summary definitions of innovation and unnovation:

- Innovation is the process of manifesting new net value through enterprise activities. To be considered manifest, the value must be measurable, verifiable (stand up to audit), and sustained (not momentary or fleeting).
- The degree of innovation success at any given point in time is measurable ROI – the value created relative to the value invested to create it. New value may be manifested in a variety of ways, including increased profits, increased business valuation (share prices) due to greater long-term strategic capabilities for value creation, competitive advantage, and customer experience of benefits. ROI is usually expressed as a percentage:

$$\text{ROI} = (\text{value created} - \text{value invested})/\text{value invested}$$

- Whether or to what extent innovation is considered successful is a relative judgment. What level of ROI is considered acceptable by any given organization, board, or investor will depend on other investment options. But if ROI is zero or low, clearly the organization will not grow in its own market valuation or ability to generate and deliver value.
- Unnovation is when the ROI is negligible or negative.

chapter 3

Value and Evaluation

"A cynic knows the price of everything, and the value of nothing."

Oscar Wilde (1892)

Defining value

Early economists defined value in monetary terms. The value of anything was defined as whatever someone might pay for it. In business today, there's still a general presumption that the value of any product should be measured, understood, and expressed in terms of money. It's further presumed that the value experienced by customers must be greater than the price they'll pay, or they would look for alternative ways to fulfill their needs. But value is thought to equate to money.

Traditional economists also assumed that people are rational, making decisions (to buy, sell or invest) based on enlightened self-interest. A more modern school of economic thought, behavioral economics, brings into focus the manifestly obvious fact that humans aren't strictly rational. Many decisions and actions people take are driven by emotions, fallacies, incorrect assumptions, and perceptions. Behavioral economics allows for a clear distinction between money and value, while accepting they're often strongly related.

So we need a definition of value that isn't tied to money.

Relationship value

An important first step is recognition that value (positive or negative) exists, or manifests, in relationships. In fact, a step further is to recognize that our ability to deliver and receive value is *only ever* in relationships – to people or things. For example, the value of money, as perceived by anyone, can *only* be understood in terms of that individual's *relationship* to money. For most of us, the perceived value of money is based on what we imagine we might use it for. In other words, it's tied up in expectations about what other relationships might be supported by the money: a relationship with a nice meal and perhaps someone to enjoy it with; a relationship with an airplane that might take us to a pleasant environment and people to share the experience with; or a relationship to an investment fund and the sense of security it might provide, feeling it's in safe hands.

Relationships are real, but only in the sense that we perceive them as real. Think about unrequited love. Perhaps you've experienced it? You loved someone, or at least the concept of who you thought they might be, or might become, in relationship to you. You might have fantasized about how it would be, what it would feel like, to be in that relationship. And yet the intended lover may have hardly been aware of your existence, let alone share your growing passion for tasting the potential relationship. Perhaps you approached them, tentatively sharing your dream. And perhaps your dream and hopes were dashed. This has happened to most of us who are over the age of 10 or so. I mention all this because it illustrates a key point: that relationships are something that exist in our minds. They are psychological, as is every single aspect of them, including, and indeed most especially, the aspect of value.

Value is psychological

The value we experience in any relationship is in our minds. It's a feeling, no doubt tied to specific neurons firing, connecting, and stimulating each other with specific neurologically active chemicals – neurotransmitters, hormones, and so on – probably within particular brain structures. Our feelings of value may be related to endorphins. Whatever the physical correlates of value experience may be, the psychological *fact* is that something has made us feel good. Of course, for good, we may substitute great, or better. Something has tipped our scales from someplace to some noticeably better place. That's *value*.

Let's consider a house. If you have your house valued or assessed by a professional, the valuation is based on an estimate of what you might sell for in the current market. But clearly, the value of your home to you and your family is not just about the money you have tied up in it. Your experience of the value of your home will also include emotional ties, memories, feelings of comfort and wellbeing, a sense of security, and so on. Value is a psychological, rather than purely financial consideration.

Innovation value

So now, let's reconsider the concept of innovation. It isn't just the delivery or provision of value, rather it is the creation and manifestation of *new* value. If we stumble across someone dying of thirst in a desert and give them water, the recipient will experience massive value, and no doubt be very grateful. With or without that gratitude, our act of kindness may also make us feel good and therefore add value in our experience of events. But this is not an example of innovation, it's just delivery.

Based on the definition in Chapter 2, innovation refers to the process or result of manifesting *new net value*. To be considered manifest, the value must be experienced by someone through their relationship with the innovation. Whether or how that value may be commercialized – priced, bought, and paid for – is another question. If new net value is experienced, it exists. If it exists, it's innovation. It's innovation whether or not that innovation is paid for. Otherwise, it would be theoretically impossible for charities, governments, or businesses providing free goods or services to innovate. That's one reason why, in my view, "commercial success," particularly if our concept of "commercial" is tied to money, is an overly limiting definition of innovation. Given that widely accepted synonyms for the word "commercial" include monetary, profit-oriented, mercantile, and materialistic, and given that the term "commercial enterprise" is often used in juxtaposition to public or social enterprises, let me conclude by rejecting commercial success as a measure or definition of innovation.

However, let's go back to the point that innovation success is defined in terms of return on investment (ROI = (value created – value invested)/ value invested), where the value must be measurable, verifiable, and sustained. How is this to be done? Let's first consider a commercial enterprise. Commercial enterprises generally measure success, failure, and anything in between in terms of money. Therefore, they would naturally tend to measure innovation ROI in exactly the same terms. But there are a number of problems associated with tying success measures strictly to financial considerations:

- What price or value should we put on improved customer loyalty, if, for example, we decide not to charge for an innovation that increases customer value?
- Most notions of commercial success tend to be short term, looking at financial measures such as net earnings within a particular time period. What if a particular innovation doesn't flow to the bottom line, in that sense, but hugely increases share prices or company valuation over the longer term?
- What if an innovation doesn't produce additional earnings or company valuation, but rather enhances long-term competitiveness, or perhaps even the ability to innovate? These sorts of strategic investments can be costly, and often have a negative impact on financial performance within time frames that investors, executives, and analysts typically care about.
- What if the innovator doesn't actually understand the value of the innovation? In many instances, enterprises investing in innovation don't fully (or even approximately) understand the customer value experienced as a result of their innovations.

The bottom line is that measuring the value of anything is extremely difficult. Value is a complex concept, with subjective and objective components. It can also be short or long term, distributed in complex ways among a wide range of stakeholders, and even experienced differently from one instance to the next, with perceptions colored by things such as service delivery. An innovation might triple a customer's value experience, while the company has decided to only double the price relative to alternatives. The company's price and earnings increase may enable it to pay employees more, or pay investors dividends, or pay a fat bonus to key executives. Clearly, companies make choices about how to price products and how to spend and allocate profits – and these decisions are essentially about how to distribute value.

Value and needs fulfillment

A core aspect of human psychology and experience is to value things that fulfill perceived or felt needs, wants, aspirations, or motivations. The sense of value is multidimensional, involving many aspects such as feelings of pleasure, spirituality, love, and the fulfillment of needs. And no, it doesn't have to be rational. Let's consider Maslow's hierarchy of needs, which he originally proposed in 1943, elaborated in 1954, and later (1964, 1970) extended to include transcendence (the need to help others self-actualize, as commonly seen in parents), aesthetic and cognitive needs.

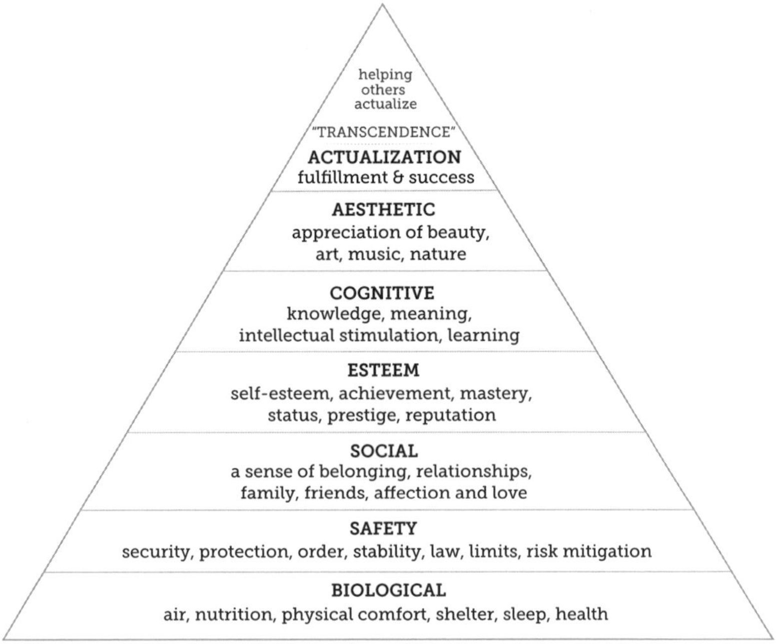

FIGURE 3.1 Maslow's hierarchy of needs
Source: Adapted from Maslow, 1970

Maslow's hierarchy has a great deal of face validity, in that we can readily see how we derive value based on the fulfillment of various needs. We work or pay to address biological needs such as eating. We pay for safety – a home to protect us from the elements, or a home security system to protect us from intruders. We place great value on love, and some people even pay for that. We pay to belong, to be members of the right clubs. We pay to build our self- and social esteem, often paying rather dearly to "keep up with the neighbors." We pay to go to and send our children to the best schools and universities. And, of course, we pay to appreciate forms of beauty such as jewelry, music, and art. Many of us are generally willing to pay huge premiums for aesthetically better designed products. We pay for self-actualization in various forms, such as self-help books, personal development programs, and gurus, churches, and spiritual pursuits.

Clearly, the fulfillment of needs can result in the experience of value, but what about the hierarchy? Maslow (1954) argued that unless our more basic needs are met, we're psychologically unable to focus on higher needs. Maslow's theory has been criticized for lacking empirical support (see Wahba and Bridwell, 1976), and in my view it lacks logical support as well. For example, do people have to feel safe to fall in love? Many personal stories of love during wars and strife completely contradict this notion.

For me, an even more basic problem is that the supposed hierarchy of needs fails to equate to value experience. There doesn't appear to be any systematic relationship between Maslow's hierarchy of needs and relative value. Will we pay more for a self-help book than sex? What about rest, also on the lowest level? If it's so low in the hierarchy, why do so many spend so much on vacations, not to mention better mattresses and pillows? If we can't find a model for value in the supposed hierarchy of needs, where can we find it? Psychologically, what *is* value if not the fulfillment of needs. How can we understand the value of fulfilling one need versus another? Are all needs created equal?

Again, back to fundamental psychological realities. Everyone is different, at least subtly. Certainly, we can find major differences in needs and values if we compare different ages, genders, cultures, and other dimensions of human diversity. Further, we see enormous differences among people who seem superficially similar. Both my twin nine-year-old boys love playing video games, soccer, rugby, cricket, swimming, and bouncing on their trampoline. But one likes toasted peanut butter and bacon sandwiches, while the other prefers French toast. One loves toy soldiers more than the other, and the other loves toy guns more than soldiers. They're different. We all are.

So the challenge for any enterprise – whether public or private, commercial or social – seeking to create, deliver, and maximize value for distribution among its stakeholders is that defining that value, or potential value, is extremely difficult. Are you ready for another "psychological truth"?

Value can only be measured or understood in relative terms. In other words, theoretically, if there were only one relationship in existence, we would have no way of assessing its value. The closest example of such a psychological reality may be that of a newborn infant. For the infant, only one relationship matters, that with the mother. Arguably, the newborn may not be aware of a separation of "self" and "m-other." The relationship simply *is*, existence simply *is*, and existence and the relationship are *one*. So when the infant's needs are met, there's contentment. When an unmet need arises, such as an empty tummy or wet diaper, the infant naturally expresses the desire for need fulfillment. And when the need is met, contentment returns. There may be a kind of blissful sense of value in the notion of contentment. But how can we understand value in this context?

As a baby develops awareness, there's no doubt that the baby becomes aware of different sorts of needs – different relationships. The relationship to the sore, bloated tummy is different from the relationship to hunger. A burp is not a bottle. A wet diaper is probably, at some stage, experienced differently than a dirty diaper. So things start to be experienced as separate, with different needs, varying degrees of discomfort or pleasure, and on it goes. The cries of infants may be different depending on what they need (but the "science" on this is currently limited).

The key point here is that enterprises must also learn to differentiate between the various "cries" of their customers and other stakeholders. They must learn the difference between a real cry for help and a cry for attention. And they must find ways to understand the relative value of things.

So, what's the best way for organizations to define, understand, measure, validate, assess, compare, and predict value? Let's break this problem down. On the one hand, we need a psychological definition of value, in terms of human experience. Then we need ways to measure it, so that we can assess the value of things. Finally, it would be extremely useful to be able to reliably predict the value of future things, as a guide for investments in innovation. We will now consider each of these objectives in turn.

The psychological components of value experience

It's helpful to break down value experience into basic psychological components, which you will see are interrelated; in effect, building on each other in specific ways that relate to fundamental human nature and the concept of creating "flow" (explained in Chapter 6). Let me start by simply laying them out in Table 3.1, and then providing more detailed definitions below.

TABLE 3.1 The psychological components of value

Value components	Psychological condition
Actualization (fulfillment)	The feeling of complete fulfillment derived from the value experience – loving it – including a sense of gratitude and loyalty to the value source, with the resulting likelihood of testimonials and referrals
Understanding	Evaluation based on rational, analytic understanding of value in terms of benefits relative to costs
Expression	Taking it to the next level – finding, learning, and expressing – articulation of value and the aspects of what is loved about the product and its source
Appreciation	Feeling the love – loving the relationship to the product and its source – appreciation of the value derived from win–win relationships
Confidence	Feeling security that our future needs will be met by the trusted source, or knowing that ongoing value delivery is secure, based on risk mitigation
Pleasure	Perceiving good feelings from value experience deriving from consumption or development
Contentment	Knowing, feeling, or perceiving that our needs are being met

Building on the above, let's revisit the question of a needs hierarchy. A fundamental premise is that humans need and want to experience value. There are two sides to this coin; we want to experience the receipt of value and also the giving – the creation. Consider the following relationship between value components and needs, or wants, or desires, or aspirations (Table 3.2). I've also added the needs identified by Maslow (1954, 1970), but in order to maintain the ordering of the value components, note that aesthetic needs must drop from second place to sixth.

TABLE 3.2 Relating value to needs

Value components	Aspirations – desires – wants – needs	Maslow's needs
Actualization	To reach one's full potential, fulfilling essential purpose and achieving success, and to help others do so	Actualization
Understanding	To know, to learn, to build intelligence and foresight, to have access to and consume information, to analyze, to develop insight and ultimately wisdom	Cognitive
Expression	To be heard, and to listen and empathize, to communicate, to find one's truth and help others do so, to express oneself through any means	Esteem
Appreciation	To feel appreciation for people, places and things, and feel appreciated by others	Social
Confidence	To feel a sense of security (risk mitigation or avoidance) in relation to ongoing receipt and provision of value	Safety
Pleasure	To enjoy, including pleasures derived from physical, aesthetic, emotional, mental, social, and creative activities and development	Aesthetics
Contentment	To feel content in any particular moment in time	Biological

Maslow's hierarchy of needs places actualization at the top, as the highest need. The concept of actualization is, of course, the fulfillment of purpose and the achievement of success. Why do humans exist if not to actualize – to reach and manifest their full potential. The very essence or spirit of humanness is to develop and grow. Maslow (1964) later added a higher need – transcendence – the desire or need to help others to achieve self-actualization. This too can easily be thought of as the fulfillment of a higher purpose. Arguably, there is no greater calling than to help others reach their full potential, so when an individual becomes self-actualized, it's only natural that they will seek to help others.

Let's consider the case for moving aesthetic needs down in the hierarchy. In our culture, which places so much value on the arts, it may seem surprising not to place aesthetic needs just below spiritual needs. But what is aesthetic value other than a form of pleasure? Clearly, aspects of art involve cognition, such as knowing about a piece of music or its history, or intellectual insights that may be stimulated by many forms of art, such as music, paintings, or poetry. But the pure aesthetic pleasure – the enjoyment, the ecstasy that we may experience listening to a performance or soaking in a painting – is, psychologically, a form of pleasure. Other forms of pleasure, such as enjoying foodie experiences, sex, and sport are, in Maslow's hierarchy, described as biological. Having a full belly, being able to breathe clean fresh air without difficulty, sleeping, and so on will, in my view, support a state of contentment, but we also derive pleasure from breathing in the scents of a fine wine, perfume, or other fragrances. Are these pleasures a lower aesthetic form than the enjoyment of music or other forms of art? Psychologically, I think not.

Further, in terms of the hierarchy, I accept the obvious point, that if we can't breathe or we're starving or dying of thirst, nothing else much matters. But is our next concern really safety, and not the pursuit of pleasure? If that is true, why do so many people risk so much in pursuit of pleasures of various kinds? People risk marriages for sex, risk life and limb to enjoy extreme sports, and risk death to enjoy artificial "highs" derived from various substances. So, the reordering of the hierarchy seems to work.

Another criticism of Maslow's hierarchy is that the need for esteem is only one aspect of the wider needs related to expression. Humans have a need to communicate, to express opinions, to listen and connect. These build on the lower needs around relationship, love, and appreciation – taking it to the higher needs around understanding, intelligence, and wisdom. So-called "esteem needs" – need for respect – are actually relationship needs. Respect and trust are foundational for any good relationship and the love and appreciation that can result. However, self-respect and self-esteem are also derived from communication, and finding one's truth. Therefore, I place esteem beside expression, with the reservation, as stated, that there is much more to expression needs than the simpler need for esteem. The need for expression was eloquently captured by Covey's eighth habit – finding your voice and helping others to find theirs (see Chapter 1).

In summary, the psychological components of positive value experience are contentment, pleasure, confidence, appreciation, expression, and, finally, actualization. However, there are two sides to every coin.

Positive, negative, and neutral value states

Corresponding with each aspect of positive value experience is a negative. Psychologically, there's an upside and a downside to each of the states or aspects of value experience. In other words, the human condition often consists of states wherein positive value is not being experienced. The value of anything can be negative as well as positive, or there can be no value at all – neutrality. So, let's consider the positive side of the "coin," as well as the negative, and neutral states for each of the psychological components of value experience.

Contentment is a resting, neutral state where we feel our needs have been or are being met. It serves as a foundation for the next level of psychological experience of value – pleasure. The opposite of contentment is discontentment. And because humans (and other creatures) are designed to adapt and survive, we also have the ability to become tolerant of states of discontent. In other words, our discontent becomes normal. We become tolerant of poor conditions, mediocrity, or difficult circumstances. We adapt, and accept the poor state of affairs as normal. This neutral value experience is "complacency."

Pleasure goes a step further than the neutral state of contentment. Pleasure moves from neutrality to positively feeling good. Interestingly, pleasure often precedes contentment. We experience the pleasure of a lovely meal, and then contentedness. We experience the pleasures of sexuality, and then contentedness. We tend to become somewhat discontent, hungry or sexually aroused, or wanting something, and then experience pleasure when we engage in relationship with what we have wanted. Of course, the opposite of pleasure is displeasure. We have various words for this – pain, disease, hunger, thirst, agony, and so on. The realm of human experience in this regard is vast, and in the same way that the Eskimos have 50 words for snow, we have many, many words for displeasure. Again, humans have an amazing ability to tolerate pain, in its various forms. We are able to adapt and, in rare cases, even transcend painful circumstances (see, for example, Frankl, 2006 for a personal account of achieving enlightenment and joy while surviving a Nazi death camp). We also adapt to pleasure, and sometimes things that initially provide great pleasure come to be taken for granted, to lose their appeal. Some psychological addictions happen because we need more and more of something to achieve the same level of pleasure. We need to take our experience, our consumption, to extremes in order to experience the same value. This neutral value experience between pleasure and pain is "boredom."

Confidence takes the value experience another level up, based on a belief or knowledge (what we think we know) that we will continue to experience the cyclical rhythms of contentment and pleasure. Note that confidence is also a complex psychological concept, based on things such as trust, beliefs, feelings of predictability, certainty, and, in some cases, a sense of power. The opposite of confidence is fear – fear that we will lose whatever is providing contentment and pleasure. This might be fear of losing power, fear that our trust is misplaced, and fear that "it might all go horribly wrong." We may also fear the continuation of whatever is preventing contentment or producing pain. And again, there's a neutral state of tolerance and acceptance of the uncertainty that exists between confidence and fear. Given that doubt is a milder form of fear, I have to point out here that the "FUD factor" – fear, uncertainty, and doubt – is at play here.

Appreciation and its highest forms – inspiration and love – require confidence, both self-confidence and confidence in the "other" – the object of our love. With the foundation of trust and confidence, a proper relationship can be built, with a two-way, win–win experience of value and connection. Of course, there are degrees of appreciation, and we use words such as love, inspiration, affection, liking, friendship, connection, support, caring, and many more besides, to describe the rich and diverse human experience of appreciation. We may love ice cream, dogs, walking, our children, our spouses, our parents, our mobile phones, and our favorite restaurants. And we have a keen ability to sense love or any other degree of appreciation from others. We can taste whether or not the bread we eat has been baked with love. We can see whether or not the chef cooked and presented our plate of food with loving care. Even if it has, we can lose the sense of love in an instant if the plate is plopped before us by someone who clearly doesn't love serving. Appreciation is a multifaceted thing, and so is its opposite – revulsion. People can feel hatred, loathing, disliking, or disapproval toward someone or something. Again, there are degrees and there is great diversity of human experience of the opposite side of appreciation. There is also a state of neutrality between the extremes of love and hate – "ambivalence."

Expression takes appreciation to new and higher levels of value experience, by expressing, articulating, describing, and giving voice to our appreciation. We're also able to express our "truths" and build appreciation for our truths among others, perhaps influencing them in the process. The two-way communication, listening and receiving as well as articulating and expressing, creates the opportunity to deepen relationship connection and also to learn from each other and build understanding. We enthusiastically express truths and build toward mutual understanding. But at the other extreme, we might express falsehoods and create misunderstanding. The neutral state between these extremes is silence, non-expression, failure to communicate. Let's call this "apathy."

Understanding is enabled by expression. If we're able to first identify, articulate, and discuss benefits and costs, we can develop a sense of understanding of value, taking value experience a level higher. This is a learning process and the result of effective learning is understanding. Understanding engages intellect, intelligence, intuition, and insight. In a sense, this takes the initial identification and expression of benefits and costs to a higher level – to analysis, assessment, and evaluation. At this level, we experience an understanding of the positive or negative aspects of our value experience in any specific relationship. We might even think of this level of experience as enlightenment, wherein we are fully enlightened about the value, benefits relative to costs, of a relationship. But there's also an opposite, negative side to this enlightenment or understanding – namely, misunderstanding. In a sense, this is a false understanding, whereby we feel we understand something, but we don't. We may be basing our understanding on incorrect data, false assumptions, faulty analyses, or misperceptions of reality. The middle ground between understanding and misunderstanding is "confusion."

Actualization is the culmination of everything above. Building on a solid understanding of value, it becomes possible to truly experience fulfillment at the highest level. We have many words for this state, including joyfulness, grace, harmony, and nirvana. At this level of value experience, there's a sense of being in the right place at the right time, oneness, or to use a Buddhist expression, being on the Tao, or path. The opposite state is one of being deeply and profoundly unfulfilled, off-track, unharmonious, out of balance, and "uncomfortable in our own skin." It is a "dis-grace," and arguably a state that is the opposite of grace. It may also be a state of "dis-ease," the opposite of ease, and when someone is profoundly disconnected from grace, the result may be various diseases threatening health and ongoing existence. If the point of existence is to achieve actualization or grace, which in some religious traditions is conceived of as being "at one with" or connected with one's spirit or a divine entity, then surely the lack of that ranges from pointlessness to being completely disconnected, for which we have words such as evil, disgraced, and fallen. The neutral state between grace-based gratitude and disgrace-based disease is arguably "pointlessness."

As you continue reading, you'll see that the above psychological aspects of the value experience relate to the seven sins of innovation and the corresponding seven entrepreneurial virtues. But for now, let's continue to consider the concept of value. We've defined value as a psychological phenomenon with specific components of human experience. So now the question is: How can we measure it?

Measuring, modeling, and predicting value

Over the years, I have tried a variety of approaches for measuring the value of things. Further, when value is measured over long periods, in a range of markets, with appropriate statistical analyses and modeling techniques, interesting trends, insights, and predictive powers emerge.

Let me start by saying that money is a useful metric (although by no means the only one) for measuring value, even though, as stated earlier, money and psychological value aren't the same thing. But the fact that money has psychological value for most people, based on what it might buy or the sense of security it might enable, means that money can be used as an indicant or measure of true value. In other words, what someone will pay for something provides a useful indication of relative value – the value of what they're paying for, relative to the potential value (or the lost opportunity cost) of whatever else the person may have done with the money.

Therefore, the real world of money, and the fact that we can measure and track it when it changes hands, provides a mechanism for assessing the relative value of things. In one sense, the world of money is a false world, full of unfairness, subterfuge, and smoke and mirrors, as seen in the build-up to and during the recent global financial crisis. We might think of Jesus in the temple, railing against the false "god" of money. Whether we buy that particular thought or not, we have already made the point that value is not only commercial and can't be directly equated with money.

However, let's not dismiss money too hastily. Money has its uses, as we all well know. Further, it has proven extremely useful in understanding, measuring, and predicting the value of things. Arguably, if one product attracts a higher price than another in a head-to-head, competitive market, then the first product is clearly more valuable. How much more valuable, we may never know. As anyone involved in pricing knows, it's not an exact science.

The importance of distinguishing between value and money is arguably best illustrated by contrasting cost-plus pricing with value-based pricing. Although it's clearly absurd, the sad fact is that most pricing decisions are still based on calculations of direct and indirect costs, and the addition of a reasonable markup, margin, or profit contribution. It's impossible to know for sure, but I estimate that about 90% of pricing is still done this way. The alternative, value-based pricing is based on the premise that value is understood and measurable. In spite of this, when I ask people how they assess value, I tend to hear a lot of waffle.

However, many techniques are used for value-based pricing, some of which I pioneered the development and usage of back in my days with Bell-Northern Research (BNR), including user needs research, choice and decision research, market research, measurement of customer satisfaction and loyalty, and other behavioral and data analytic approaches to getting a handle on value. Let's briefly consider the various options for measuring value.

Needs research

User or consumer needs research analyzes the needs of people who may use a particular product, enabling product designers to focus on the all-important question of how to deliver benefits that users will value. Needs assessment can take a variety of shapes, including subjective surveys, interviews or focus groups, and objective analyses of behavior or product attributes. For example, if the objective is to design a better dental X-ray machine, the behavior of dentists and patients might be observed and documented to help generate ideas for improving usability, and existing X-ray devices and results might be analyzed to identify further areas for design improvement. Dentists, patients, and perhaps additional groups of users such as dental assistants might also be asked for opinions that can inform new product design or development. Understanding the needs and potential benefits associated with fulfilling those needs is notoriously difficult. Done properly, the research must be based on a detailed and thorough understanding of the entire business being observed – in this case, what the dentist is doing and why, the purpose of X-rays within that wider context, how the X-rays are used, current limitations, risks, costs, options, and alternatives. To add yet another complexity, it must be understood that the user or consumer of any product may or may not also be the chooser or purchaser of the product.

Chooser decision research

A variety of specific techniques are used in an attempt to understand buying behavior, including focus groups, surveys, tracking behaviors in shops and online, and attempts to portray the shopper journey, from couch (watching TV) to counter (point of sale), trying to understand how TV or other advertisements, in-store promotions, and so on may or may not have influenced purchase decisions. Obviously, the simplest case is where the consumer and purchaser are one and the same, but this is not the case for all commerce. In many cases, one family member will do the shopping, influenced in varying degrees by other family members. And when organizations are the unit of analysis, purchasing behavior can be far more complex. The decision process can be highly complex, involving many parties including decision makers and a variety of influencers, such as consultants, analysts, and industry experts. There's a whole realm of psychology focused on choice behavior, decision theory, and gaming – all aimed at understanding how rational and irrational thoughts, feelings, perceptions, and misperceptions influence our decisions. Getting people to make real decisions in unreal environments, such as simulations, games, and hypothetical scenarios, can be highly informative for understanding how and why they'll buy, how they choose among competitive alternatives, or indeed the alternative of choosing nothing, and what prices they may pay. However, this is also notoriously difficult. People will say one thing and do another. In groups, they'll influence each other, they may also be influenced by the facilitator who may be less than neutral, by subtle biases in how questions are asked, or by assumptions (right or wrong) about who's asking. Highly professional, double-blind, meticulously unbiased one-to-one questioning may be useful, but arguably the best way to research choice behavior is a real-world trial in a test market. There's nothing like watching how people actually spend money to get a handle on how people will spend money.

Market research

Both user and chooser research might be considered types of market research. However, I only consider a study to be an example of market research when statistical comparisons are made across different markets or market segments. The broad intent is typically to determine whether or not there is a market for a particular product, to roughly estimate what portion of a population might buy the product, or to help the product's marketers decide where to focus and target their efforts, in terms of segments of the population.

Customer satisfaction research

We've all been asked to rate how we feel about an enterprise or its product, from poor, fair, good, very good, to excellent. Other five-point scales can be employed, looking at accuracy, importance, usefulness, value, quality, excellence, satisfaction, and so on. Enterprises that have built a large database of such feedback, over a long period, often find the data useful for predicting future events, such as loss of custom and declines in sales or profits. But more often than not, enterprises simply aggregate and summarize the data for senior executives or boards to satisfy a reporting requirement. They often combine the top two ratings (4 and 5) because then the results look better. However, the underlying psychological reality is that 4s and 5s are very different beasties. Enterprises combining their data in such ways are often lulled into an entirely false and dangerous sense of complacency, and would be well advised to stop doing so (see Lee, 2004).

Customer loyalty research

Enterprises that have shifted from only asking customers to rate them (as above) to also answering questions about whether or not they would (or will) continue doing business with them have discovered that loyalty data is a far more powerful predictor of future buying behavior. The ratings might still be useful for identifying specific areas requiring improvement, but statements of loyalty are a better predictor of actual loyalty.

The Net Promoter methodology, initially pioneered by Enterprise Rent-A-Car and further developed by Reichheld (2006), is a specific form of loyalty research, focused on whether and the extent to which someone may recommend a business or a product to a friend, and why. Two simple questions shed a huge amount of light on any enterprise or product:

1 How likely, from zero to one hundred percent, would you be to recommend us or our product to a friend who has the same needs as you?
2 Why?

Obviously, answers to "why" questions can provide valuable insights regarding value, and serve as a valuable source of ideas for innovation.

Net Promoter proponents – Bain & Company (netpromotersystem.com) and Satmetrix Systems (netpromoter.com) – advocate focusing on Net Promoter Scores (NPS), defined as the percentage of promoters (scoring 9 or 10 on likelihood to recommend) minus the percentage of detractors (scoring 6 or below). There's no compelling evidence or logic behind this simplistic approach (Keiningham et al., 2008; Hayes, 2009). Clearly, equating scores of 9 with scores of 10 is every bit as problematic as lumping 4s and 5s in customer satisfaction research, not to mention treating scores from 0 to 6 as equivalent. However, the simplistic NPS approach, especially when used to benchmark against competitors within industries, is quite useful. But the most useful insights, in my view, come from understanding the "why?" answers.

Competitive research

As stated above, NPS is useful for understanding competition, but it's just one form of competitive research. It's always fascinating to know what our customers think of us, but even more useful to know how they, and our competitors' customers, view us relative to the competitors. The best way to obtain the data, for yourself and your competitors, is through a neutral agent. Someone phones or otherwise connects with customers to explore satisfaction, loyalty or recommendations, but it isn't you, because the fact that it is you may bias the results. Further, the neutrality allows researchers to explore customer feelings about directly competitive options (such as different makes of cars), as well as indirect alternatives (such as walking, biking, or using public transport).

Another form of competitive research is spying. For example, in the early 1980s, we discovered that a competitor was booking seats on flights that were heavily and regularly used by BNR and Nortel executives, hoping to hear conversations or see documents being read. Spying can take many forms, some of which are immoral and illegal. But they happen. Hacking into ICT systems, burglary, and bribery are clear examples of illegal activities. There are also gray areas, such as job interviews to prise interesting tidbits from applicants who may be overly eager to impress. There are also activities we might prefer to think of as looking rather than spying, such as noting what competitor products might be on our customer's warehouse or store shelves, looking at their websites and other external communications, and (as discussed above) simply asking our customers what they think of the competition.

Trade shows and conferences are also great for competitive research, particularly if you can (legitimately or otherwise) get a press pass. It's amazing how much people will divulge to the press, or indeed any complete stranger, as long as they're not wearing a badge of an archrival.

A further technique is to simply phone competitors and ask questions. Amazingly, people will often say a great deal before even stopping to ask who they're speaking with.

One of my favorite approaches is getting the competition drunk. I once found myself in a bar with a horde of employees of a Scandinavian competitor, who were already "three sheets to the wind" before I joined them. It was one of the most illuminating bar experiences ever, and they even bought the drinks.

Data mining

The fact that many enterprises use data on customer satisfaction to predict future performance has already been mentioned, and is an example of mining data for insights. The broader point is that when enterprises invest in building vast databases of information about customers, competitors, and markets, various opportunities are enabled for exploiting the data. Insights (or "gold nuggets") can be found – business intelligence emerges and evolves.

Data modeling and simulation

When truly rich collections of big data have been developed, patterns understood, hypotheses tested, and theories have emerged, it becomes possible to develop accurate mathematical models that demonstrate, simulate, and predict the behavior of complex systems, including customers, markets, and competitors. Of course, this sort of research requires all of the above, but arguably takes it all to a higher level of intelligence.

Evaluation research

It's one thing to attempt to simulate reality (such as a future reality), but quite another to actually try something. There are various ways to enable customers or potential customers to experience a product or potential product – all of which I'm calling "evaluation research." Prototype products can be developed and provided to potential users or choosers for assessment. Some products may even be simulated (not to be confused with the above data simulation). For example, complex online services or software products may be simulated, as in made to look like the real thing, but are actually just a technical emulation. In short, by putting the product or a reasonable facsimile of the product in the hands of users or choosers, the product's producers have a golden opportunity to evaluate, that is, assess, the value of the product.

I've performed a variety of evaluations, mainly of complex office systems and specific business services, but also of some devices such as business phones and multimedia devices, based on free or paid-for trials, at various stages of development (sometimes distinguished with words such as alpha, beta or field trials). We found evaluation research extremely valuable for understanding customer value, helping set pricing strategies, competitive positioning, avoiding launches of market duds, developing marketing strategies centered on value, and, perhaps most important, identifying design improvements to enhance customer value.

Evaluation research is arguably the pinnacle among powerful techniques for producers of value to assess or predict the value of products or potential products. But it's also the penultimate customer experience of value, as seen above. Researchers and organizations must always remember, it's one thing to perform research in an attempt to measure value and quite another to experience it as a customer, consumer, or recipient.

Performance and results

Real-world performance and results are, of course, the ultimate form of understanding value. When organizations build vast pools of knowledge from the above forms of research, and also tie that to knowledge about accurately measured and tracked aspects of business performance, wisdom can emerge.

The aspects of business performance that matter may vary from one organization to the next, but may include various balanced scorecard indicators, including:

- Financial measures such as profitability, share price, relative revenue (market share), and the plethora of ratios that finance people love to use as key performance indicators – ROI, already defined, and many more.
- Customer measures such as Net Promoter Scores, and all the other ways of measuring customer value experience, already discussed.
- Operational measures designed to provide objective measures of quality (defect rates) that can correlate with customer measures (such as subjective perception of quality), productivity (unit rates of manufacturing, billable hours, or whatever matters to the organization), and even innovation (number of new products introduced, rates of success commercializing new ideas, and so on).
- Organizational psychology measures designed to get a handle on cultural factors, such as morale, motivations, attitudes, beliefs, cohesion, communication, shared values, leadership qualities, and so on.

Bottom line value

When organizations invest in building intelligence, connecting most or all of the above types of information, it not only becomes possible to measure and predict value, but also to understand how to manage and optimize value creation and delivery among stakeholders.

It's important to note that value, particularly as it relates to enterprise and entrepreneurship, has many aspects or sides to the "coin" (see Figure 3.2): customer perception and experience of value in the relationship with the product and enterprise providing it, partly influenced by the value proposition or USP and how they're marketed and sold, and how the value is delivered and made manifest through the organizational "business (or value delivery) model," all underpinned by the all-important core values of the enterprise.

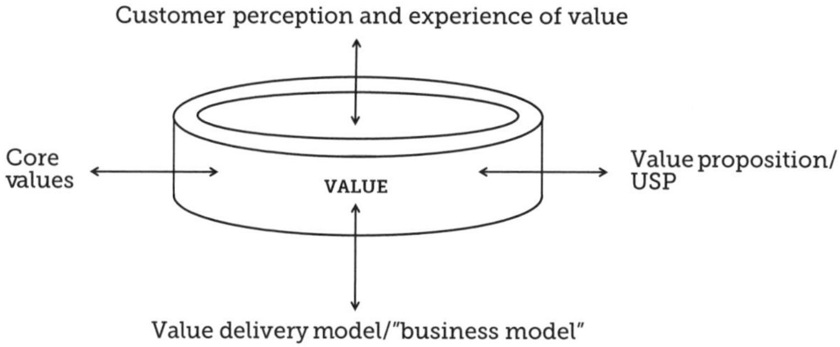

FIGURE 3.2 The many-sided value "coin"

Now that we've defined innovation and value, we can proceed to define entrepreneurship and entrepreneurial flow (Chapter 4), and then consider and define a new strategic model for entrepreneurial innovation (Chapter 5), before considering a phenomenon I call "innovation zoning" (Chapter 6), and how to do it – the art and science of "bridging" (Chapter 7).

chapter 4

Entrepreneurial Psyche and Flow

"Imagination is more important than knowledge. For knowledge is limited, whereas imagination embraces the entire world, stimulating progress, giving birth to evolution."

Albert Einstein (1931)

Defining entrepreneurship

Let's begin with some personal questions:

1 Are you an entrepreneur?
2 Have you ever been one?
3 Do you perhaps want to become one?

How you answer these questions depends on your definitions and perhaps also your self-beliefs. Let's consider some definitions of an entrepreneur:

- Oxford International: a person who sets up a business or businesses, taking on financial risks in the hope of profit.
- Wikipedia: an individual who organizes or operates a business or businesses.
- Free Dictionary: a person who organizes, operates, and assumes the risk for a business venture.

- Merriam-Webster: one who organizes, manages, and assumes the risks of a business or enterprise.
- Dictionary.com: a person who organizes and manages any enterprise, especially a business, usually with considerable initiative and risk.
- BusinessDictionary.com: someone who exercises initiative by organizing a venture to take benefit of an opportunity and, as the decision maker, decides what, how, and how much of a good or service will be produced. An entrepreneur supplies risk capital as a risk taker, and monitors and controls the business activities. The entrepreneur is usually a sole proprietor, a partner, or the one who owns the majority of shares in an incorporated venture.

These definitions have several things in common. An entrepreneur is a person, an organizer (as Oxford's "set up" could be considered equivalent to "organizing"), and a risk taker. But this seems to be an overly limited definition that fails to capture the true spirit of entrepreneurship. Let me remind you that another word for "spirit" or "soul" is "psyche" – the root word for psychology. To understand entrepreneurial psyche, let's first go back to basics.

The term "entrepreneur" was first introduced by Richard Cantillon, in a manuscript written around 1730 and published in 1755. Arguably, the term was derived from the French word, *entreprendre*, meaning to undertake, also a root of the English word "enterprise." Cantillon, considered by many to be one of the earliest significant contributors to monetary theories and economic cause-and-effect methodologies, defined an entrepreneur as an opportunist and risk taker, buying things at certain prices, hoping to sell at a profit. A prevalent entrepreneurial business model in his day was shipowner entrepreneurs, buying commodities or other goods in one port, hoping to sail part way around the world where they might be sold for a profit. In another model, factory owner entrepreneurs would pay laborers wages to produce goods, in effect buying the goods at determinate prices, hoping to sell the goods later to consumers for higher prices.

In the 19th century, Jean-Baptiste Say (1803) more extensively developed and used the concept of entrepreneurship, now in relation to the more strongly emerging entrepreneurial model of the Industrial Revolution. Say defined an entrepreneur as a producer and seller of products, seeking profit beyond the costs for utilizing the required resources (labor, materials, facilities, capital). According to Casson (1982):

> The term came into much wider use after John Stuart Mill popularized it in his 1848 classic, *Principles of Political Economy*, but then all but disappeared from the economics literature by the end of the nineteenth century.

Early in the 20th century, Knight (1921) defined entrepreneurs as those who "attempt to predict and act upon change." Later, Schumpeter (1934) equated the entrepreneur with the innovator, creating new products, new methods of production, new markets, new supply sources, or new organizations. Finally, Drucker (1985) refined and adopted the foregoing definitions and defined an entrepreneur as a change agent who employs innovation to create new value.

In my view, successful entrepreneurship and successful innovation are one and the same thing – the creation of new net value. An entrepreneur is someone who attempts to engage in innovation, and a successful entrepreneur is one who innovates successfully. But are the terms "innovator" and "entrepreneur" synonymous? What about the element of risk taking, which many argue is an essential aspect of entrepreneurship? Are all innovators "entrepreneurs"?

This brings us to consider the distinction between intrapreneurship and entrepreneurship. Gifford and Pinchot (1978) first introduced the notion of "intrapreneurs," referring to entrepreneurial innovators employed by corporations. The essential distinction (see McCrae, 1982) has to do with personal risk. An organization engaged in innovation is taking risks, and therefore the employees of the organization who are proposing and managing the risks, who are usually rewarded or punished accordingly, do so as agents of the company. But are they entrepreneurs? Do they instead have to be self-employed, or have their homes mortgaged on behalf of the company?

In some cases, when champions for innovation can't gain internal acceptance, they leave, taking their entrepreneurship elsewhere. For example, in the early 1990s, a survey of the Ottawa area, known as Silicon Valley North, indicated that about 80% of local technology businesses were started by former BNR (then the largest private R&D organization in Canada) employees. So, while much innovation was being spawned within

BNR, and ultimately commercialized by its parents (Nortel Networks and Bell Canada), a lot of innovation "leaked" into the local community in the form of new startups. A key example was Mitel. The founders initially tried to champion their idea for a new switch design internally, and after failing to gain approval to proceed, they left. A few years later, headquartered just down the road from BNR and populated by thousands of former BNR employees, Mitel had become a successful rival on a global basis. Intrapreneurship can clearly lead to entrepreneurship.

Also in the 1990s, many organizations, including those that formed the MIT Innovation Lab, engaged in organizational "reengineering" designed to encourage more entrepreneurship, thereby improving business results and, most especially, innovation. In some companies, executives were tested, and those who exhibited entrepreneurial characteristics and a willingness to take on greater personal risks and potential rewards were empowered to operate parts of the business as their own. They were given P&L responsibility for specific products, markets, or both. Having worked as both an intrapreneur and entrepreneur, many of us will have personal, subjective opinions about the differences. My overriding view is that the distinction is unnecessary, but that the concept and associated mindset of intrapreneurship can limit entrepreneurship.

I agree with Drucker's (1985) view that high risk is erroneously associated with entrepreneurship. Rather, an appetite for risk is more often associated with failed entrepreneurship – those lacking the experience, resources, and leadership qualities that contribute to successful innovation. Successful entrepreneurs hate risk, have a heightened sense of risks, and a disposition toward managing them carefully (see also Brown, 2013). As Gladwell (2010) said:

> Entrepreneurial spirit could not have less in common with that of the daring risk-taker of popular imagination. Would we so revere risk-taking if we realized that the people who are supposedly taking bold risks in the cause of entrepreneurship are doing no such thing?

So, dispensing with the myth that entrepreneurship is about taking risks, we might drop the distinction between entrepreneurs and intrapreneurs. Both are engaged in innovation, managing the inherent risks, and working to maximize ROI for their benefit and that of other stakeholders.

My definition of an entrepreneur is anyone engaged in entrepreneurship, which I define as an act or quality of leadership applied to the creation and manifestation of value. In other words, we're back to Schumpeter's (1934) and Drucker's (1985) definition: entrepreneurs are innovators. An entrepreneur's success or failure – how "good to great" they are – can be defined by their track record of innovation ROI. If you are trying to make the world, even a little corner of it, a better place, then you're an aspiring entrepreneur. The spirit of entrepreneurship is improvement. It is the attempt to create more from less – to create new value. Entrepreneurship can come in many specific forms – commercial, social, and even governmental or public. Any leader, of any type of organization, who is seeking to innovate – to manifest new net value – is imbued with entrepreneurial spirit, soul, and psyche. In conclusion, an entrepreneur is anyone trying to innovate. A successful entrepreneur is someone doing it well – achieving ROI.

Now that we've defined entrepreneurship, and its spirit, essence, or psyche, I hope you consider yourself one, whether or not you answered the questions at the start of this chapter in the affirmative. Let's now consider the entrepreneurial psyche in greater detail and, in particular, an important psychological concept, that of "flow."

Flow psychology

The concept of psychological "flow" was developed by Csikszentmihalyi, a psychologist concerned with happiness, creativity, and performance. Csikszentmihalyi (1990) defined flow as an exceptional state of high performance where the performers become totally absorbed in a very challenging activity at which they are highly skilled. We can all probably think of personal instances where we became so engrossed in an activity that we lost track of time and self-awareness, becoming "at one" with the activity. Further, we can probably think of times when we admired athletes, musicians, or other performers who seemed to be in a state of flow, making their incredible performances look effortless.

Beyond telling us what it subjectively feels like to be in a state of flow, and suggesting what we need to be like to be more likely to experience it, "flow psychology" has not, in my view, provided any real insights into or recommendations on what people can do to tap into flow. Csikszentmihalyi

(1996) focused on creativity, suggesting that creative flow results from motivation, defining an "autotelic" personality type as someone who finds a particular activity inherently (intrinsically) motivating, rather than needing external rewards such as money or approval to drive them. But telling people to change their personality or motivations might be seen as not very useful for someone who might want to create more flow in their life or business.

Flow in business

My interest is the application of the concept of "flow" to business, and most particularly to the business of entrepreneurship. And when I say "application," I don't mean I'm satisfied to find some subjective correlations between entrepreneurial characteristics and aspects of "autotelic personality," such as curiosity, persistence, and humbleness. What I want to know is how to apply this knowledge to create more entrepreneurism in businesses, and to make such efforts more successful – to create more entrepreneurial flow. What enterprises and leaders need, and what this book provides, is a systematic approach, built on a new psychological and strategic framework for entrepreneurial innovation, for innovation.

Csikszentmihalyi's (2004) prescriptions for how to create flow in organizations are "clear goals that can be adapted to meet changing conditions; immediate feedback to one's actions; and a matching of the challenges of the job with the worker's skills." While I agree with each point, this falls far short of delivering a model for how to create flow in businesses.

I've also been disappointed by the so-called "flow movement" (see flowidealism.org/Vision/overview). In my view, it has failed to link its work to flow psychology, and offers nothing substantive on how to create more entrepreneurial success, other than the already prevalent and hardly new or unique view that entrepreneurs and businesses should try to make the world a better place. Agreed, but "ho hum." Positioning flow as a global "movement" does not satisfy my desire to understand how to create more entrepreneurial or business flow.

However, I remained convinced that the concept of flow would be highly valuable in the world of business – to understand entrepreneurship and innovation, and the wider phenomenon of value. For example, for years I intuited that "value flow" would be far more accurate and powerful than the metaphor of "value chains" for describing business models.

Chakras

The concept of "chakras" originated in the 8th century, and is popular in New Age spirituality, deriving from earlier Buddhist and Hindu philosophies. The basic idea is that chakras are energy centers, connected together in a particular way, and loosely corresponding to specific areas of the body's anatomy. Each of the chakras is thought to be a center for a specific type of energy, and the premise is that if one or more of our chakras are relatively closed or constricted, the flow of vital energy within ourselves, our psyche, and our lives is thereby limited. Figure 4.1 defines the seven chakras.

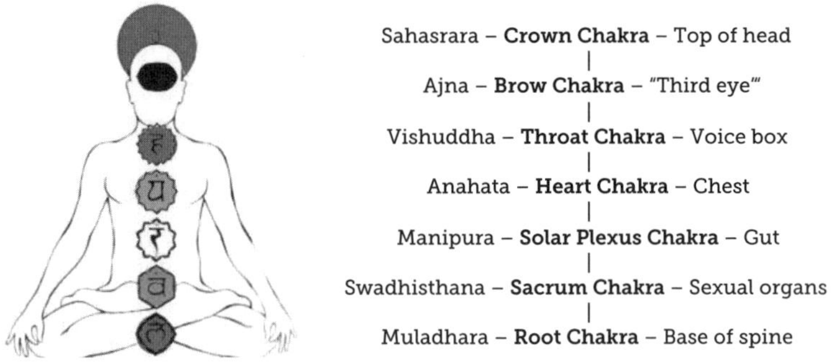

FIGURE 4.1 Chakras
Source: Wikipedia & Wikimedia Commons

An entrepreneurial interpretation of chakras

In building toward a definition of entrepreneurial flow, let me first translate the chakra definitions into psychological terms applicable to the task at hand, shown in Table 4.1.

TABLE 4.1 Psychological translation of chakras

Chakra	Approximate meaning (see http://en.wikipedia.org/wiki/Chakra)	Psychological translation
Crown	Spirit: essential purpose	Spirit, passions, and purpose
Brow	Third eye: developing intellect and insight	Insight, vision, and goals
Throat	Voice: finding and speaking your truth	Integrity and influence
Heart	Heart: finding and cultivating love	Collaboration and partnering
Solar plexus	Power: finding and manifesting power	Responsibility and empowerment
Sacrum	Creation: finding and channelling creativity	Creativity and ideation
Root	Root: underlying potential, ego, survival	Drive, expertise, and mindset

Entrepreneurial functions

Let's now consider how the above translations of chakra energies apply to entrepreneurial psychology and, in the first instance, to the psychological functions required of entrepreneurs:

1 A "root" functional requirement for entrepreneurship is the right **mindset** based on a combination of domain expertise, skills, drive, and a restless discontentment with "what is." Not everyone can be an entrepreneur, just by wishing for it.

2 The next requirement is **ideation** – the ability to generate and develop ideas. Arguably, successful entrepreneurs must have their "big idea" – their great product or way to make the world a better place.

3 To turn ideas into reality, entrepreneurs require the ability to take personal responsibility and to attract, engage, and empower whatever other resources (including investment or R&D) are required to bring their ideas into being. Effective **empowerment** goes "hand in glove" with responsibility. On the one hand, taking personal responsibility requires self-empowerment, and on the other, the only responsible way to empower others is to hold them responsible and accountable for their results.

4 The ability to form win–win collaborative **partnerships** by connecting and developing functional relationships with customers, investors, partners, and all other potential stakeholders is the next fundamental requirement for entrepreneurship to succeed.

5 The ability to **influence**, with integrity, through articulating and communicating the big idea or USP, the essential "truth" being offered to the world, is the next key requirement for entrepreneurial success.
6 Insight connecting to an audacious **goal** (or cluster of goals) is a starting point for entrepreneurship, illustrating the fact that the seven aspects of entrepreneurial psyche are not sequential, but are simultaneously required to achieve flow and success. The entrepreneur must have strategic insight, a big idea for how to create value, and a specific vision of what success entails.
7 Last, but not least, the entrepreneur must have a strong sense of **purpose** – of the "why" for their big idea – essential entrepreneurial spirit.

I find it useful to view the psychological elements of entrepreneurship in a pyramid (Figure 4.2).

FIGURE 4.2 Psychological elements of entrepreneurship

The entrepreneurial brain

It's also interesting to speculate that there may be two sides to each of the above "coins" of entrepreneurial psyche, possibly related to left- and right-brain function (see Bolte Taylor, 2008 for a fascinating descriptive case), as illustrated in Figure 4.3.

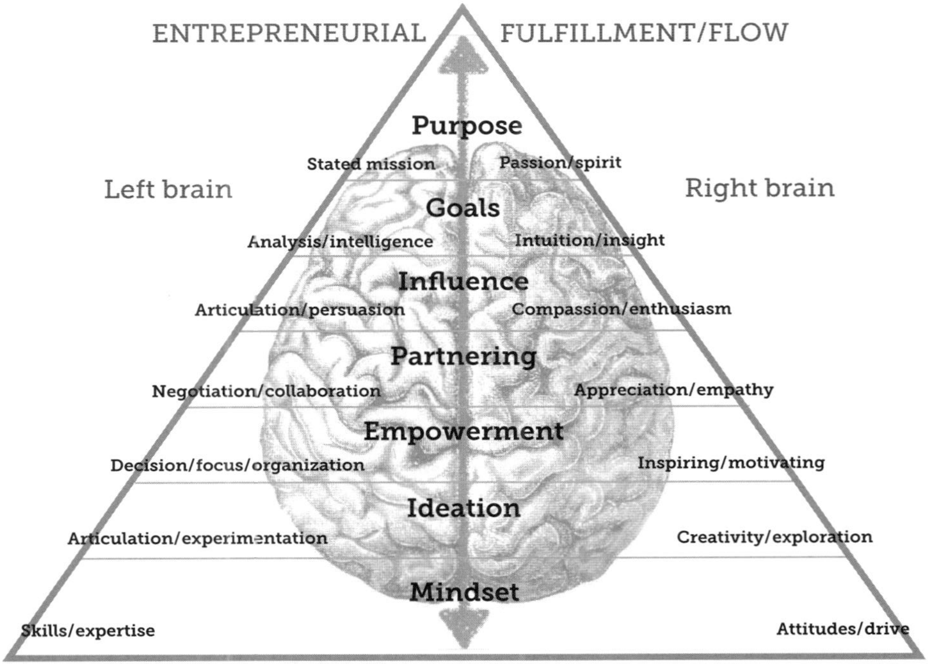

FIGURE 4.3 Possible left- and right-brain aspects of entrepreneurial psychology

Source: Brain image from Wikimedia CC BY-SA 3.0

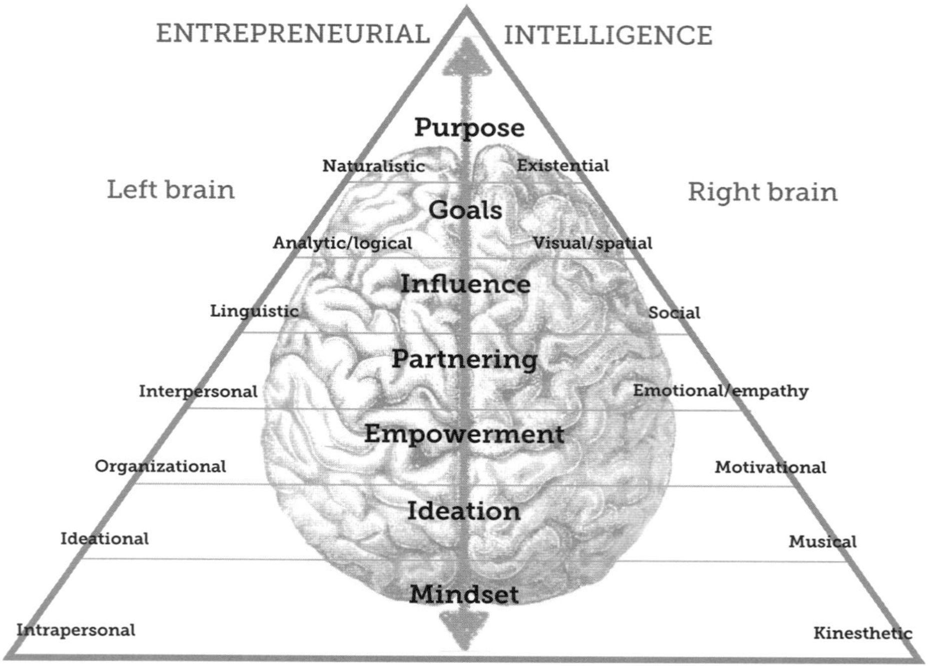

FIGURE 4.4 Possible left- and right-brain aspects of entrepreneurial intelligence

Source: Brain image from Wikimedia CC BY-SA 3.0

Entrepreneurial intelligence

It might also be of interest to consider various aspects of intelligence, whether or not we agree with Gardner's (1983) theory of multiple intelligences, as opposed to a more holistic model of general intelligence. Gardner initially proposed eight, and later added a ninth intelligence. In Figure 4.4, I've indicated how I think these aspects of intelligence may relate to the left- and right-brain aspects of the entrepreneurial psyche centers. But in order to complete the model, five additional aspects of intelligence are required. Emotional and social intelligence, missing from Gardner's list, are well defined and researched (as discussed previously). However, I see three additional aspects of intelligence needed to complete the model: two related to what we might consider "leadership intelligence," the ability to organize and motivate resources, and a third, left-brain function, the ability to generate and work with creative ideas, which we might term "ideational intelligence."

Entrepreneurial functions and inspirations

Let's take a moment to consider the entrepreneurial psyche centers, alongside the crucial functions and sources of inspiration for the functions (see Table 4.2). Note that each function is essential for the corresponding virtue, and in turn draws on – is inspired by – specific further aspects of psychological makeup:

1. Entrepreneurial **spirit**, and the sense of purpose that results, is inspired by **passions** and **love**.
2. An entrepreneur's **insight**, and resulting goal, is inspired by **belief** in and/or **intuition** about what's possible.
3. **Integrity**, and the resulting ability to influence others and the world toward manifesting their strategic intent (purpose and goals), is inspired by **enthusiasm** and **compassion**.
4. **Collaboration**, and the resulting ability to partner effectively, is inspired by **attraction** to others and/or their toys (resources) and is the **inspiration** for developing a win–win relationship.
5. **Responsibility**, and the resulting ability to empower resources effectively, is inspired by **courage** and **accountability** of self and others.
6. The **creativity** that generates ideation, the formation and development of the entrepreneur's idea(s), is inspired by **receptivity** and **openness** to ideas from within and without.

7 Last, but not least, the entrepreneur's underlying **drive**, and resulting mindset, is inspired by a fundamental **optimism** and **hope** that "what is" can become better.

TABLE 4.2 Crucial functions and inspirations of entrepreneurial psyche

Entrepreneurial center	Crucial functions	Sources of inspiration
Purpose	Spirit	Passions and love
Goals	Insight	Belief and intuition
Influence	Integrity	Enthusiasm and compassion
Partnering	Collaboration	Attraction and inspiration
Empowerment	Responsibility	Courage and accountability
Ideation	Creativity	Openness and receptivity
Mindset	Drive	Optimism and hope

Entrepreneurial drivers and needs

Now let's consider (see Table 4.3) how the functional centers of entrepreneurship are powered by underlying drivers that each relate to specific psychological needs and components of value. These drivers, needs, and values function as the sources of motivation for entrepreneurship:

1 Spirited purpose is underpinned by effective **championship**, motivated by the indomitable human drive toward **actualization** – the fulfillment of the essential purpose of our entrepreneurial spirit.

2 Insightful goals require underlying knowledge and intelligence based on the results of **learning** – motivated by a need or desire for **understanding**.

3 Integrous influence requires an ability to **persuade** others – to sell them on supporting, investing in, or adopting the entrepreneur's dream or innovation, motivated by a desire to **express**, or to be heard.

4 Collaborative partnering ability requires underlying emotional intelligence, or **empathy**, which is motivated by a desire to form a mutually **appreciative** relationship.

5 Responsible empowerment requires **change agency**, motivated by **confidence** that something better is possible, and by the desire to achieve confidence in the ongoing benefits of change through appropriate risk avoidance and mitigation.

6 Creative ideation, to be effective, must be solidly underpinned by some sort of domain **expertise** from which the entrepreneur derives and is motivated by **pleasure**.
7 The driven entrepreneurial mindset derives from an underlying **discontentment**, motivated by a desire for **contentment** that will arguably never be achieved, in that the entrepreneur's glass will always be only half-full, no matter how full it may get (the glass expands).

These relationships are summarized in Table 4.3.

TABLE 4.3 Drivers and needs underlying entrepreneurial virtues

Functional centers of entrepreneurship	Entrepreneurial drives	Psychological value/ needs
Spirited purpose	Championship	Actualization
Insightful goals	Learning	Understanding
Integrous influence	Persuasion	Expression
Collaborative partnering	Empathy	Appreciation
Responsible empowerment	Change agency	Confidence
Creative ideation	Expertise	Pleasure
Driven mindset	Discontentment	Contentment

Entrepreneurial virtues

Entrepreneurial flow can occur when the seven aspects of psyche are bridged effectively – aligned, mutually supportive and effective, or open. We can therefore describe healthy, high-functioning entrepreneurial psyche centers as "entrepreneurial virtues":

1 **Spirited purpose:** An entrepreneur's essential mission, inspired by passions and love, driven toward fulfillment and actualization – the search for meaning and the desire to make the world, or some small part of it (such as the entrepreneur's business), a better place. As Robert F. Kennedy said: "The purpose of life is to contribute in some way to making things better."
2 **Insightful goals:** An entrepreneur's desire for and dream of success exists in the form of goal(s) based on insight, which are therefore

specific, measurable, attainable, relevant, and time bound (SMART). As Walt Disney said: "If you can dream it, you can do it."

3 **Integrous influence:** An entrepreneur's ability to give voice to or express the core value proposition or USP of the intended innovation – the ability to market and sell it, influencing others to value it and potentially to help bring it into being – all with integrity, enthusiasm, and compassion, or caring for the needs of others, driven by the fundamental need for expression and the ability to persuade or "sell." As Drucker (1985) said: "The purpose of a business is to create and keep a customer."

4 **Collaborative partnering:** An entrepreneur's ability to engage relevant stakeholders in win–win relationships, connecting, first and foremost, with the intended customer – manifesting value for all stakeholders based on the ability to empathize and the fundamental need for appreciation – inspired by mutual attraction or chemistry, and the inspiration to form a win–win relationship. As Tapscott (2013) said:

> Collaboration is important not just because it's a better way to learn. The spirit of collaboration is penetrating every institution and all of our lives. So learning to collaborate is part of equipping yourself for effectiveness, problem solving, innovation and life-long learning in an ever-changing networked economy.

5 **Responsible empowerment:** An entrepreneur's ability to marshal, attract, inspire, lead and manage all the resources required to develop and deliver their offering – empowering them to get the job of innovation done. Responsible empowerment requires a combination of ensuring that those empowered have the resources, skills, and "rope" to be effective, and that they're held accountable. Empowerment is driven by entrepreneurial "change agency" and confidence, and motivated by a desire to avoid and appropriately mitigate and manage risks, but also inspired by courage and the ability to take appropriate risks. As Dwight D. Eisenhower said: "Leadership is the art of getting someone else to do something you want done because he wants to do it."

6 **Creative ideation:** The process of having an idea and then developing it is underpinned by mastery – domain expertise or an area of skill and knowledge that serves as the focus for creativity and the source or basis for ideas. Mastery drives toward the psychological value component of pleasure, in that an entrepreneur's greatest pleasure is arguably the creative process, and especially the moment a "great idea" is formed.

The rest is hard work. The underlying inspiration for creative ideation is hope for improvement – for innovation. As Benjamin Franklin said: "Without continual growth and progress, such words as improvement, achievement, and success have no meaning."

7 **Driven mindset:** An entrepreneur's underlying discontentment, and the inherent need or desire to move toward contentment, is an essential restlessness that serves as the "root" ingredient of an effective entrepreneur's psychological makeup. The glass is always only ever half-full. But underneath this is the entrepreneur's paradox; the fact that the entrepreneurial mindset is based on restless discontentment and also inspired by optimism that the glass can always be filled a little or a lot more. As Thomas Edison (*c.* 1930) said: "Restlessness is discontent – and discontent is the first necessity of progress. Show me a thoroughly satisfied man – and I will show you a failure."

Entrepreneurial competencies

Dyer et al. (2011) offer fascinating insights into the behavioral skills or core competencies of successful innovators. Based on interviews with various types of entrepreneurial innovators (startup, corporate, product, and process), they identified five behaviors that differentiated them from non-innovators. Unsurprisingly, these behavioral skills relate to five of the entrepreneurial virtues identified above. Additionally, there are important skills not identified by Dyer et al., which I believe highlights the weakness of interview research – hearing what one expects or wants to hear. The seven constellations of behavioral skills associated with the entrepreneurial virtues above are as follows (with the five from Dyer et al. identified in bold):

1 Purposefulness as a core competency manifests as being results driven, fueled by clear strategic intent. Such individuals tend to clearly convey their sense of purpose and passion to others. Their restless discontentment with "what is" tends to be obvious, as is their ability to champion their cause. These behavioral skills are readily apparent when looking at the individuals Dyer et al. interviewed or referred to, such as Steve Jobs (Apple), Jeff Bezos (Amazon), and Richard Branson (Virgin), and also apparent in others I've worked with, such as Larry Ellison (Oracle) and John Roth (Nortel), but were not identified as a core competency for

entrepreneurship. That said, as we progress through the list, you will appreciate that all the core competencies are interrelated, and therefore elements of purposefulness can be seen in skills that Dyer et al. identified.

2 Being visionary is a core competency that links to purposefulness through the strategic intent manifested in championship, and underpinned by intelligence. Dyer et al. got it half right, in identifying the skill of **observing** as a key entrepreneurial competency. Observing reflects the intellectual curiosity of entrepreneurs that serves as a foundation for their arsenal of business intelligence. But the other key aspect of being visionary is dreaming the audacious goals for a better world, which are achievable when founded on intelligence. Being visionary only works well when underpinned by learning and understanding – a solid foundation in observed reality.

3 Communication as a core competency links to vision through intelligence – the ability to influence, infecting others with enthusiasm for the vision and value of innovation. Dyer et al. identified **questioning** as a key skill, which is an important communication skill, along with listening, articulating, clarifying, and expressing enthusiasm. To be effective, all of it requires integrity, compassion, and a strong base of core values.

4 The ability to meaningfully engage others in win–win innovation is another core competency, supported by the skill of **networking** identified by Dyer et al. They position networking as building rich, diverse networks, attending conferences, building creative communities, and engaging outsiders and experts – all to stimulate new ideas. Networks can serve as a source of ideas and connections for collaborations, but the ability to build solid partnerships also requires emotional intelligence (empathy) and the ability to attract and inspire others.

5 Leadership as a core competency, based on responsible, effective empowerment of resources, requires a range of specific skills, attributes, and behaviors including courage, resolve (change agency), and emotional intelligence – none of which Dyer et al. identified, although few people would see the entrepreneurs they interviewed as anything other than highly impressive leaders.

6 Creation – the ability to generate and exploit ideas for improvement and change and the development of winning capabilities and advantages – is supported by **association**, which Dyer et al. identified as a key skill. The ability to link ideas is a fundamental human cognitive skill supporting creativity, along with being open to new ideas, receptive to the wellspring

of creativity that exists within us all, and developing mastery and domain expertise within an area for our entrepreneurial focus and innovation.

7 Last but not least, the driven mindset of an effective entrepreneur links to purposefulness through the dance of discontentment/contentment, the drive to act – to perform, to achieve desired results. The core competency is arguably nothing less than the persona of the entrepreneur – the holistic reflection of their being, attitudes, motivations, aspirations, and hope. The drive to act, to make things happen, and to try things out is supported by the skill of **experimenting**, identified by Dyer et al. Additional skills important to any given entrepreneur also include expertise related to the enterprise domain, and the HR management ability to create a culture that reflects the entrepreneur's personal psyche. As Dyer et al. point out, the most innovative organizations are the ones that get the right people in place, establish processes for manifesting all the key entrepreneurial skills (questioning, observing, networking, brainstorming, and prototyping/experimenting), and manifest a philosophy (culture) of innovation (as everyone's job, being "disruptive," establishing innovation teams, and taking smart risks).

Entrepreneurial DNA and flow

What emerges from the foregoing consideration of the entrepreneurial psyche is a simple human truth. There is nothing more natural than to aspire, desire, want, and need to become a successful entrepreneur. It is in our DNA, as well as in the psychic DNA of human cultures and organizations (some more than others). When the elements of entrepreneurial DNA (illustrated in Figure 4.5, which also compares the "innovator's DNA" according to Dyer et al.) are effectively functioning *and* aligned, supported by core competencies and the specific associated skills, the "magic" can happen – entrepreneurial peak performance, or flow.

The concept of entrepreneurial flow is simply this: making the most of what one has. Naturally, all entrepreneurs are not "created equal," some achieve greater value flow than others. Entrepreneurs experience widely divergent rates of innovation success, compared to others and often within their own careers. And there are important qualitative differences, whereby the success of some entrepreneurs tends to be thought of in more commercial terms, while others clearly made the world a better place, brought highly valued new products into being, or in some cases drove social innovations of various kinds. Some of my favorite examples of social innovation and entrepreneurship include Mahatma Gandhi, Martin Luther King Jr, and Emmeline Pankhurst. All successful entrepreneurs have the seven virtues in common: driven persona, creative ideation, responsible empowerment, collaborative partnering, integrous influence, insightful goals, and spirited purpose.

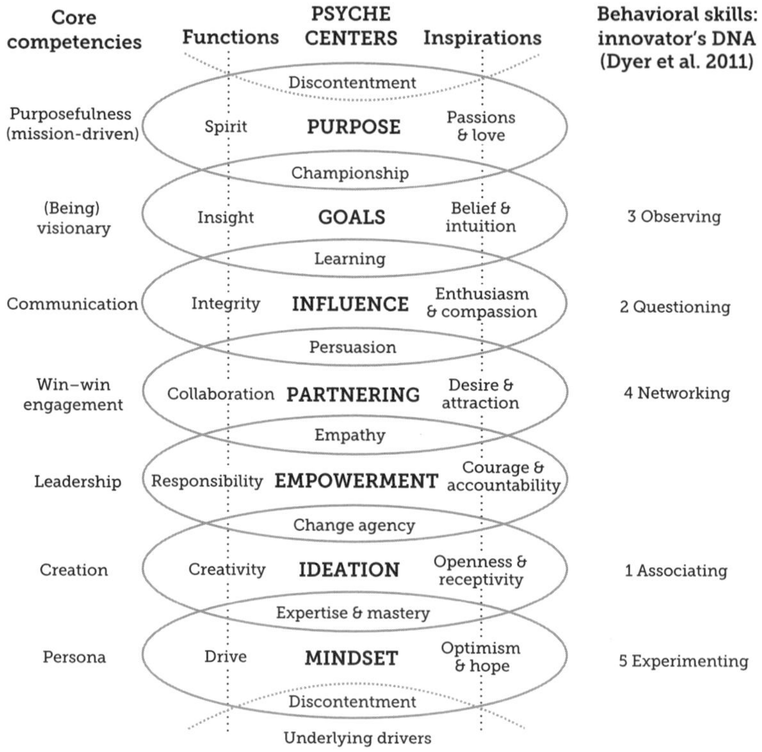

FIGURE 4.5 Entrepreneurial DNA

So the question becomes: How can we develop entrepreneurial psyche and culture, and translate these into successful innovation? We'll turn to the answer in Chapter 5. What we need is a strategic model for entrepreneurship, one that enables bridging between the soft stuff of entrepreneurial psyche and culture and the hard stuff of strategy and innovation.

chapter 5

Strategy

"Nothing is more difficult than the art of maneuvering for advantageous position."

Sun Tzu (6th century BC)

The elements of strategy

For many years, I've struggled to use various frameworks for strategic planning and management. I'm not saying I struggled in the sense that I failed to create and implement strategies to achieve success. I was involved in quite a few successful strategies, and, of course, some spectacular failures. My point is I tried many different approaches for formulating, organizing, and implementing strategies, and found most of them lacking in a number of key respects.

Most strategy frameworks seemed to lack coherence, in that the various elements of strategy didn't seem to hang together in a logical way. Some frameworks placed vision at the top of a strategy pyramid, which seemed to make sense. What better to place at the top than a definition of success – the mountain to be climbed, and a sense of what it will look and feel like to get there? And yet it somehow didn't seem right to place mission below vision. Without a clear mission or purpose, how can one define "success"? You need to know what game you're playing before you can envision the win. Even more confusing were structures suggested by the Balanced Scorecard Institute (see http://balancedscorecard.org/Resources/AbouttheBalancedScorecard), seeming to suggest that vision and strategy are two distinct but related things, while vision is obviously a core aspect of strategy and is usually positioned as such by strategists.

Over the years, I eventually created my own sense of structure among what I considered to be the key elements of strategies and plans:

1. **Mission**: Strategy starts with purpose, defining why we exist, what war we're trying to win, what game we're playing, and essentially what we exist to do.
2. **Vision:** Then we need to know exactly what we're trying to achieve, what it means to win, and how we'll know when we've won – how we'll measure it, or what it will look and feel like. Note how these top two elements of strategy are inextricably linked. Understanding what war we're fighting and what it means to win are inseparable.
3. **Communication:** The next essential element of strategy is communication with a specific purpose – to influence – and specifically to market and sell. Marketing and selling have external and internal aspects. Success requires influencing customers and markets to adopt the products and innovations created by the enterprise. It also requires internally marketing and selling the strategy. For example, communicating the mission and vision is vitally important. If anyone in an enterprise doesn't understand the mission or vision, they can't possibly contribute effectively.
4. **Engagement:** Collaborative win–win stakeholder engagement is inextricably linked to communication; in fact, it starts with communication but extends to all aspects of relationships, including relationship building, partnering, and relationship management. Value is manifested, delivered, and experienced in stakeholder relationships – to the greatest extent when the relationships are collaborative. The entire pattern of operational value delivery and stakeholder value experience is one way of thinking about an organization's business model.
5. **Leadership:** The next element of strategy is essentially the plans and actions for how resources will be applied to achieve the overall strategy. This must be based on understanding what resources are available, deciding how to apply the resources – creating vital focus, directing as well as motivating and inspiring them. I think of this as "resource empowerment" – putting resources in motion, "powering" or "empowering" them, and holding them responsible and accountable. Leadership is also about self-empowerment and responsibility, and in the best organizations, it's about enabling leadership to happen at all levels throughout the organization.

6 **Creation:** The realm of ideas and creativity is linked to leadership through change agency and transformation. Ideas for improvement must be generated, developed, mixed with other ideas, or rejected in favor of better ones. Driving from ideas to reality is a vital aspect of strategy, linking to the final element.

7 **Culture:** The final element of strategy is where the rubber meets the road – organizational culture. This is where potential is translated into performance. This is the "coalface" level of individual egos, team dynamics, and behavior. It's where individual psychologies meet and mingle in the "soup" of organizational psychology. Organizations are made up of people – individual psychologies that communicate, interact, behave, and misbehave in complex ways we might think of as group psychology, or "culture." This is the "root" realm of potentiality or capability to implement strategy – the abilities, skills, expertise of individuals and organizations, put into action and shaped by mindsets (personalities, motives, beliefs, and attitudes). This is also the realm of "action in the now," where performance translates into strategic results to be monitored and assessed.

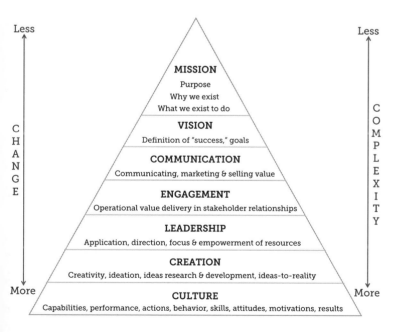

FIGURE 5.1 Elements of enterprise strategy

I find it helpful to conceptualize the elements of strategy as a pyramid, as illustrated in Figure 5.1, because it conveniently and simply shows the relationship of strategy elements. There's also a logic underlying the pyramid shape, based on the fact that there is much greater detail and complexity involved lower in the hierarchy, and also much more churn or change required.

Strategy and the entrepreneurial virtues

You've probably already noticed that the elements of strategy relate directly to the seven entrepreneurial virtues, as per Table 5.1.

TABLE 5.1 Entrepreneurial virtues related to elements of strategy

Elements of strategy	Entrepreneurial virtues and related aspects of strategy to be defined and realized
Mission	Spirited purpose: why and what we exist to do
Vision	Insightful goals: what it means to win and achieve success
Communication	Integrous influence: communicating, marketing, and selling value
Engagement	Collaborative partnering: stakeholder engagement and value experience
Leadership	Responsible empowerment: directing, organizing, and applying resources
Creation	Creative ideation: creativity, ideas for improvement and value creation
Culture	Driven persona: psychology, personality, beliefs, attitudes, motivations, skills and expertise, behavior in action

Strategy nesting

In fact, each of the elements of strategy is and must be supported by nested elements related to smaller units of the organization, down to the level of all individuals involved in any aspect of strategy planning or implementation. Figure 5.2 illustrates the "nesting" of missions.

The overall organizational mission must be supported by the missions of specific divisions, subsidiaries, or operating units, which, in turn, must be supported by the missions of specific functions, departments, or teams, which must also be supported by the missions or purposes of each team member, each individual in the organization.

FIGURE 5.2 Nested missions

There can be many levels and a great deal of nesting required in large, complex organizations. Or there might be only two levels in a small organization, one for the organization, and one for the individual partners or members of it. Regardless of size, if any of these missions are out of alignment, then the lower missions won't support the overarching mission.

Note that vertical connections from lower to higher missions can be thought of as representing aligned support, while horizontal links can be thought of as representing coordination or interdependence of lower level missions.

Exactly the same points can be made for the other elements of strategy:

- The overall vision of organizational success must be supported by more specific visions for parts of the organization, and should ultimately be supported by the aligned goals of individual contributors.
- The organization's overall communication, marketing, and sales strategies must be supported by lower, aligned communications right down to the level of individual influence.
- Overall stakeholder engagement must translate into more specific stakeholder engagement at lower levels, all the way down to individual relationships.
- Leadership must also cascade down into the organization, all the way to individual empowerment and management of resources.

- Overall creation within an organization must also be supported by creation at every level, all the way down to the creativity and ideas of specific individuals.
- Finally, the overall organization's culture consists of individual psychologies, mindsets, skill sets, personalities, and personas meeting and mingling at various levels such that specific subcultures may exist within distinct teams or units.

Demystifying strategy

I've met quite a few SME owners who don't have explicit strategies. In some cases, they gloss over the issue with statements such as "our strategy is to make money," or "we're just trying to survive in these tough times." I've also met business owners and senior executives of large enterprises who are cynical about strategy, feeling that it's simply a way for consulting firms to sell services, which results in little more than glossy documents that end up adorning shelves or drawers, with little practical relevance to the day-to-day operations of their enterprises. Perhaps, therefore, it may be useful to demystify the concept of strategy:

- **Planning:** At a basic level, strategy is nothing more than thinking ahead – having and using a plan. The plan may be to win or survive, grow or retreat and exit as gracefully as possible. A strategy exists if there is strategic intent to do or achieve something, and any sort of planned, directed action engaged in for that purpose.
- **Learning:** Another example of strategy is the act of consciously trying things out and learning from results, versus just bumbling along.
- **Coordination:** Strategy is also in action when there is any effort to coordinate interdependent activities based on formal agreement, resource commitments, and accountability for outcomes.
- **SWOT management:** Looking for ways to exploit opportunities, counteract threats, manage risks, develop new strengths, and eliminate weakness and waste are also examples of strategy in action.
- **Leading:** Any attempt to lead and manage resources with the intention of achieving specific goals engages strategy.
- **Innovation:** Focusing on maximizing the value that's created and delivered by an enterprise is a final example of strategy.

- **Change management:** Anyone consciously dealing with change is employing strategy. Strategy is about being proactive as well as reactive, responding to, driving and managing change – anticipating versus always being surprised.

The cyclicity of strategy

The process of developing and implementing strategy is and must be cyclic, as shown in Figure 5.3. Many organizations engage in cycles of strategic planning: a board retreat in January (somewhere nice and warm, with great golf, food, and wine to fuel the creative juices), February edicts to divisional managers, March development of strategic delivery plans, April budgets, and so on, with the whole thing ending up in a neatly bound document, in the front left-hand drawer of the CEO's desk. Instead, effective strategy is more about doing, rather than planning.

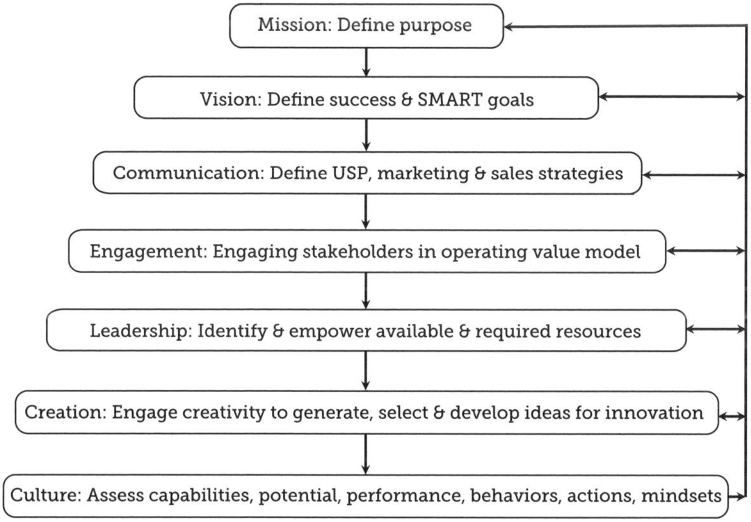

FIGURE 5.3 Strategy as a process

All the elements of the planning and implementation process are linked. A mission may require reconsideration based on the emergence of a new vision for success. The vision will need to be changed if marketing, sales, stakeholder engagement, and resource application reveal that it's not achievable or perhaps not audacious enough. As real-world performance and results kick in, it may emerge that more resources are required, which then either need to be applied, or if not available, goals and targets may need to be reconsidered, perhaps even calling the overall vision and mission into question.

Strategic dreaming

In one sense, strategy is about dreaming a new reality (vision) while staying true to purpose (mission). An exciting new dream might lead to reconsideration and perhaps expansion of purpose. Then, as we get into the realities of implementing our dream, it may need to change.

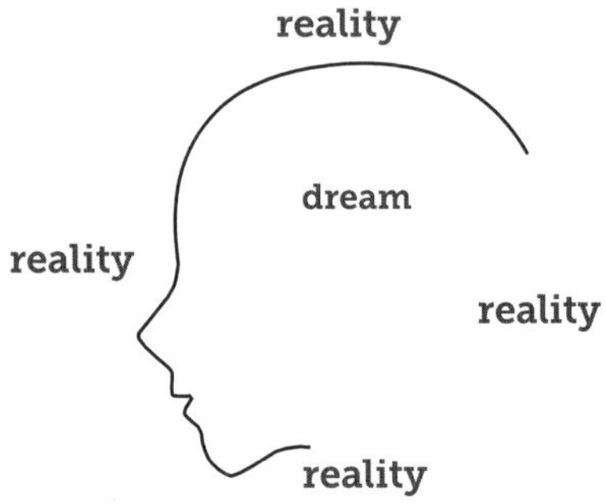

FIGURE 5.4 Strategy as dreaming

The cyclicity of strategy can also be seen in the "dream" metaphor (Figure 5.4). We may find our dream is ahead of its time – that there's no way to manifest it in a feasible business or value delivery model. Perhaps the market, regulators, investors, or employees aren't ready to engage and enable the dream. Or perhaps in the process of defining specific objectives in relation to stakeholders, we find that some are clearly not achievable, requiring us to reconsider the dream. Maybe we simply don't have the required resources, requiring us to either get more, or if we can't, reconsider our objectives. Or we may find we're stymied by lack of ideas, obstacles to change, or organizational inertia. And, of course, ultimately, when the "rubber meets the road" of strategy implementation, we may find reality really "bites." Our performance as individuals, teams, or whole organizations may simply fail to work, requiring us to come up with new ideas, apply new resources, or reconsider even higher elements of the strategy.

The cyclical nature of strategy as a process should now be clear, so finally we consider how the elements and process of strategy relate to the psyche centers of entrepreneurial flow, defining what I think of as "strategic DNA."

Strategic DNA

One thing that struck me early on was the obvious similarity between the aspects of individual entrepreneurial psyche and the elements of organizational strategy. I started to see these as existing in a kind of "dance," a highly interactive double helix of DNA (see Figure 5.5). I see this as the DNA of enterprise function, of psychology and strategy. Of course, the "dance" of relationship is also a form of bridging between individual entrepreneurship and organizational strategy, where both are aimed at innovation.

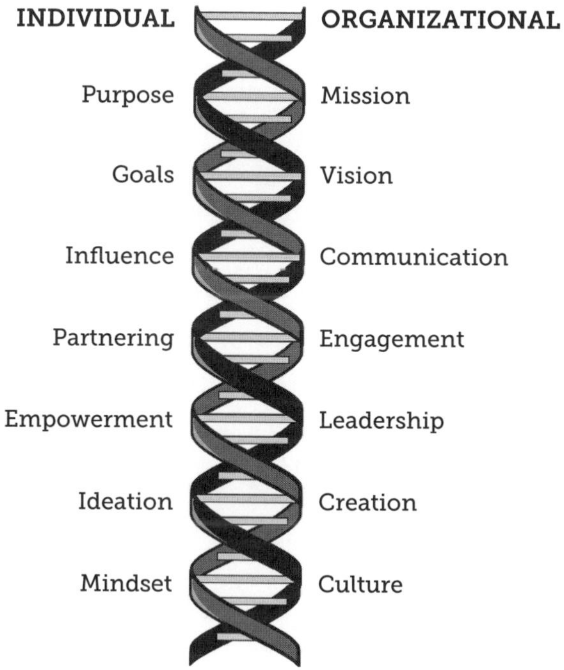

FIGURE 5.5 Strategic DNA

Source: Strand image adapted from www.clker.com, user OCAL

With the framework for strategic entrepreneurial innovation defined, we can now consider the phenomena of "innovation zoning" (Chapter 6) and "bridging" (Chapter 7) – how and why some entrepreneurs and organizations get it fantastically right. Then in Part II, Chapters 8–14, we consider the seven sins of innovation – how and why things go horribly wrong – and what to do about it.

chapter 6

The Innovation Zone and Innovation Zoning

"The greatest danger for most of us is not that our aim is too high and we miss it, but that it is too low and we reach it."

Michelangelo (*c.* 1530)

The zone

What does it mean to be "in the zone"? In terms of individual psychology, it means doing, being and feeling good, or great. It means being in a state of flow. This is also true for organizational psychology and the phenomenon of innovation zoning. I define "innovation zoning" as:

- Maximizing innovation ROI – new net value manifestation – as measured and tracked in relation to relevant stakeholders.
- Doing innovation effectively, actively engaged in it, trying, experimenting, perhaps even failing at times, but learning and improving.
- Being an innovator, and ideally an innovation leader within a particular industry, market, or area of human enterprise.
- Being in a state of entrepreneurial flow.
- Feeling good or great about the tangible, measurable results, such as return on innovation investments, competitive advantage, and the resulting growth of share and profits.

- Feeling the love, in terms of customer appreciation, feedback, value, advocacy, and loyalty. These good feelings will extend to boards of directors, owners, employees, and other stakeholders. Love has a tendency to spread. It's infectious.

Based on previous definitions of innovation, the innovation zone can now be defined as new net value creation, and value defined as a psychological state deriving from fulfillment, entrepreneurial flow, and entrepreneurial strategy.

As Figure 6.1 suggests, potential innovation ROI is exponentially driven by "bridging" – a phenomenon detailed in Chapter 7. The underlying reality is that the value that is experienced in any relationship increases based on the *quality* of the relationship, which, in my view, is determined by bridging. Therefore, the value created and manifested by an enterprise through innovation increases based on the enterprise's effectiveness at building, managing, and optimizing all the relationships within which the value is to be created and manifested.

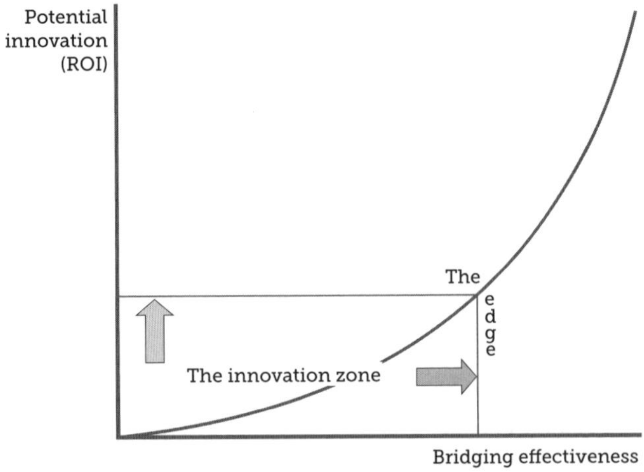

FIGURE 6.1 The innovation zone

There are various aspects to effective bridging, including bridging between entrepreneurship and strategy, between individual and organizational psychology, and between the psyche centers. Individual entrepreneurs must bridge aspects of their own psyche – functions, drivers, motivators, fundamental needs, and desired outcomes. Similarly, organizations must bridge across functions and specific strategic agendas, in order to achieve desired outcomes and overall success.

In the broadest sense, bridging is also about building effective relationships – engaging people, and their diverse perspectives, values, disciplines, and thoughts. Collaboration, creative conflict, customer-driven design, open innovation processes, creative partnering, successful commercialization of technologies, successful change management, "blue ocean" strategy, and other realizations of human potential are key examples of successful bridging. A systematic, strategic approach to bridging the vital hard stuff and soft stuff is required to achieve entrepreneurial innovation and strategic success.

The innovation zone reflects an organization's ability to create, produce, and deliver value within specific relationships (bridges), such as the all-important relationship with customers. Note that the innovation "zone" is different from innovation "zoning," which is all about maximizing – being on the cutting edge.

The innovation zone might also be thought of as the innovation "sandbox" within which the enterprise "plays." The point about "innovation play" is that enterprises won't, indeed can't always get it right. There will inevitably be initial faltering steps, false starts, blind alleys, and failed experiments. No play, no gain. As Thomas Watson of IBM said (cited in van Oech, 1983): "If you want to increase your success rate, double your failure rate."

Appropriately led organizations, those driven to live on the edge, will expand and indeed maximize their innovation zone, as illustrated by the arrows in Figure 6.1, representing efforts to expand organizational innovation zones. Such organizations will develop long-term, sustainable advantages. They'll tend to achieve superior innovation results, in terms of value creation and ROI. And, over time, they will benefit from ongoing work to expand their innovation zones. I call this "learning on the edge."

Zoning

In contrast, innovation "zoning" is the result of being on the "edge," maximizing value creation, by optimizing entrepreneurial flow and strategy and consistently hitting the sweet spot – the cutting edge, as shown in the upper right-hand corner of the innovation zone in Figure 6.1. In that sense, innovation zoning is about innovation leadership – leading on "the edge," prompting me to offer the following modification of the well-known quote (about living on the edge), from an unknown source: "If you're not living, leading, learning, and loving on the edge, you're taking up too much space."

chapter 7

The Art and Science of Bridging

"Whenever you're in conflict with someone, there is one factor that can make the difference between damaging your relationship and deepening it. That factor is attitude."

William James (1890)

Psychological bridges

Let's consider the various bridges that need to be built and driven across to succeed at entrepreneurial innovation. Let's also explicitly recognize that unlike physical bridges that are built and might last for years, the psychological relationship bridges we're considering here need to be continually created, re-created, developed, and optimized over time.

One of the key aspects of bridging is between individuals and organizations; on the one hand, the ability of individual, entrepreneurial champions to engage teams and organizations, and on the other hand, the ability of organizations to engage individuals in innovation and strategy and develop entrepreneurial cultures.

Another vitally important set of bridges is between or across the psyche centers. As reflected in successful entrepreneurship, peak performance, and innovation zoning, flow happens when there's effective alignment and bridging across all seven psyche centers. Further, the central bridges that connect the psyche centers are, in effect, critical success factors. Collectively, they are the "critical path" for successful strategy, innovation, and entrepreneurship.

The bridging model

For each of these critical path connections, there are clear needs and desired outcomes, for individual entrepreneurs and organizations wishing to innovate.

For individuals, specific needs and desired outcomes have corresponding entrepreneurial drivers. In effect, these drivers "bridge" between individual needs or desired outcomes and the psyche center connection points. There are also key psychological functions centered between groups of drivers and outcomes. All these are shown in Figure 7.1.

The concept of a bridge is a useful metaphor for any relationship. I use the term "bridging" to refer not only to building relationship bridges, but also to maintaining them, strengthening them, and enabling greater flow of "stuff" over or through the bridge. The stuff that should ideally flow over relationship bridges includes information, communication, appreciation, and value. As stated earlier, value can only be delivered or experienced in relationship to people, products, organizations, or indeed anything. Therefore, the very notion of value and the related notions of innovation and entrepreneurship are inherently about bridging. Many specific bridges are required to achieve success.

Another bridge that must be effective for successful entrepreneurial innovation is the bridge between entrepreneurship and innovation – the ability for an aspiring entrepreneur to build an effective personal relationship with the innovation process.

Innovation is only rarely an individual effort. Therefore, bridging between individual psychologies and the resulting "stew" we call organizational culture is of paramount importance. In a sense, there's a bridge connecting each of the psyche centers in the double helix of the innovation dance between individuals and between individual and group psyches.

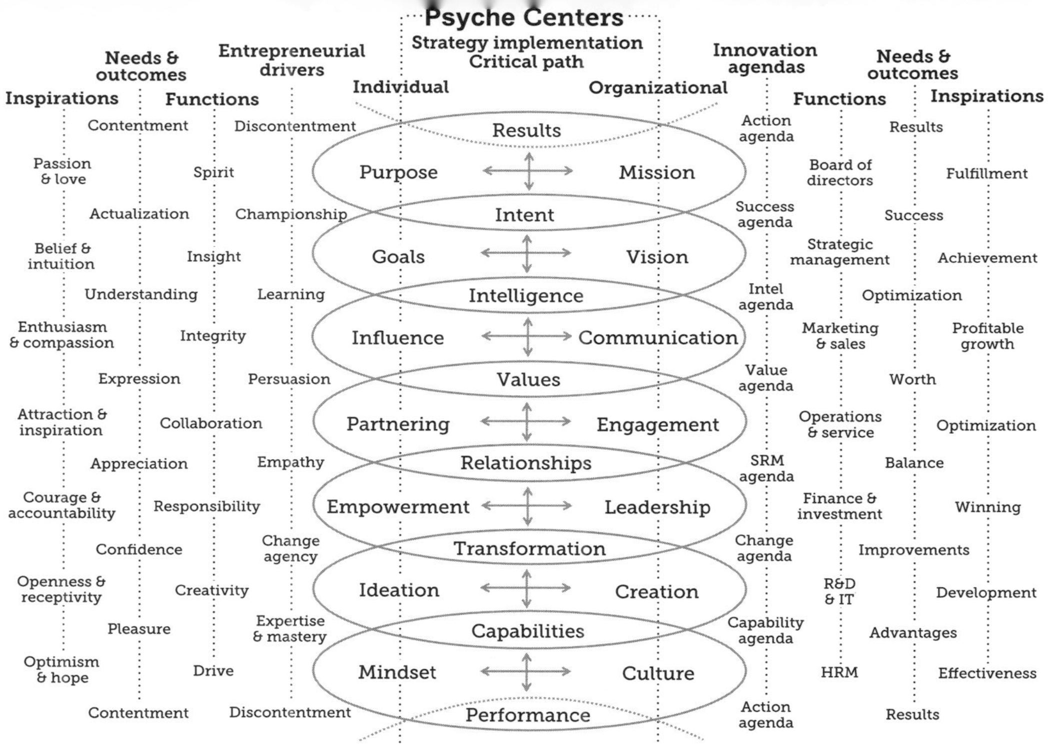

FIGURE 7.1 Bridging individual and organizational psychology

Another vital bridge is between innovation and customers (see Prahalad and Krishnan, 2008). This relationship is the acid test for innovation, in terms of whether any new net value is actually manifested. Further, if the innovation is not informed by customer needs, wants, aspirations, and, ultimately, values, then it's likely to fail.

Last, but not least, a critical determinant of success is the ability of entrepreneurs and enterprises to bridge between the soft stuff of psychology and culture and the hard stuff of performance, results, innovation, and strategy.

Bridging virtues

Bridges also exist, and must be optimized within each entrepreneurial psyche center, as a basis for entrepreneurial virtue. Referring to Figure 7.1, let's start at the bottom and work upward:

1. The root driver for entrepreneurship is discontentment (motivated toward contentment), which is met by (bridged with) expertise and mastery (motivated toward pleasurable development and demonstration of skills) and manifested as drive fueled by optimism, forming the entrepreneur's driven mindset.
2. The same expertise and mastery forms the basis for creative ideation – skills and domain expertise supporting the capability or potential to create. This bridges (or meets and mingles) with the entrepreneur's sense of transformative change agency (motivated by a desire for confidence, and therefore the careful mitigation and management of risks) to manifest, based on receptivity to ideas from within and outside, as creative ideation.
3. Change agency meets emotional intelligence or empathy toward others (motivated by a desire for mutual appreciation), based on appreciation of their needs, perspectives, and motives to manifest as responsible (based on courageous accountability) empowerment of others – giving them what they need to enable contribution (as resources) to the intended innovation, the idea rising from below (per above point).
4. Empathy bridges with persuasiveness (motivated by the need for expression, to be heard) to serve as the basis for collaborative partnering – the ability to inspire and engage within truly powerful, win–win relationships with all relevant stakeholders.

5. Persuasive ability to sell the big idea or the value to be delivered by the innovation meets with the ability to learn (motivated toward understanding and intelligence) in the form of integrous influence.
6. Learning bridges with championship (motivated toward actualization and success) to support the insightful goal(s) that form an entrepreneurial vision for what might be possible.
7. Championship meets the discontentment to bridge into the entrepreneurial spirit fueled by love and passion – spirited purpose.

In summary, what emerged for me, over time, is an image of how entrepreneurial flow psychology relates to the successful implementation of strategies for innovation. Individual and organizational psyche centers relate and interact, while also driving upward and downward, and, in doing so, connecting and interacting with neighboring psyche centers (see Figure 7.1). They are as follows:

1. **Mindset/culture:** Individual mindsets meet and mingle in cultural soup. Downward, touching the pavement, is the realm of performance – behavior in action. Further downward, this loops around (it's cyclic), connecting with the top psyche center – purpose and mission. Performance becomes results. We'll come back to this, but let's look "upward" from mindset/culture to what it creates – potential or capability.
2. **Ideation/creation:** A key potential in relation to innovation is the possibility of generating ideas and the creative development of those ideas. Driving upward, this leads to transformation – change and improvement. Driving downward, the ideation/creation dance also drives the development of greater potential, capabilities for innovation, and the creation of competitive or other advantages.
3. **Empowerment/leadership:** Empowerment and leadership derive a vital kind of energy from the realm of transformation, namely, change agency and change management, and that continues the flow upwards, driving commitment among stakeholders to do whatever they must to contribute to success. The downward flow of energy can be thought of as the leadership team's commitment and support from the realm of stakeholder (including the wider team) engagement toward successful transformation, in all its forms.
4. **Engagement/partnering:** Stakeholder engagement rests on specific commitments and drives them, requiring trust and accountability. In

these stakeholder relationships, value is manifested and experienced through collaborative partnering.

5 **Influence/communication:** Influence and communication are partly about managing the value experience and appreciation downward, and partly about articulating and expressing the value upwards. It's about measuring and appreciating value, building intelligence about what customers and other stakeholders need and value, what competitors are doing, and what's happening in the wider world. That intelligence also drives or flows downward, directing sales and marketing efforts in the never-ending quest for growth.
6 **Goals/vision:** SMART goals and vision require a base of intelligence, a grounding in reality, and also drive the intelligence engine to focus on developing insights and understanding related to strategic intent and direction. They direct learning and intelligence gathering. Upward, goals and vision connect to purpose and mission – both driving and deriving from each other.
7 **Purpose/mission:** At the top, purpose and mission define "fulfillment" and success – why the organization exists, what it exists to do, in a sense what war or game it's playing, which defines (downward) what it means to win. Upward, the purposeful mission-driven focus of the organization drives results and performance – measurable outcomes. In this context, we can see "performance management" as a purpose/mission-driven effort to drive psychological and cultural advancement.

Agendas motivating innovation strategy

As discussed in relation to entrepreneurial psyche and flow, there are specific needs and desired outcomes associated with each of the connections of the psyche centers. Similarly, organizations have strategic needs or desired outcomes corresponding with each of the psyche center connections, as seen in Figure 7.1. Further, there is an organizational driver associated with each needed outcome, in the form of a specific agenda within the overall strategy or innovation agenda:

1 **The action agenda driving for results:** Connecting purpose/mission and persona/culture is the realm of performance and results, driven by an action agenda – who is doing what, when, why, how, with whom,

and so on. The action agenda must be time specific, and is often phrased as 30-/60-/90-day action plans. Upward, it connects to capability – you can only do what you're capable of – and downward it connects to strategic intent – the point of the actions.

2 **The success agenda driving for success:** Connecting goals/vision with purpose/mission is intent, driving toward the successful fulfillment of mission and the achievement of the organization's vision – the two sides of the "success coin." Upward, intent "connects with" (intends) results, and downward it is underpinned by intelligence. Intent without intelligence is just a "brain fart."
3 **The "intel" agenda driving for optimization:** Bridging between influence/communication and goals/vision is the realm of intelligence based on internally and externally derived knowledge and assessment of strengths, weaknesses, opportunities, threats, and all sorts of data (Net Promoter, employee skills and motivations, and so on) important to supporting intent above, and the manifestation and measurement of value, below. The right intelligence enables optimization, making the best of the organization's current situation.
4 **The value agenda driving for worth:** Bridging the realm of partnering/stakeholder with influence/communication is the realm of value – manifesting it, expressing it in the marketing mix and selling process, and delivering it in the operational business model, supply and value chains or flow, customer service, and experience. Value, and in particular evaluation, drives into intelligence upward, and downward into the engagement of stakeholders, those whose values and value experience matter for the overall maximization of worth, the value (valuation, if relevant) of the organization.
5 **The stakeholder relationship management (SRM) agenda driving for balance:** Connecting empowerment/leadership with partnering/stakeholders is the realm of engagement – engaging stakeholders and partners, as well as engaging staff and other resources – driving upward toward value manifestation, and downward toward transformation – the realm of balanced scorecards, balancing across (seeking the right balance among) financial, market or customer, cultural, and operational considerations of organizational engagement in strategy.
6 **The change agenda driving for improvements:** Bridging between ideation/creation and empowerment/leadership is the realm of transformation – driving upward toward the engagement of those

involved in the change journey, and downward to capability, the capacity for sustainable change and improvement.

7 **The capability agenda driving for advantages:** Relating persona/ culture and ideation/creation is the realm of potentiality or capability for the creation of strategic advantages of all kinds – driving upward to continuous improvement, change and transformation, and downward to performance and results.

Strategy planning and implementation

Figure 7.2 shows how the elements of strategy link together in the formulation of strategic plans, and how the areas of overlap – the bridging innovation agendas that drive strategy implementation – also relate to organizational functions that are arguably all concerned with all aspects of strategy, but in a sense more centered, concerned, and associated with each of the psyche centers.

One aspect of the model that perhaps bears a "sanity check" – in that of all the links between elements and functions, it is arguably the least obvious – is the connection between leadership and finance and investment. I tend to think of and experience leadership as being most manifest within the executive management team of any organization. However, leadership of resources is specifically concerned with focusing, directing, inspiring, and empowering them – in every sense of that word – to achieve what's desired. We could call this "resource management," but the reality is that the qualities of leadership, in the truest and fullest sense, are what's required here as a critical success factor. The key insight, perhaps, is that when it comes to the financial budgetary decisions that organizations make, which ultimately translate into how they choose to focus their limited resources of funds, people, systems, and tools, this is where leadership is most needed and, all too often, is sorely lacking. However, we'll get into this next, when considering the sins of innovation. For now, let's just say it's clear that more organizations need to invest in developing key leadership qualities within the organizational functions, most typically product management or product marketing and finance, which control budgets and investment.

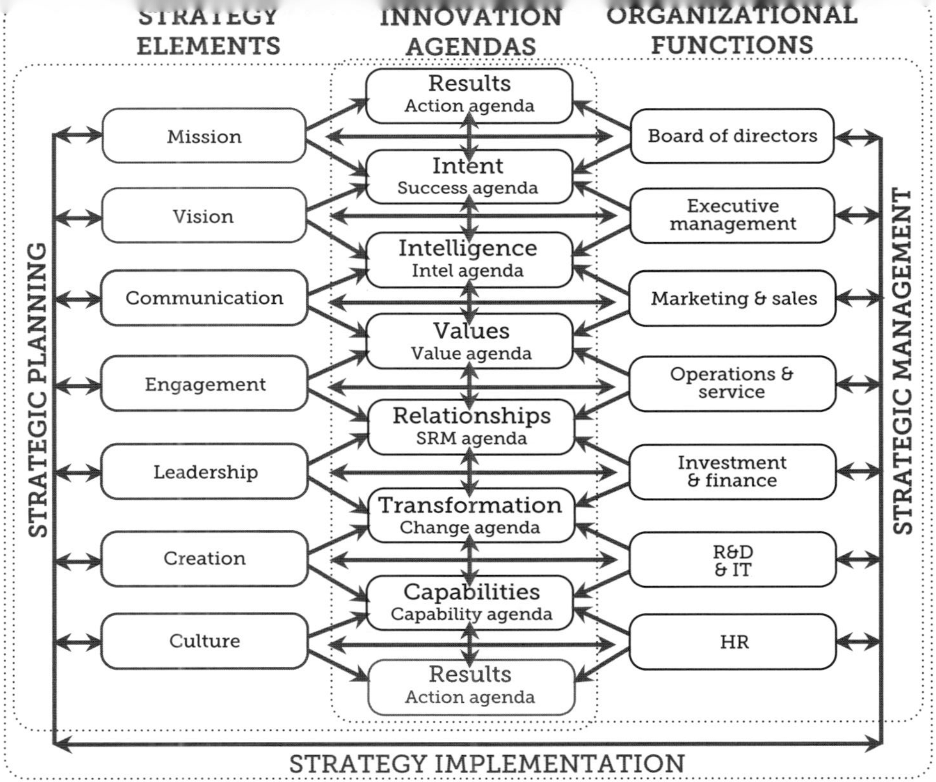

FIGURE 7.2 Bridging innovation agendas in planning, managing, and implementing strategy

Bridging thought leadership

With the organizing framework for strategic bridging in place, I began seeing correspondences between the model and various thought leadership offerings related to strategy, innovation, and entrepreneurship. A few of the most well known are now considered, before turning to Part II, which will define and discuss the seven sins of innovation.

Leading change

Kotter's (1996) seminal book on leading change identified eight errors that leaders commonly make, and offered a corresponding eight-step process for effectively driving strategic change. Although there is a suggested order to Kotter's process, we might note that the elements of strategy need to be managed simultaneously, even if they might be conceived of in a different order. In my view, Kotter's eight factors relate to the seven elements of strategy, as shown in Figure 7.3.

Blue ocean strategy

Kim and Mauborgne (2005) defined "blue ocean" strategy as a "game-changing" way to redefine an enterprise's paradigm, making the existing competition irrelevant, at least for a while. Their concept of using a strategy canvas to identify and deliver new values to achieve differentiation starts, in my view, with bridging from insightful goals and vision, through the intelligent analysis of customer and market needs and competitive offerings, to the new values and value delivery models. Of course, success then depends on aligning and implementing all the innovation agendas.

Good strategy

Rumelt (2011) characterizes "good strategies" – a mix of thought and action – as strategies that achieve two key things:

1. Coherence based on alignment of the key elements of the strategy.
2. Power based on focusing resources and actions, and sometimes developing key new strengths and competitive advantages from the insightful ("blue ocean") reframing of the problem or situation.

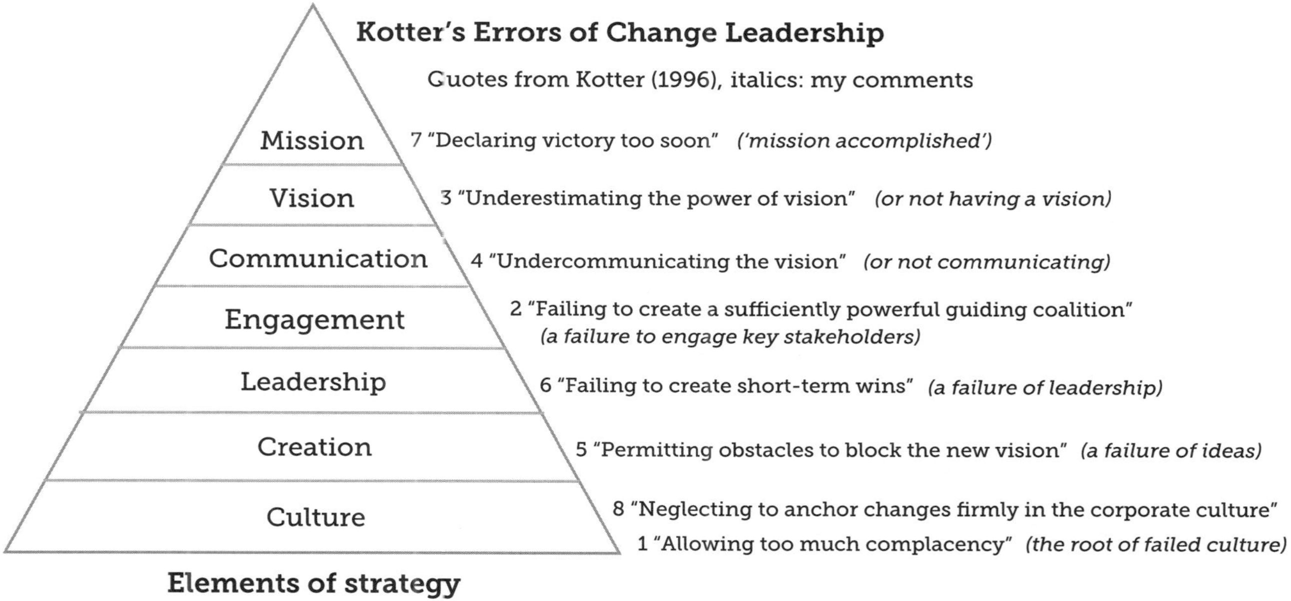

FIGURE 7.3 Relating errors of change leadership to the elements of strategy

New-found powers to overwhelm the problem, competitor, or obstacles to success are all about bridging from the leadership and focused empowerment of resources, to the development of advantageous capabilities, through successful, transformative leadership of change. Coherence is about aligning all the action agendas and aspects of organizational psyche and behavior, in order to achieve flow, peak performance, and desired results.

Innovation personas

Kelley with Littman (2008) defined ten innovation personas. I have placed these ten personas, along with the devil's advocate persona they eschew, on the framework in Figure 7.4, along with three further personas that are vitally important in the innovation process. This is the complete list:

1. **Anthropologists:** keen observers who often provide key ideas based on insights.
2. **Experimenters:** develop ideas through trying things out.
3. **Cross-pollinators:** advance thinking by juxtaposing concepts and ideas.
4. **Hurdlers:** see solutions to problems, ways around obstacles, or ways to do more with less.
5. **Collaborators:** bring people together to get things done and stir the pot.
6. **Directors:** map and drive projects and bring out the best in people.
7. **Experience architects:** design experiences that will create improvement and value.
8. **Set designers:** create real and virtual spaces for innovative culture to flourish.
9. **Caregivers:** support and foster, in Kelley's terms, "human-powered innovation."
10. **Storytellers:** galvanize teams through a persuasive vision of past, present, and future.
11. **Devil's advocates:** positioned by Kelley as the innovation nasties, who, if unchecked, block the valiant efforts of the ten innovation personas. However, in my experience, devil's advocates play a critically important creative role in pointing out risks and pitfalls that we ignore at our peril.
12. **Marketers:** missing from Kelley's list, yet in my experience, innovations rarely succeed without engagement of the marketing perspective, and not just experience architects, from the beginning to the end.

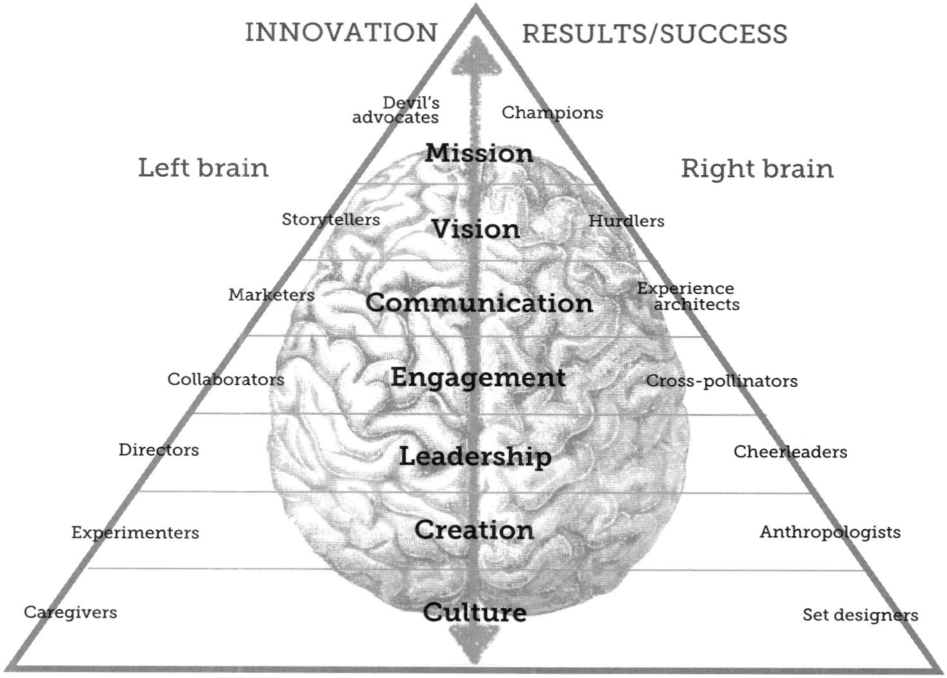

FIGURE 7.4 Relating innovation personas to entrepreneurial psychology

Source: Brain image from Wikimedia CC BY-SA 3.0

13 **Champions:** also missing from the innovation personas put forward by Kelley and IDEO, yet, in my view, absolutely vital to the innovation process from inception to conclusion.
14 **Cheerleaders:** or what Kotter (1996) calls a "coalition of support for change" – are vital in that few champions can "go it alone" particularly when large or complex organizations try to innovate.

Note that I am not implying, in Figure 7.4, that each of the innovation personas doesn't have a functioning left and right brain, or indeed all seven functional centers of psyche; merely that, arguably, the key strength of each persona seems to be centered in one of the seven centers of the entrepreneurial psyche. The other message, reiterating the value of diversity, is that fourteen brains are better than one.

3M seven pillars of innovation

Another view on what it takes to innovate successfully comes from 3M, a global innovation leader. Its "seven pillars" of innovation are related to the organizational factors within the present strategic model. The quotes in the following list are from an article by Arndt (2006), in an interview with Larry Wendling, vice-president of 3M's corporate research lab:

1 **Mission** – 3M 1: "From the chief executive on down, the company must be committed to innovation." 3M's mission statement is: "To solve unsolved problems innovatively" (3m.com).
2 **Vision** – 3M 6: "3M tallies how much of its revenue comes from products introduced in the past four years to judge whether its R&D money is being spent wisely." The strategic intent to deliver value through innovation is clearly tied to reality and metrics. No doubt this aspect of vision ties to wider, specific aspirations about growth and industry leadership.
3 **Communication** – 3M 4: "Talk, talk, talk. Management at 3M has long encouraged networking – formal and informal – among its researchers. Wendling calls this 3M's secret weapon." Internal networking is also a "secret weapon" at Google (among others), and is a centrally important communication activity, along with external networking, marketing communications, and more besides.
4 **Engagement** – 3M 7: "Research must be tied to the customer. Employees spend a lot of time with customers to understand what their needs are so they can go back to the labs to come up with valuable

products." Engagement isn't just about customers, but the all-important customer relationship should be at the heart of it.

5 **Leadership** – 3M 5: "The folks who call themselves 3Mers take pride in discoveries that lead to real-world products. Management reinforces this by fostering a dual-career ladder so veteran researchers can continue to move up without becoming managers." Again, this is one aspect of leadership and empowerment of resources, making them feel valued no matter what their chosen career path.

6 **Creation** – 3M 3: "3M claims to have leading know-how in 42 diverse technologies. That allows researchers to take an idea from one realm and apply it to another. For example, 3M scientists have used a technology behind layered plastic lenses to make more durable abrasives, more reflective highway signs, and golf gloves that allow you to get a tighter grip without squeezing as hard. Companies that remained 'unidimensional', as Wendling puts it, typically run out of ideas after their first success." Technology platforms can be vitally important to enabling creativity, but, again, are just one aspect of it.

7 **Culture** – 3M 2: "The corporate culture must be actively maintained." 3M's commitment to fostering an effective organizational culture, maximizing potential for performance and innovation results, is aptly reflected in these words.

It might help to see the 3M lineup graphically, as in Figure 7.5.

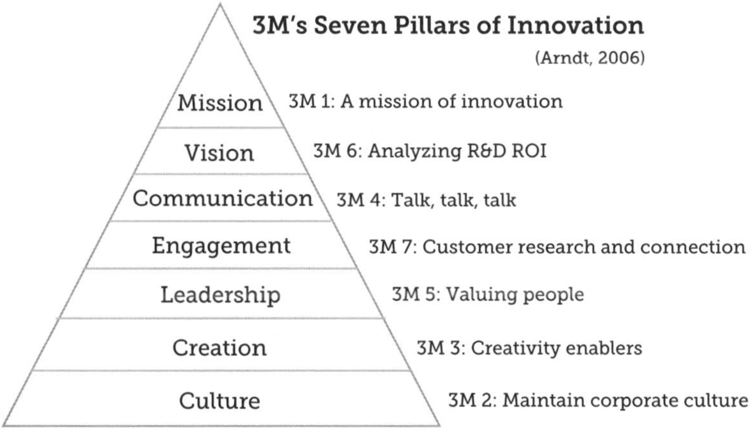

FIGURE 7.5 Relating 3M's pillars of innovation to the elements of strategy

Google's eight pillars of innovation

Susan Wojcicki (2011), Google's senior vice-president of advertising, described Google's eight pillars of innovation as follows, which I have related to the present framework:

1 **Mission** – Google 1: "Have a mission that matters."
2 **Vision** – Google 6: "Spark with imagination, fuel with data ... recruit people who believe the impossible can become a reality."
3 **Communication** – Google 5: "Share everything ... our employees know pretty much everything that's going on and why decisions are made."
4 **Engagement** – Google 7: "Be a platform ... openness helps to move the needle forward for everyone involved."
5 **Leadership** – Google 2: "Think big, but start small ... No matter how ambitious the plan, you have to roll up your sleeves and start somewhere."
6 **Creation** – Google 4: "Look for ideas everywhere."
Google 3: "Strive for continual innovation, not instant perfection ... Our iterative process often teaches us invaluable lessons. Watching users 'in the wild' as they use our products is the best way to find out what works, then we can act on that feedback. It's much better to learn these things early and be able to respond than to go too far down the wrong path."

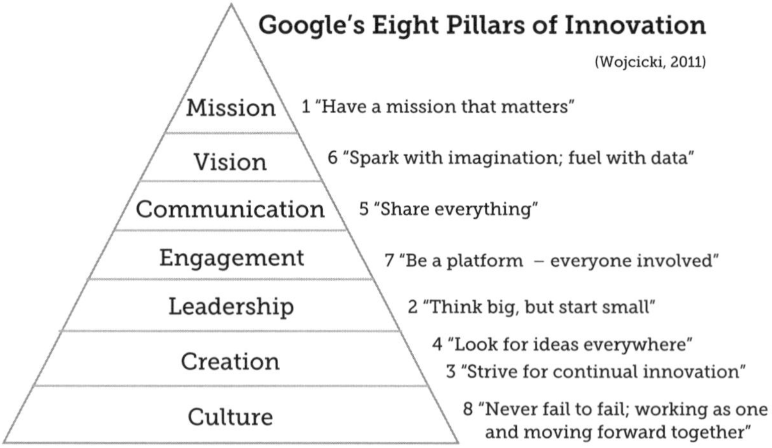

FIGURE 7.6 Relating Google's pillars of innovation to the elements of strategy

7 **Culture** – Google 8: "Never fail to fail … It's okay to fail as long as you learn from your mistakes and correct them fast … Our growing Google workforce comes to us from all over the world, bringing with them vastly different experiences and backgrounds. A set of strong common principles for a company makes it possible for all its employees to work as one and move forward together. We just need to continue to say 'yes' and resist a culture of 'no', accept the inevitability of failures, and continue iterating until we get things right."

Google's eight pillars relate to the seven elements of strategy, as illustrated in Figure 7.6.

Steve Jobs' seven secrets of success

A final confirmation that my model for strategic entrepreneurial innovation might be "more or less right" came when Steve Jobs' seven "secrets" of success were published (Gallo, 2010). I hope Steve wouldn't mind that I've changed the order of his "secrets"; this is because, although his secrets are numbered, I derive no sense of order or sequencing from Gallo's presentation of them.

1 **Mission** – Jobs 1: "Do what you love – follow your passions – don't settle for anything your heart isn't in."
2 **Vision** – Jobs 2: "Put a dent in the universe – have a big, bold, clear and concise vision."
3 **Communication** – Jobs 7: "Master the message – creating excitement and buzz."
4 **Engagement** – Jobs 6: "Create insanely great experiences to create an emotional connection with customers." And I would add other stakeholders.
5 **Leadership** – Jobs 3: Focus – "Say 'no' to 1,000 things – focus on key relationships." To me, focus is a key aspect of leadership, to ensure appropriate investment of energy and time in the relationships and resources that most matter.
6 **Creation** – Jobs 4: "Kick start your brain – get out of the box – make unexpected connections." Again, this isn't the only important aspect of creativity, but it is vital.
7 **Culture** – Jobs 5: "Sell dreams not products." To me, this is the essence of Steve Jobs' mindset, and Apple's brand and culture.

FIGURE 7.7 Relating Steve Jobs' secrets to success to the elements of strategy

Now that we've defined the concept of innovation zoning, and the underlying phenomenon of bridging various aspects of entrepreneurial and organizational psyche, Part II considers the seven sins of innovation, which lead to unnovation.

part II

The Seven Sins

"We are not punished for our sins, but by them."
Elbert Hubbard (1906)

The seven sins of innovation represent the major obstacles to innovation success. The sins derive from the seven key aspects of individual psychology, and their counterparts in organizational psychology. They happen when specific psyche centers are blocked, preventing entrepreneurial flow and innovation success.

Again, it is worth noting that blockages have a multiplicative effect. Consider a hypothetical example with two centers 90% blocked:

100% x 100% x 100% x 100% x 100% x 10% x 10% = 1%

The psyche centers interact and resonate together in ways described in this part of the book. When they're out of alignment, flow can't happen. When one center is unhealthy, it affects the other centers and the overall psychological function of individuals and organizations. The centers and their characteristics, associated drivers, motivations, and emotions interact, producing the seven sins of innovation.

It might help to list the sins, showing their relation to the entrepreneurial virtues, as illustrated in Figure II.1.

Entrepreneurial virtues ←	**Strategy elements**	→ **Innovation sins**
Spirited purpose ←	Mission	→ Pointless purpose
Insightful goals ←	Vision	→ Impaired vision
Integrous influence ←	Communication	→ Apathetic miscommunication
Collaborative partnering ←	Engagement	→ Ambivalent disengagement
Responsible empowerment ←	Leadership	→ Frightfully disempowered followership
Creative ideation ←	Creation	→ Painfully boring uncreativity
Driven mindset ←	Culture	→ Comfortable complacency

FIGURE II.1 Innovation sins, entrepreneurial virtues, and strategy

It's also worth reminding ourselves of the entrepreneurial blockers, the opposite of the virtues, as these underlie the innovation sins, as shown in Figure II.2.

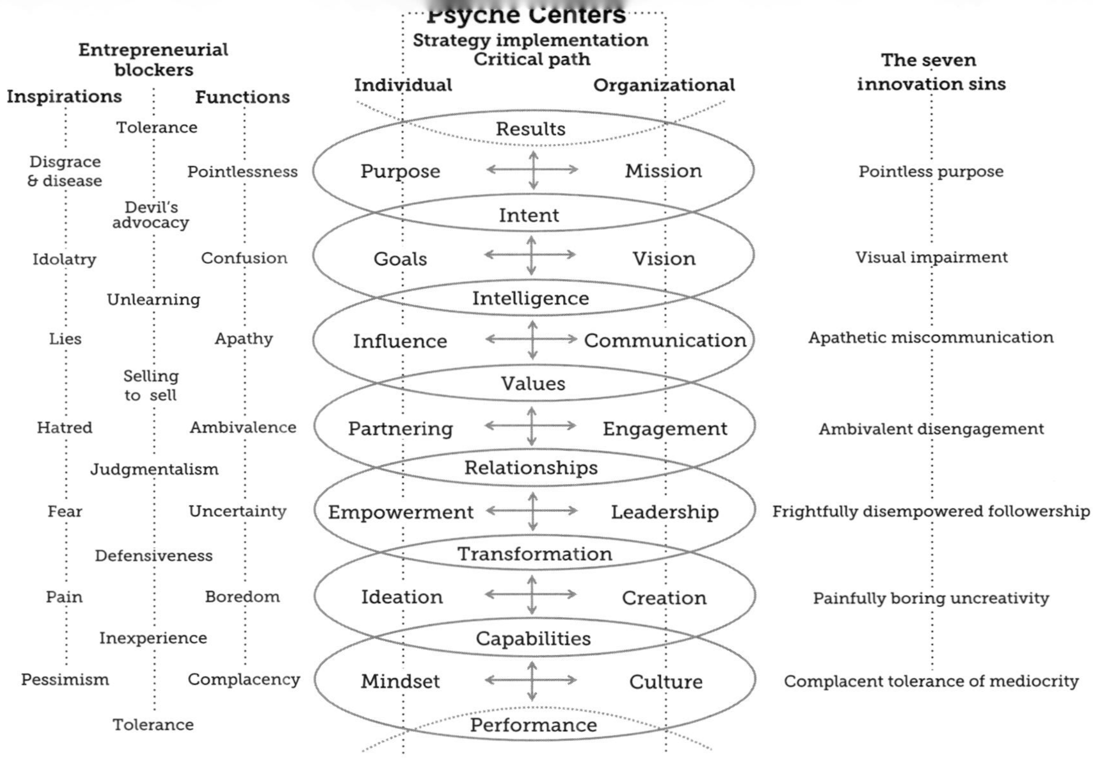

FIGURE II.2 Entrepreneurial blockers leading to innovation sins

chapter 8

Pointless Purpose

"To forget one's purpose is the commonest form of stupidity."

Friedrich Nietzsche (*c.* 1880)

The first sin

Pointless purpose is the first sin of innovation. It comes in several main forms.

Technology push

A potential innovation without a clear and compelling purpose means, at best, that the innovation is a case of "technology push" – a solution in search of a problem. "If we build it, they will come" is the development mantra. In technology push, the entrepreneur, engineer or some other form of technocrat has produced a solution, and it becomes the job of someone else, typically marketing and sales, to find the problem, and someone willing to pay for its solution. Technology push is arguably the most common form of pointless purpose.

Lust for money

Another form of entrepreneurial stupidity is entrepreneurship inspired by the love of money, a point made brilliantly by Kao et al. (2002). "I work so that some day I won't have to." Does the person saying this inspire your confidence as a nurse, pilot, or leader? It doesn't inspire me when I hear aspiring entrepreneurs say such things either. In the same vein, if an organization's stated purpose is to enrich its owners, enabling them to enjoy a nice lifestyle, would that inspire us as customers to seek its products?

People and companies working purely for the money don't inspire us at any level, because money is not connected to purpose, it's simply an economic exchange mechanism. For anything to have value, it must connect to purpose. Money only has value as a trading mechanism, whereby we can exchange it for something of intrinsic value. Forms of money have not been inherently valuable since the days of coins made of precious metals, jewels, beads or cowrie shells, which had perceived uses and therefore value other than as a measure of wealth or mechanism for exchange.

So let's be absolutely clear: the purpose or underlying reason for entrepreneurship is *not* to make money. Yet, paradoxically, the core objective of many aspiring entrepreneurs is to make bucket loads of money. As discussed in Chapter 3, wealth, status, and financial security are among the many factors that motivate people. But motivation and purpose are *not* the same thing, and we confuse them at our peril.

If an entrepreneur's primary driver for creating a new company is self-enrichment or self-aggrandizement, the enterprise is unlikely to succeed. The best enterprises are created by entrepreneurs who start with clarity about the value they intend to deliver to customers, rather than the value they hope to personally derive from the process. The best entrepreneurial ideas are focused on fulfilling a customer need, solving a customer problem, and/or delivering customer value.

Unclear need

I've met numerous entrepreneurs who struggle to articulate the need, problem, or value addressed by their "big idea." In fact, a majority of the entrepreneurs I've met or been approached by tend to struggle to explain their idea other than in "geeky" terms. They dive into technical details about what their invention does, how their technology works, or how their website or e-business model will function. They usually fail to start from the customer's point of view, describing how their idea addresses a customer need, problem, or value. This is classic technology push.

Great entrepreneurs have invariably started with understanding a need, and the objective of addressing it. Ford wanted to provide mobility. Disney wanted to make people happy. Pasteur wanted to save lives. They, and other successful entrepreneurs, were clear on what they wanted to accomplish, why their enterprises should exist, and what they would exist to do. In not one case was the focus just to make lots of money.

Delayed traction

Entrepreneurs who struggle to articulate their ideas in customer terms also fail to engage partners, investors, colleagues, and other stakeholders who might otherwise help them. Whether the entrepreneur is trying to champion an idea for innovation in an organization, or an individual trying to do a startup, the result of inarticulate purpose is the same – slower engagement. Slower engagement translates into higher development costs, and also less traction in the marketplace when the idea is eventually commercialized. In the MIT Innovation Lab, looking across companies and many R&D programs, we saw that a six-month delay in a "go/no-go" decision resulted in more or less doubling development costs (due to drift of key resources and dependencies, and longer, drawn-out projects with greater net overheads), and more or less halving the eventual market impact (due to greater direct competition and market alternatives to the eventually delivered products), effectively killing the ROI and business case.

If an idea is delayed too long, it may as well be killed, unless it's one of the small minority of ideas "whose time has yet to come." An inarticulate idea or champion of the idea has the same effect as a delayed "go" decision. The idea can't get going, can't gain traction as quickly, and therefore loses vital momentum, and eventually achieves nothing at all, or only a small level of the success that might potentially have been achieved with an articulate champion, with a clear and compelling idea connected to purpose.

Bottom line

Here's a test for any aspiring entrepreneur with an idea, whether it might be for a new business, a new product, or a business improvement. See if you can explain it to your mom, or someone else's mom or dad. Make sure the person you're explaining the idea to isn't too much like you, with similar training, perspective, and industry knowledge. Explain your idea to them, and if they haven't got a clue what you're talking about, try again. Once you've practiced with moms, dads, a spouse or your children, the real acid test is to try explaining it to potential customers.

The bottom line – the first, and arguably the deadliest of the seven sins of innovation – is not having a powerful, compelling, and clear sense of purpose for the intended innovation. Innovations need champions, and effective championing requires compelling purpose, articulated with clarity and passion. If you haven't got it, get it.

The psychological roots of pointless purpose

Let's consider how pointless purpose can result from deficiencies, blockages, stifling or misalignment with the various psyche centers.

Misaligned missions

Of course, the top psyche center has to do with purpose, so blockage here may mean there is simply no identified purpose for the innovation, such that it is inherently pointless. I also consider this "disgraceful" – the opposite of "grace," a state associated with being fully on track in living and fulfilling a higher purpose.

However, a far more pervasive problem is when the purpose or point of an intended innovation is not aligned with higher purpose. If an innovation isn't connected to the entrepreneur's overall sense of purpose or passions, it's unlikely to be championed effectively, or attract cheerleaders or wider support in the organization. Similarly, an innovation that isn't in synch with the fundamental mission of an organization is unlikely to achieve traction.

Even a potentially great innovation, if it doesn't contribute to the essential purpose or mission of the organization, is pointless with respect to that organization. Perhaps it needs to find a home elsewhere.

Purpose misaligned with vision

If the intended innovation doesn't connect to a vision for success, with clarity about how the innovation actively contributes toward success and how that will be measured and verified, then the suggested purpose of the innovation is unlikely to inspire investment or other needed support.

Even if there is a clear vision for a specific innovation, but the vision isn't aligned with the "parent" organization's definition of and plan for creating success – if it isn't part of the grand plan – then the innovation's purpose will be pointless with respect to the organization's vision.

Ineffectual communication and influencing

If the purpose for an innovation is ineffectively articulated and communicated to potential stakeholders, if it's not marketed and sold internally and externally, it will not achieve traction and is probably destined for pointlessness.

Another way that many specific innovation initiatives fail is when their purpose does not inspire and thereby make it into the plans of the marketing and sales functions in the wider organization. In this sense, the first task of an innovation champion is arguably internal selling and marketing, especially to the sales and marketing people, who ultimately have to embrace, market, and sell the innovation.

Poor stakeholder engagement

Purpose will be compromised if there isn't a solid understanding of the partners, colleagues, investors, or other stakeholders who need to be effectively engaged to deliver the innovation, and an understanding of the purpose of the innovation in relation to their needs and aspirations. All stakeholders need to have specific purpose in relation to the overall purpose, or their involvement is pointless and, in that sense, they're not really stakeholders.

Another way stakeholder misalignment can undermine purpose is when the stakeholders for a specific innovation are different from the wider organization's stakeholders, particularly if they have needs or agendas that conflict.

Ineffectual leadership

Pointless purpose will also result from a lack of clarity regarding how the innovation will be purposefully led, including who will do what, what resources need to be applied and managed, and how they'll be motivated and empowered to succeed.

Within organizations, a common reason for failure is the inability to attract the necessary resources. Resources are always limited, so unless the purpose of an innovation inspires the decision to invest the resources, and also inspires the human resources themselves, it is likely to end up on the garbage (or rubbish) heap of pointlessness. Consider this comment about founder entrepreneurs, equally true of entrepreneurial champions: "The lovestruck founder is blinded by innovation. They're so hooked on their idea they hope budget lines will be created to fit their product. They want to bend others to their will and wait longer than is healthy for this to take place" (Cain, 2014).

Further, if the point of the innovation isn't focused on leadership, as well as connected or aligned to it, it is arguably pointless. What's the point of innovation that isn't purposefully aimed at achieving leadership within a market, industry or sector of human enterprise?

Misaligned creativity

Purpose will be pointless if there isn't a strong creative element, in terms of bringing some new value into the world, transforming or improving something that in some way makes the world a better place. If the purpose isn't driven by an exciting "big" (or small) idea for innovation, the purpose will be stunted, probably in proportion to the quality and psychological "size" of the idea.

Another way in which creative misalignment can occur in organizations is when the idea for an innovation is out of synch with prevailing ideas. Even perfectly great ideas can wither and die in a sea of discordant or incompatible ideas, particularly if lacking effective, purposeful championship.

Cultural disconnect

Last, but not least, if there is no underlying capability, performance potential, ability, or capacity to deliver the innovation, such that it's arguably a nonstarter, it might also be said to be pointless.

Another way of saying this is that the purpose of an innovation must, in some sense, connect to the motivations, beliefs, attitudes, skills, domain expertise, and mindsets of the champion and the prevailing organizational culture.

Spirited purpose

In summary, if there is constriction or ineffectiveness in any of the foregoing aspects of individual or organizational psychology, the result will be the first deadly sin of innovation – pointless purpose. The opposite of the sin – the first entrepreneurial virtue – is spirited purpose, required to drive effective innovation.

Any entrepreneur must have spirited purpose that resonates in all the individual psyche centers:

1. The fundamental point of "purpose" is about fulfillment of the human psyche, or "spirit" – one's higher purpose.
2. There is absolute clarity of purpose in terms of what successful fulfillment of purpose will look like – the impact of the intended innovation.
3. The purpose and value of the innovation is clearly and effectively articulated, voiced, and communicated.
4. There is a solid understanding of the partners, colleagues, investors, or other stakeholders who need to be effectively engaged to deliver the innovation, and a plan to do so.
5. There's a powerful sense of how to lead the innovation from idea through to fruition – to deliver, marshal, and lead the required resources through development to successful delivery.
6. There's an essential, "big" (or small) idea for the creation of new value (innovation).
7. There is an underlying potential, ability, or capacity to deliver the innovation based on domain expertise, relevant skills, motivations, drive, and the underlying restless discontent that is a core aspect of the entrepreneurial spirit or psyche, connecting it to higher purpose – improving the world, at least one little piece at a time.

We can also consider how spirited purpose resonates in all the centers of organizational psychology, or culture, in relation to any specific innovation, or the more general problem of driving innovation in organizations:

1. The fundamental point of any innovation needs to resonate with the fundamental purpose or mission of the organization – what it exists to do.
2. The purpose of the intended innovation needs to connect to the organization's vision for success, with clarity about how the innovation

actively contributes toward success, and how that will be measured and verified.

3 The marketing plan – the full marketing mix of what's going to be delivered to customers and how, pricing, distribution, and so on – needs to be understood, including the core value proposition for the innovation.
4 There is a stakeholder engagement plan – understanding all the bridges that need to be built to deliver, and how to create the love for the innovation – from within the team delivering, all the way to customers, investors, and other stakeholders.
5 It is understood how the innovation will be led and managed, including who will do what, what resources need to be applied, and how the innovation will result in leadership within a market, industry, or sector of human enterprise.
6 There is a creative purpose for the innovation, in terms of bringing some new value into the world, transforming something that in some way makes the world a better place.
7 The purpose of innovation is reflected in the beliefs, attitudes, mindsets, motivations, character, and behavior of key people within the organization.

In conclusion, entrepreneurs achieve a state of actualization and grace – fulfillment of higher purpose – when they are in a state of flow in relation to purpose. In contrast, when one or more aspects of psyche within the entrepreneur or the wider organization are misaligned, the first deadly sin of innovation – pointless purpose – will undermine efforts to innovate.

Purposeful innovation agendas

Spirited purpose is supported by and key to successfully driving the specific innovation agendas of any enterprise:

1 Ensuring purpose will be fulfilled through achieving the goals and overall vision that, together with purpose, define strategic intent – the "success agenda."
2 The enterprise's "knowledge agenda" supports spirited purpose with up-to-date intelligence answering the vital question of why the organization exists, and why the innovation matters. Also, the intelligence efforts should be focused and driven by overall enterprise purpose.

3. Purpose connects with the "value agenda" defining the value sets to be delivered, and how that delivery represents fulfillment of purpose.
4. An effective "stakeholder relationship management agenda" requires understanding stakeholder purposes in relation to the enterprise, and how serving their purposes helps fulfill that of the enterprise.
5. Any "change agenda" should be driven by purpose that's aligned with the enterprise's overall mission, and missions may themselves encompass a sense of dynamism and change, for example when missions embrace the innovation imperative.
6. A powerful "capability agenda" for developing winning advantages contributes to and is guided by purpose.
7. Finally, purpose motivates action and through the "action agenda" results are achieved in relation to purpose.

Entrepreneurial actualization

In conclusion, entrepreneurs achieve a state of actualization and grace – fulfillment of higher purpose – when they are in a state of flow in relation to purpose. In contrast, when one or more aspects of psyche within the entrepreneur or the wider organization are misaligned, the first deadly sin of innovation – pointless purpose – will undermine efforts to innovate.

chapter 9

Impaired Vision

"Every man takes the limits of his own field of vision for the limits of the world."

Arthur Schopenhauer (1851)

The second sin

The second sin that blocks innovation is a lack of vision, unclear, confused or otherwise impaired vision, or a vision for success that is unattainable or hopeless. Impaired vision has to do with failure within the psyche center associated with insight, foresight, intuition, intelligence, and championship intent. Let's consider various forms this particular sin takes.

Misaligned visions

Any vision is a goal, or set of goals rich and big enough to be considered a vision. Another way of saying this is that big visions and goals can be rollups of smaller visions and goals. Figure 9.1 illustrates how a BHAG (big hairy audacious goal; Collins 2001) or vision might consist of and be supported by smaller goals or visions. Problems occur when the visions of individuals, groups, or various stakeholders are out of alignment, or in conflict.

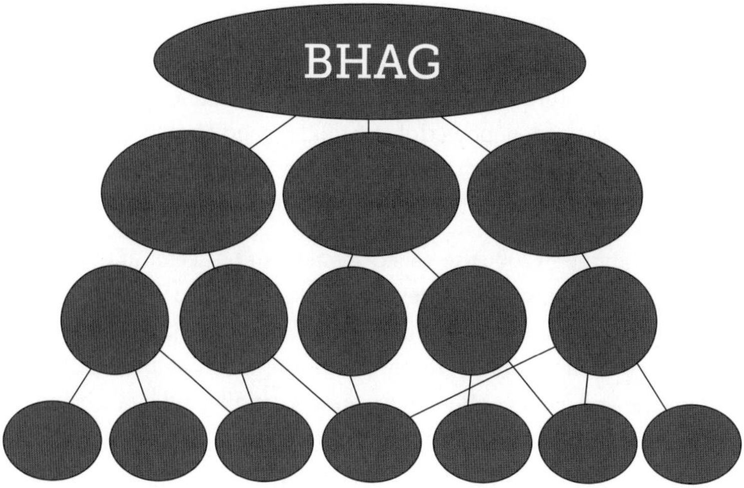

FIGURE 9.1 Nested visions

Bad red oceans

Impaired vision is what "red ocean" (Kim and Mauborgne, 2005) and "bad" (Rumelt, 2011) strategies are inherently about – a failure to see what's possible. When leaders are able to look above the fray, firefights, and day-to-day operations, they have the opportunity to envision new potential, new dreams, and new future realities. As Drucker (1985) said: "The best way to predict the future is to create it."

Visions typically consist of goals. Stated another way, a BHAG can in most (if not all) cases be broken down into various subgoals. A vision for dominating the world can be broken down into a series of smaller goals or steps, defined in discrete terms even if there are complex interdependencies among them.

Business as usual

For many enterprises, the problem with vision is simply that it fails to look beyond "business as usual." As Cooper (2014) says:

> Way too many businesses are just trying to get by. They aim to do just a bit better than last year … and if they do, they're thrilled. They've become mediocre and they have no vision as to what an extraordinary future could be.

Unlucky victims

Rich, audacious visions are better than impoverished, sparse ones. In fact, the "success literature" argues that a richly detailed vision, with many specific subgoals, is more powerful as a guiding and attracting force than a less elaborate vision. The argument is that the law of attraction works best with clear, detailed visualization of the desired outcome.

In my view, Byrne's (2006) so-called "secret" isn't a secret at all. The fact that negative thoughts, attitudes, and beliefs tend to lead to negative outcomes, and that the opposite is true for positives, isn't magic. It's psychology in action. Our attitudes shape the world around us, because other people and even nonhuman organisms are affected by the subtleties of how we feel, what we think, and the attitude we bring to life and relationships. Even relationships to inanimate objects can be affected by attitude. Just think about a tennis player's relationship to racquet, ball, net, and court – very different on "good or bad days," as defined by attitude rather than these objects.

I believe we create our own luck. When we're positive, we're more attractive. With a positive outlook, we tend to attract help toward positive outcomes. Serendipity happens, not by chance, but by design. We're psychologically wired to be attracted to positive people and causes. We just don't always get it right.

Our vision can become impaired in various ways. In life, we can develop a victim mentality, coming to believe that the way things are is because of this or that person, or this or that story of how we were victimized. We can lose the ability to dream, to think positively, or to see what might become a new reality if we work toward it.

Whose vision is this?

We can become confused regarding what we should aspire for. We can take on the goals or visions of others, making them our own, even if they ultimately don't sit that comfortably with us. We can get all the way through a specialist university degree and then realize it was perhaps a parent's dream. And we all tend to be affected by our consumerist culture of craving wealth and conspicuous consumption.

Myopia

A key way in which vision is impaired within entrepreneurs and organizations is being myopic, or short-sighted. Many organizations are so short term in their thinking, and in the demands and conditions they set for entrepreneurship and innovation, that they inherently bias their thinking and behavior toward short-term incremental improvements, rather than bold, audacious breakthrough innovations.

Big breakthrough innovations typically require greater investment and sustained effort over longer periods than is required for the smaller, more immediate gains available from continuous improvement. There's nothing wrong with continuous improvement, and a vision that consists of thousands of tiny little goals for improvement may seem exciting for some. But it's always more rewarding to be the game changer, than to continuously improve within industries or businesses that get left by the wayside.

Organizational churn is a root cause of short-termism. When CEOs consider their term leading an organization, they typically have incentives tied to delivering results within a relatively short time span, often just a few years. So, when faced with the choice between short-term investment in relatively immediate results, or investing in a game-changing innovation that they might not even see delivered within their tenure, with relatively high risk and deferred reward, their choice is unfortunately clear, but short-sighted. They, and their boards, need distance glasses.

Hyperopia

Long-sightedness (hyperopia) can also be a significant visual impairment. Many entrepreneurs suffer from having too grand a vision, and not seeing the merits in smaller, shorter steps, celebrating along the way. Getting early traction and early revenue from smaller, shorter term wins is often a better route to the longer term, grand vision than an attempted fast run up a slippery slope, as illustrated in Figure 9.2.

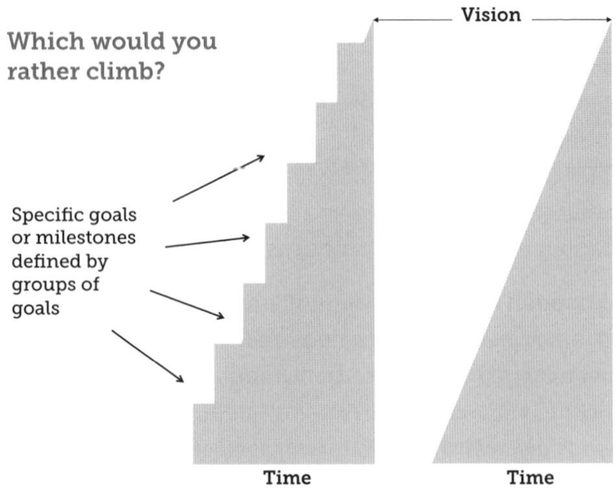

FIGURE 9.2 Goals shaping vision

Inability to focus

Vision can also get confused, blurred – seeing double, triple or worse. Clear vision requires focus, not trying to do too much, too soon. It's also impossible to look in two very different directions and see clearly. Sometimes, entrepreneurs and organizations need to choose one direction over another.

Strategic choices or decisions often need to be made at the level of vision – choice of direction – and also implemented at the level of resource investment, application, and focus. Various strategic choice frameworks illustrate this:

- Ansoff's matrix, considering whether to focus on new or existing products, or go into new or existing markets (Ansoff, 1957).
- Boston Consulting Group's advantage matrix (Lochridge, 1981).
- Porter's generic strategies matrix, for considering whether to focus on differentiation, segmentation, or cost leadership (Porter, 1980).

The key principle underlying all the suggested frameworks is to focus, based on making intelligent choices.

Just plain dumb

In fact, intelligence is a key requirement and foundation for good vision. A good dream is based on a clear understanding of reality; intelligence about what is, internally and externally, and intelligence about what might be, and the ability to connect the dots, to learn, to see patterns, to anticipate the unexpected. Some frameworks are useful for organizing intelligence, and identifying gaps in insight that require further analysis:

- SWOT analysis is particularly useful when one asks what key strengths should be applied to address opportunities and threats, and what weaknesses must be overcome to do so.
- Porter's five forces, and Porter's four corners, for considering competitive position and possibilities (see Porter, 1980).
- PESTEL analysis, looking at how various external factors such as political, economic, social, technological, environmental, or legal trends may affect strategies (see CIPD, 2013).

Without intelligence, and the ability to learn, digest, and understand relevant information, and then turning it into insights, vision will be just plain dumb.

Psychological vision blockers

As with all the other psyche centers, impaired vision can be considered in terms of the causes and effects associated with aspects of individual psychology, as well as the causes and effects of organizational psychology. Each of these resonates by interacting with all the other psychological centers.

Vision will be impaired when:

1. Success is defined in terms that don't resonate with individual and organizational purpose.
2. Not striking the right balance between ambition and realism; for example, if the vision isn't at least somewhat audacious, a stretch, or if it's not built on insight, intuition, and intelligence, it may be infeasible or unrealistic.
3. Not articulated and expressed effectively, with a clear and powerfully articulated sense of what success will look, feel, and be like.

4 Not based on clarity regarding who needs to be engaged, and what they need to contribute to achieve the vision for success, and how each will derive value from the "success scenario."
5 Not underpinned by focused, directive, and empowered leadership dedicated to achieving the vision by making the right decisions to ensure allocation and focus of the resources required to win.
6 Not visualizing a specific and significant improvement.
7 Not rooted in the right mindset and culture, including an unshakable belief that the vision can be achieved, based on the capability and potential to manifest the vision in reality.

In summary, blockages in any of these aspects of the psyche will result in impaired vision, leading to unnovation.

Insightful goals

Insightful goals are the basis for vision that's clear, distant, focused, and visionary. This second entrepreneurial virtue is achieved by:

1 Ensuring goals/vision are aligned to purpose/mission, together forming clear strategic intent in the form of a "success agenda," defining precisely what success the enterprise must work toward.
2 Basing goals and vision on complete, accurate, and up-to-date intelligence on customer needs, direct and indirect competitive ways of fulfilling customer needs, SWOT and other relevant analyses to form the enterprise's "knowledge agenda," which is designed to optimize achievement through time and every situation.
3 Ensuring that goals are clearly tied to a "value agenda" defining USPs, plans to maximize customer value experience, and the value ("business") model, all underpinned by the enterprise's values, and designed to drive the maximization of enterprise worth or valuation.
4 Identifying specific goals in relation to every important cluster of stakeholders in the form of a "stakeholder relationship management agenda," which defines the SMART goals to be achieved within every vital relationship internal and external to the enterprise, and is designed to optimally balance the priorities of the organization's various stakeholders.

5 Ensuring clarity of goals for enterprise transformation within a "change agenda" defining precisely what improvements are required, when, how, and by whom they will be achieved.
6 Defining specific goals for the organizational development of the key capabilities required to achieve overall success within a "capability agenda" focused on developing winning advantages.
7 Identifying specific results to be achieved by individuals, groups, and the enterprise as a whole through an "action agenda" focused on maximizing performance.

Balancing dream and reality

Again, defining goals and visions is about finding the balance between dream and reality. By rooting the dream in reality, we must, in a sense, be awake. Thus, I appreciate the following quote: "Your vision will become clear only when you look into your heart … Who looks outside, dreams. Who looks inside, awakens" (Carl Jung, 1963).

chapter 10

Apathetic Miscommunication

"The single biggest problem in communication is the illusion that it has taken place."

George Bernard Shaw (1912)

The third sin

Apathetic miscommunication is the third sin of innovation. We've already seen, in the first two sins, that failures to communicate purpose and vision can block entrepreneurial efforts. But there are many additional ways that miscommunication can undermine efforts to innovate, and arguably the worst is when the poor communicators don't even care, when there's apathy on top of incompetence. Let's consider the various forms.

The role of communication

Enterprises thrive or perish based on communication and miscommunication. Communication isn't just about carefully crafted press releases, websites, brochures, blogs, or speeches. It's often what we *don't* say that counts most. We communicate through everything we do, how we do it, and how we do nothing. Our body language reflects attitudes and feelings, which may not support our spoken word and the messages we want to convey. Tone of voice, pauses in conversation, and the presence or absence of social "niceties" can shape customer experience more than the actual service provided. A delay in follow-up, noncommunication, may result in a loss of opportunity. So can following up too quickly, by coming across as desperate.

The world of business communication is full of paradoxes that boggle the mind, and trip up the most competent executives and companies. But let's step back and consider the role of communication in enterprises. In terms of strategy, communication sits as a bridge or glue between the top layers, mission and vision – the twin aspects of strategic intent – and the lower layers, beginning with engagement in relationships. Communicating intent gives purpose and direction to engagement. Further, the communication arising from the engagement becomes an expression of value, which is psychologically essential to the experience of value. And as communication bridges higher, into the realm of strategic intent, it becomes the expression of intelligence to guide and direct strategy.

Communications poverty

Various forms of miscommunication are a root cause for failure and mediocrity. Given that mental life arises from communication and that most of our life is spent in relationship, communicating with others, why are we so bad at it? Clearly, we're evolving, but as a species we have a long way to go. We can all think of remarkable examples of leaders who influenced and changed the world through their written or spoken word. People like Gandhi, Churchill, and Mandela come to mind as great leaders and great communicators. But less obviously, if you look at what underlay the success of Apple, 3M, or indeed any noteworthy enterprise, communication played a central role from initial developments in labs, to global market dominance. Genius rides on effective communication. And yet, the reality is that most people aren't great communicators, and poor communication is rife.

Ineffectual marketing and sales

Communication at the most basic level consists of a message and a medium, along with a messenger and an audience or recipient. The role of enterprise communication is to:

1 articulate the offering
2 express its potential value to the intended recipients of the value

3 influence them to purchase or in other ways engage with the enterprise, which is the central purpose of marketing and sales.

One of the most common forms of apathetic miscommunication in enterprises is the failure to appreciate that everyone in the enterprise is involved in marketing and selling. Many people react to this statement with disbelief and even distain. They feel "selling" is beneath them, probably because their image of salespeople is based on incompetent ones.

We've probably all met a proud salesperson claiming to be able to sell ice to Eskimos. But selling someone something they don't need is simply stupid. It's unsustainable, not to mention immoral, wasteful, and bad for the environment. It's also a classic example of apathetic miscommunication. We should only open our mouths, laptops, or mobiles when we have something worthwhile to say or to offer. If it isn't from the heart, true, honest, and designed to help the recipient, pack it in. My mom used to say: "if you can't say something nice, don't say anything." I say, nice or not, if what you say isn't honestly intended to help someone in some way, say nothing.

Effective selling is about creating win–win relationships, and when done right, the salesperson becomes a consultative, trusted partner. When everyone in an enterprise realizes exactly how they directly or indirectly touch customers, and when they take the further mental step of viewing everyone (internal or external to the enterprise) they interact with as a customer, they properly appreciate their role in marketing and selling the enterprise, themselves, and the value they are seeking to provide. Marketing and selling aren't dirty commercial activities beneath most people, but essential acts of connection and positive influence intended to provide value. Therefore, marketing and selling are everyone's job, and yet this attitude is far from prevalent, even in commercial enterprises, but most especially in public and professional service enterprises.

Due to ineffectual marketing and sales, great innovations that are fully productized and ready to roll can fail to deliver ROI, based on various dysfunctions, such as underinvestment in marketing or sales, the wrong people or approaches, failure to anticipate or respond to competition, and the wrong pricing, distribution or service strategies. But apathetic miscommunication can kill innovations long before they are delivered to the marketplace. Let's consider the many ways this happens.

No flow zones

Miscommunication takes various forms that can stifle or kill innovation. I'm not simply referring to erroneous communication, but broadly to communication that is lacking in any way. One of the most common ways communication is lacking in organizations is when it simply doesn't happen, when vital information does not flow to the people who need it, or when people feel disengaged because they don't know "what's going on," or lack a sense of direction.

A few further examples of ways in which miscommunication or a lack of communication can harm innovation initiatives include:

- Innovation teams' efforts not being tuned into changing customer and market requirements, and what competitors are doing.
- Management not knowing what's really going on within an innovation initiative, such as the fact that it will be late, over budget or off track in terms of delivering what's expected.
- Not managing critical dependencies or requirements for coordination across innovation initiatives.
- Not knowing when additional resources need to be applied to avoid delivery delays or failures.
- Manufacturing, operations, or suppliers not receiving early sight of requirements needed for production of the intended innovation.
- Marketing not knowing what customers require, perhaps due to poor communications with frontline sales or service.
- No one listening to customers or understanding what they really require.
- Sales not having any idea what innovations might be coming "down the track."
- Finance, HR, or IT functions not knowing enough about an intended innovation or the details of the development program to anticipate and contribute to its success.
- Executives not really knowing what's going on in parts of their organizations.

Pointlessness

Some people seem to like the sound of their own voice, but apart from their own enjoyment, if their communication lacks purpose, it's pointless.

If unclear about purpose, we rarely achieve desirable results. Everything we do, including communication, should have a specific purpose. Any communication that lacks a reason for it to happen is simply useless noise. Therefore, if we stop to think and fail to identify a desired outcome to result from a specific communication, the intended communication is a waste of your time and the time of any intended recipient.

Jumbled thoughts

The realm of thought is also often full of useless noise. If a person's stream of consciousness, of thoughts, is disorganized, random meandering, that person is unlikely to be very clear or articulate. Thought is a form of communication, an internal conversation. If our thoughts are pointless, distracting or defocusing, we're unlikely to inspire or influence our own behavior let alone the thoughts or actions of others. Further, when we're attempting to listen, our thoughts, feelings, worries, judgments, and so on can create so much mental clutter we hardly hear what's really being said.

Most mental chatter is from ego. The ego mind focuses on survival, relative position, sense of worth, and the desire to be appreciated and loved. If we can relax the ego "muscle" even a little, the benefits are noticeable to others and ourselves.

Failure to listen

Another impact of ego on communication is preventing effective listening, and therefore proper two-way conversation. An imbalanced ego wants to be heard, but rarely does it truly care about or accept influence from "the other."

Covey (1989) said: "Seek first to understand; then to be understood." If we don't understand our audience, we won't be effective at targeting them with relevant, powerful, action-generating, influential communications. Talking less and listening more, we're more likely to perceive what's going on – the subtleties of reality. In the silence or gaps we allow, we're more likely to learn or appreciate something new. We are more likely to see beyond our own ego structures and perceptions. Further, if we chatter and babble less, our communication is likely to improve. Less is more, and when the quiet one speaks, people tend to stop and listen.

The truth gap

It's one thing to improve our ability to communicate, but first we need something to "shout about" – something worth saying. Arguably, the most important element of communication in relation to entrepreneurship is a crystalized value proposition that powerfully attracts potential customers. Without a clear proposition, an "essential truth," or a persuasive, enthusiastic "voice," ideas and potential innovations fall flat.

To succeed in generating market success and ROI, an innovation must be based on a solid marketing strategy, and effective internal and external communications from its inception through to delivery into the marketplace. Poor articulation of value can kill innovation before it starts.

The essence of effective voice is the communication of value – the marketing message and connection to potential customers, and the selling – influencing them to buy or use the product. If the potential value of an innovation is miscommunicated, or perhaps not conveyed at all, the innovation will fail to attract support from within or from potential customers or other external stakeholders such as investors, suppliers, or partners.

Information overload

Equally, too much information – another form of noise – results in a failure to see (or hear) the wood for the trees. Good communication is about content, as well as timing and the medium chosen for delivery.

Wrong choice of media

Marshall McLuhan, Canada's famous communication theorist, said: "the medium is the message." The medium we choose to express an idea is as important as the idea content.

For example, before you hit the send button on your next email, ask yourself whether you should simply pick up the phone and call the person. How much time can be saved by instantly exchanging and clarifying information, versus the back and forth of email exchange?

And before you press the dial button on your phone, ask yourself whether you should just walk down the hall, or even get on a plane, to meet face to face. Human beings are creatures of habit. To be the best possible communicators, we need to avoid letting habits select our communications media. Email and phones are great inventions, but there's no substitute for *being* together and all that involves – exchanging glances, talking, eating, and drinking.

You've got junk mail

The reality of our email-saturated world of enterprise communication is that much of it is pointless junk, distracting and detracting from the real work of creating success, reflecting our cluttered minds, lives, and work spaces. It's yet another form of noise.

Atos, Europe's largest IT company, caused shock waves in late 2011 by announcing it would ban the use of email. Try finding a news update on this now. It wasn't very shocking, considering the issues and alternatives. It wasn't even very newsworthy, considering the qualifiers – banning *internal* email (only) by *2014* (yawn). A decade ago at Oracle, we looked critically at how email was used and misused, as a vital tool and, simultaneously, as a huge cause of lost productivity. Our studies showed that many of our knowledge workers spent a third to half of working time on emails, or compulsively checking for new mail. The keyword here is "spend" rather than "invest," given that most emails are ineffectual, time-wasting, and pointless.

Countless unnecessary, time-consuming, and costly email communications happen every second of every day because the original email wasn't clear, raised more questions than it answered, required follow-up questions, or didn't properly state what was being asked or actioned. Before hitting "send," ask yourself why the email is needed in the first place, what is required as a response (decision, acknowledgement, and so on), who needs to get it, and who doesn't. Does the CEO really need to be copied in, and if everyone copies them in, will they have time to be a CEO? In short, ensure that every email makes sense and is correctly addressed. Gaining control of email communications is arguably the first important step any individual or organization can take to reduce miscommunication.

Lack of clarity

Most people don't take the time to properly plan or execute their communications. Whenever you speak or write, try to be as concise as possible. Fewer words are always *better* words. Time is money. Fewer words ensure crisper, cleaner, clearer messages. Think about it. Before you hit the send button, reread, edit, and cut out unnecessary words/phrases. Do the same before opening your mouth. Get rid of clutter. If our minds, mouths, and emails are cluttered, we come across as less organized, less convincing, less articulate, and less attractive to do business with. I could go on, but you get the point – less is more.

Influencing without integrity

The ultimate goal of communication is influence. But influencing without integrity is never a basis for win–win. Lacking integrity, communication is more likely to support evil than good. So what is integrity? It is defined in terms of honesty, morality, ethics, righteousness, sincerity, nobility, decency, and honor. Structurally, and psychologically, it also refers to a state of unity, coherence, cohesion, wholeness, solidity, and soundness. People and enterprises lacking any of the attributes or aspects of integrity have a fatal flaw with respect to innovation. Lacking integrity, they cannot influence with integrity, except perhaps by accident. More likely, their attempts to influence will be selfish, mean or nasty, and therefore of inherently limited value.

Psychological blocks to effective communication

Innovation will be hindered by miscommunication or ineffectual communication. Because of blockages or constrictions of the psyche centers in individuals and organizations, innovation will be undermined by communication if or when it is:

1. Not clearly tied to the essential purpose of conveying the value, benefits, or problem solution to be delivered by the innovation.
2. Not provided by and founded on intelligence and insights on customer needs and experience, market trends and segmentation, competition, relevant regulations, and anything else that might affect successful marketing and sales.
3. Not based on truth and values including honesty and authenticity, such that the innovation is the real deal and says what it does "on the tin" – something worth shouting about, and a way to do it – a message and an appropriate medium or media.

4 Not based on proper, two-way listening as well as expressing win–win engagement in every vital relationship, including the intended customer, and all other key stakeholders.
5 Not enabling the effective inspiration and management of the resources required to deliver the innovation.
6 Not offering clear, and clearly creative ideas.
7 Not connected to the mindsets of individuals or the collective culture, such that, in reality, there's no potential for performance or results.

In summary, if any of the above aspects of psychology are constricted, miscommunication will be a major impediment to innovation. In contrast, effective, timely, clear, and influential communication will tend to result from the third entrepreneurial virtue – integrous influence.

Integrous influence

Effective communication has specific purpose in relation to the listener. Before communicating, state your purpose, restate it, and work at articulating it clearly, succinctly and powerfully. It's not about you. Design messages for listeners, conveying useful information, value, benefits, and calls to action. Pitching a product or service should relate to the listener's problems or requirements, the solution, and what's so unique or special about your offering. Practice pitching in 30–60 seconds, as if on an elevator. Design pitches to attract, convey passion, excite interest, and encourage questions and conversation. End with a call to action – at least get a number and permission to call. View the pitch as the start of a beautiful relationship. It's a pickup, not a stick up.

Influencing effectively and with the required integrity can be achieved by ensuring effective bridging with each of the strategic innovation agendas. Communication should be:

1 Driven and powered by strategic intent.
2 Knowledgeable, both in terms of intelligent presentation and content tied to understanding the recipient.
3 Value based, conveying value and benefits.
4 Audience-centric, linked to the specific stakeholder receiving the communication.

5 Change and improvement oriented.
6 Based on the capability to deliver and follow through on what's promised.
7 Results oriented, tied to strategic intent, with a specific call to action.

Get out more

Although part of the problem is communication clutter, the reality is that most enterprises would benefit from more communication, provided it meets the criteria above, for achieving integrous influence. There's no substitute for wandering around, chatting, asking questions, connecting, and exploring. Drop in on people. Go to networking events. Meet and talk with people you don't know. Creatively explore how you might help each other, points of common interest, and people you might know in common. Get online, join interest groups, engage in dialogue, and work the net(work). The next person you talk to might either know or be someone who will change your world forever.

Silence is golden

Silence is a source of wisdom. Wisdom can arise from improved listening and understanding of the other party. But wisdom also arises from within. A practiced mind can become a powerful source of inspiring, useful, and creative thoughts – ideas that can start a business, create value, transform relationships, or change the world. The word is mightier than the sword. In ancient Vedic cosmology, the initial "big bang" began with a word, "spoken" in thought.

Improving communication

In summary, there are simple yet powerful things we can do to improve communication. If we do, we improve personal effectiveness as leaders and change agents. We improve teams and organizations. We improve our ability to turn ideas into reality. We improve our lives, and the world we live in. We powerfully and positively transform relationships with colleagues, customers, and loved ones. Perhaps most importantly, we transform our most essential relationship, that between our consciousness and the unconscious wellspring of thoughts and ideas.

chapter 11

Ambivalent Disengagement

"The meeting of two personalities is like the contact of two chemical substances: if there is any reaction, both are transformed."

Carl Jung (1933)

The fourth sin

Ambivalent disengagement with and among key stakeholders is the fourth deadly sin of innovation. Missing or ineffectual relationships with any stakeholders for an innovation will limit or completely block success. Let's consider various ways in which disengagement undermines the success of organizations, entrepreneurs, and innovation efforts.

Ignoring key relationships

Successful innovation requires the effective engagement of all relevant stakeholders. At the most basic level, user and chooser "customer perspective" is essential to ensure the innovation is targeted at solving a problem, delivering benefits, meeting needs. Otherwise, it's an innovation nobody needs.

Engagement is about bridging vital relationships. A starting point is to relate the innovation to customer needs, and to identify interesting, novel, better, or less costly ways to fulfill the needs.

Consider some of the relationships that are vital to innovation success, and typical ways in which unnovators get it wrong:

- Customers are a fabulous source of ideas for innovation (von Hippel, 1988, 2005), intelligence (Gale, 1994) and insight (Stone et al., 2004), and yet, amazingly, they are usually grossly underutilized, misunderstood, and even ignored.
- Partners such as suppliers, sales or distribution channels, logistics or outsourced manufacturers are often vitally important to an organization's ability to deliver innovations, but frequently aren't consulted early enough in the process, resulting in delays or an inability to deliver innovations as planned.
- Innovation teams, referring to anyone within an organization who needs to contribute to an innovation, are often not effectively engaged, with a resulting lack of cohesion, communication, creative conflict, clarity of purpose, direction, and teamwork.
- Investors need to be engaged effectively, or entrepreneurial champions will fail to attract and maintain required levels of investment support.
- Regulators or other governmental agencies can make innovations difficult or even impossible if they are not actively considered and appropriately engaged.
- Communities, society, and the environment are often overlooked; and yet, if they're affected by a potential innovation, ignoring their interests could jeopardize the innovation.

Imbalance

Effective stakeholder engagement requires a balancing act – juggling and sometimes making tough choices among (balancing) stakeholder interests. As Bennis (1989) said: "Find the appropriate balance of competing claims by various groups of stakeholders. All claims deserve consideration but some claims are more important than others." In addition to balancing between stakeholders, there are many other aspects of balance required to achieve success from the perspectives of all stakeholders.

Balanced scorecard

Because of its enormous popularity, the first aspect of balance I consider is the balanced scorecard (usually abbreviated to BSC, although for reasons that may become obvious, I will abbreviate it BS).

The highly popular BS approach was founded on the recognition that strategies must achieve a balance between financial and nonfinancial aspects of performance. Noncommercial organizations especially welcomed a framework for engaging strategy that wasn't entirely driven by considerations of shareholder value, bottom line profits, or other measures of financial success. Customer value and other aspects of customer and market performance were clearly more important than financial performance to organizations such as government agencies, public utilities, and many NGOs.

Kaplan and Norton (1992, 1996), who borrowed their ideas from their client Arthur Schneiderman of Analog Devices (see Schneiderman, 2006), suggested that organizations need to consider financial/shareholder, customer/market, operational/quality, and organizational/cultural aspects of performance. Each group reflects a cluster of factors that might be considered. Kaplan and Norton have been criticized for failing to cite the originator, and indeed any previously published literature on strategy. Perhaps more important, the model presupposes that a strategy (especially mission and vision) exists, such that the BS is simply a model for implementing strategy, rather than creating it.

As stated above, my view is that the development and implementation (or planning and execution) of strategy are and must be interwoven as a creative, cyclic process. Therefore, taking strategy as a "given" is a fatal flaw in the BS approach.

The BS approach has also been criticized for being unable to address the new innovation economy. According to Voelpel et al. (2006):

- Financial measures should focus on network stakeholder value rather than just shareholder value.
- Customer focus should aim to improve customer success and partnerships rather than just satisfaction and relationships.
- Process improvement should focus on optimizing network collaboration and strengths.
- Efforts toward learning and growth should look system wide, rather than just within the organization as the unit of analysis.

In my view, there is value in focusing on the entire system and networks an organization may exist in rather than only on the performance of the organization. There is also value in focusing on all stakeholders rather than just shareholders, and in recognizing that all stakeholders, including customers, will have financial interests as well as other qualitative and quantitative interests in organizational performance. But, to me, these are, more or less, semantic differences rather than a step change from the BS to a substantively better approach. And the newly proposed approach is just as fuzzy and illogical as the BS. For example, how can the financial measure of customer value, which surely must be included under network stakeholder value, be separated from customer success, a customer dimension?

The bottom line on the BS and "systemic" scorecards is that they are fundamentally wrong as vehicles or frameworks for engaging strategy. However, the BS and related approaches make three important points:

1. Strategies should consider and achieve a kind of balance across financial and nonfinancial aspects of organizational performance, because not everything can be measured in financial terms.
2. Strategies should recognize that organizations have different kinds of stakeholders, such as owners, employees, and customers, and each of these stakeholders is likely to have interests that can be expressed in financial and nonfinancial terms.
3. Strategies should not only identify key objectives (critical success factors, the vital elements of vision), but also ways of measuring progress against each objective (key performance indicators for each critical success factor), and specific targets and initiatives toward their achievement.

Let's consider additional aspects of balance that must be achieved in relation to various stakeholders.

Short- versus long-term interests

Shareholders clearly have short- and long-term strategic interests, which can conflict in strategically significant ways. For example, many fund managers tend to want short-term results, and, given the magnitude of their holdings, have been known to influence strategic management to make decisions that can have negative longer term consequences. Effective bridging with the shareholder, investor, and analyst community is a "tricky business," a delicate juggling act that can pay off when it goes right and be extremely painful when it goes wrong.

Employees want remuneration, good working conditions, and so on in the immediate term, and also security, career development, and further financial rewards in the longer term. Clearly, all other kinds of stakeholders, governments, communities, suppliers, partners, and so on, have short- and long-term interests. But there is a more interesting point to be made; namely, that while short-term stakeholder interests may diverge, long-term strategic interests will tend to align. Therefore, getting stakeholders to see this can benefit the strategic management of organizations.

Organizations must, from time to time, make tough decisions that require balancing across stakeholder interests. Let's consider an example. Employees usually want higher pay and other incentives for great performance in the short term, which probably come out of profits, and therefore reduce the short-term rewards for investors. Even though short-term interests conflict, it is arguably the case that long-term interests are aligned. Incentivizing employees is part of a strategy for long-term success and value creation, clearly of interest to owners. Similarly, taking lower pay or bonuses in order to improve their company's financial position, valuation, and ability to attract investment may be a good long-term strategy for employees.

I've seen organizations go to great lengths to keep their stakeholders as distant and apart from each other as possible. I believe this is driven by a desire to avoid conflict, but it's also based on short-term thinking. Building bridges among stakeholders, such that there is communication about long-term interests and their alignment, is likely to create and underpin more effective strategies for balanced success across the entire spectrum of stakeholders.

Strategy versus tactics

Distinct from short- and longer term strategic considerations, strategic versus tactical balance refers to the need to achieve the right level of focus on each.

Definitions may be in order. Strategy refers to the strategic plan and its overall implementation, the plan to win the war. Tactics refer to an aspect of strategy implementation, specifically to the detail of implementing a particular agenda that is a component part of the overall strategy. This might be the execution of a particular battle that is part of the overall war strategy, or managing an aspect of the capability agenda, such as engaging in succession planning.

If management focuses exclusively on high-level strategy, without giving due attention to the lower level tactical implementation, they will fail. The more typical case is for management to be so focused on tactics that they fail to properly plan and execute strategy. Terms such as "firefighting," "working in versus on the business," and "heads down management" all conjure up the image of the manager too busy to strategize. The manager may be efficient, for example climbing a ladder quickly, but not effective, deciding if the ladder is positioned to climb the right wall (Covey, 1989). Clearly, any enterprise that isn't guided by strategy, flying blind, is doomed to failure, at least (even if "lucky" enough to survive) in the sense of not living its full potential.

Existing versus potential stakeholders

A common error of strategy is to focus on the known stakeholders, ignoring the unknown, unthought of, or forgotten stakeholders. Who is more important, your biggest customer or your future biggest customer? What about the future partner who will help you survive an unforeseen shift in your industry, rendering your existing production or delivery techniques obsolete? Do you know what next generation employees will need and want for you to be "an employer of choice" a decade from now?

The point is that strategic planning and management require as much intelligence as possible regarding stakeholders, past, present, and future. We can learn from the past and present. We must anticipate the future, and manage the present. Doing this effectively, given limited time and resources for analysis and planning, requires some balance in considering the stakeholders we are currently engaged with, and the ones we might, for some reason or other, want to become engaged with in the future.

Risk taking versus risk mitigation

A key aspect of balance in strategy in general, and entrepreneurial innovation in particular, is between risk taking and risk mitigation. Any deployment of resources involves a degree of risk. Any enterprise activity, and life in general, involves risk. But taking the time and committing resources to potential breakthrough innovations, audacious goals, and winning visions typically involves a much higher degree of risk than, say, continuous improvement initiatives, incremental growth, or business as usual. We've all heard the expression "no risk, no reward."

The point is to find the risks worth taking and then mitigate the downside of the things that might happen, that is, manage the risks so as to minimize the probability of "bad" things happening and their impact or consequences. These days, the discipline of risk management also tends to focus on maximizing the chances and impacts of good things happening as well (see ISO, 2009 for a comprehensive definition).

Tried and true versus experimentation

There's wisdom in the saying: "If it ain't broke, don't fix it." However, trying new approaches, which risks failure, means we may find something that works better, or learn from the failure. The following quotes sum this up brilliantly:

- "I have not failed. I've just found 10,000 ways that won't work" (Thomas Edison, *c.* 1920).
- "Success does not consist in never making mistakes but in never making the same one a second time" (George Bernard Shaw, 1912).
- "Anyone who doesn't make mistakes isn't trying hard enough" (Wess Roberts, 1987).
- "I am glad that I paid so little attention to good advice; had I abided by it I might have been saved from some of my most valuable mistakes" (Edna St Vincent Millay, *c.* 1940).

Continuous versus breakthrough innovation

We've already discussed the levels of risk and reward involved in continuous, incremental or sustaining innovation activities relative to breakthrough, audacious, visionary innovations. But quite apart from risk, any organization with finite resources, that is, all organizations, must strike the right balance between investing in big and small gains.

If an enterprise focused exclusively on coming up with the "next big thing," and failed to improve, reduce costs, improve quality assurance, or add value to existing products in other ways, they may well fail before getting their new technologies out the door.

Conversely, and far more commonly, if organizations focus exclusively on incremental innovation without considering potential breakthroughs or at least more significant advances, they may be left in the dust. This is tied to short-termism and risk aversion, which combine to ensure that the vast majority of leaders and enterprises never rise to the challenge of leading innovation. They are innovation followers, late adopters, and plodders, rather than trailblazers.

The familiar versus the new

Also tied to trailblazing, risk, and the question of existing versus future stakeholders is the larger challenge of achieving balance between the familiar versus the new. For the vast majority of us, it is human nature to gravitate toward the known. Relatively few of us are drawn to paths we've never trodden, dark corners, people we don't know, or, in a more general sense, the "unfamiliar." And yet, for some, the unfamiliar has a distinct allure. Further, most people tend to like something new; as long as the idea of it is somewhat familiar, new and improved, we want it.

Therefore, a further aspect of balance to consider is whether you are overly tied to the familiar, or perhaps overly drawn to the new. Are you balanced?

Stabilizing versus disruption

Somewhat related to (overlapping with) the concept of breakthrough innovation is that of disruptive innovation (breakthroughs aren't always disruptive, but disruptive innovations are generally "breakthrough" rather than incremental in nature). Disruptive innovations, first defined by Bower and Christensen (1995; also see Dyer et al., 2011), are ones that make existing products, production or delivery techniques (business models), enterprises or parts of them, and sometimes whole industries obsolete or irrelevant.

Disruptive innovation has become a kind of mantra, chanted in especially loud and strident ways by leaders in stale or stuck realms of innovation. The presumption is that resistance to change, or the stabilizing forces of inertia within the "system" require disruption. This may well be true, to an extent, but I find these voices a little too shrill, and the specifics of their message a little too devoid of specific suggestions for what should change, other than change for the sake of it.

There's no doubt that disruption can be "good," but so can stability. Some innovations can stabilize enterprises, making them more resilient and able to weather the storms of change. A broad example is diversification strategies; simply put, not having all your eggs in one basket.

Again, the overall point is the need for balance. Humans and enterprises need a degree of stability, and to embrace change. Within an enterprise, there will typically be some stakeholders who want more or less of each, and balancing their perspectives and requirements is key. This doesn't mean managing by consensus. If stability is required, it should be achieved without "turning off" change agents – making them feel change is impossible. Helping those who desire change understand that it may be a question of when or how the change will come about may keep them motivated. On the other hand, if change is required, discussing the concerns or fears of those not wanting the change may help them see the need for it, and considering their issues may support risk management. Either way, balance requires engagement.

Creation versus destruction

Related to but, again, subtly distinct from the ideas discussed above is achieving the right balance between the forces of creation and the forces of destruction. Sometimes, things need to be destroyed to make way for better things. Sometimes, it is right and useful to criticize existing institutions, leaders, practices, and policies. Sometimes, specific people need to be torn down and ripped out of the enterprise. New institutions or new leaders may be required.

Creation and destruction are another kind of dance, and therefore another aspect of the balance required. Finding the truth, the right balance for any given organization at any given point in time, is probably as much a mystical as a strategic process. But whatever the underlying process, the reality is that when it's time for something or someone to go, the "system" often knows. It's as if the "writing is on the wall."

Competition versus collaboration

Most organizations must compete, and all organizations would benefit from more, or more effective collaboration. Within an individual mindset, and within the group psyche or organizational cultures, the instinct to compete and the instinct to collaborate are at odds. Should I share my idea, in the hope that this person may help make it better, or might they simply steal it, claiming it as their own? Should we develop our idea into something to beat the competition with, or do they have expertise or other resources we lack, such that together we might make something even better? Should we spy on them, acquire them, or ask to collaborate?

Again, the challenge is to achieve balance. So, in seeking improved balance, it is important to remember that most people and organizations are firmly rooted in a competitive mindset.

Ambivalent disengagement

Ambivalence is the neutral value state between attraction and repulsion – the dance we experience as chemistry between people, or indeed anything we might be in relationship to. Ambivalent disengagement happens when there are blockages or failures to resonate in each of the psychological centers:

1. Stakeholder purposes are disconnected, misaligned, or unclear.
2. Visions for and definitions of relationship success are not shared or mutually supportive.
3. Miscommunication weakens the relationship fabric, through misaligned values, lack of trust, mismatched expectations, or misunderstanding.
4. There's no essential cohesiveness within the relationship – no attraction, no chemistry, no empathy, no or limited potential for value delivery, or no appreciation – or there's a failure to negotiate the right balance and win–win deal structure or framework within the relationship.
5. Leadership is disengaged from the rest of the organization – failing to inspire, provide direction, motivate or otherwise empower resources – or members of a leadership team are disengaged from each other, resulting in a lack of cohesion, coherence, or coordinated strategy and action, and usually setting a standard for poor engagement throughout the enterprise, at every level.
6. There's no engagement in creative conflict, collaborative learning (experimentation, mistakes, and improvement), idea co-development, and co-creation.
7. There's no synergy or alignment of motivations, attitudes, abilities, or potential to perform.

In summary, if any of the above aspects of psychology reduce the effectiveness of key stakeholder relationships, the fourth sin of innovation, disengagement, will block or counter success. On the other hand, appropriate stakeholder identification, consideration, and engagement will tend to result from the fourth entrepreneurial virtue – collaborative partnering.

Collaborative partnering

Collaboration is the "new competition." More to the point, achieve collaborative advantage, and sustainable competitive advantage will follow.

Strong collaborators are likely to benefit from exposure to more ideas early on, and they will also more readily develop their initial ideas into robust, winning ideas. A collaborator will happily share a half-baked cake and with the help of someone else's ingredients, turn it into something more beautiful and powerful. People or organizations disposed to "go for it" on their own may succeed, but not as often, or as well. And they won't have half the fun doing so. Collaborators have more fun and, in the process, they transform a higher-than-average portion of good ideas into great ideas and projects.

Another advantage collaborators possess over loners is a wider worldview, based on more complete information and intelligence. Loners tend to live in mental holes.

Even if a collaborator and a loner are both in possession of an equally great idea (perhaps the loner stole it), such that we now have, at least theoretically, a level playing field, the collaborator still enjoys distinct advantages. One key advantage the collaborator will enjoy is greater emotional intelligence, the stuff that makes for an excellent collaborative capability in the first place. In general, the collaborator is more likely to build the broad coalitions of support and stakeholder partnerships needed for ultimate success. In other words, a great collaborator is more likely to be an effective champion and attract support from others. It's viral.

Steve Jobs (2003) said: "to turn really interesting ideas and fledgling technologies into a company that can continue to innovate for years, it requires a lot of disciplines." Innovation requires the input of many disciplines. The idea that benefits from being touched and developed by many diverse disciplinary perspectives will win over other, less fortunate ideas. To build a better mousetrap, don't hire a bunch of mechanical engineers. Hire one of those, a few other types of engineers, a marketer, and most especially a mouse, or someone capable of seeing the world through a mouse's eyes. The key is to engage as many and as rich a diversity mix as possible. Again, the natural collaborators have a critical edge.

One also has to be multidisciplined in terms of the innovation process. Unnovation drivers such as a delayed decision to launch or kill projects cause enormous waste. Here, too, collaborators will have the edge over noncollaborators. We certainly don't need decisions by committees, but the collaborator will be more likely to hold all the key facts than the noncollaborator. Collaborators spend more time looking in "the mirror of other people." The individual or company that has lots of solid relationships will be better able to ask for mirroring, better able to really listen to and understand the feedback, and also better able to engage in partnering to help move from their niche into other valuable realms. Advantage, collaborators.

A healthy organization needs a range of offerings, as well as constant investment in keeping the offerings fresh, but not at the expense of focus. A discordant portfolio is the worst of all worlds. If you have a great idea for something that doesn't fit your existing portfolio, give it away. Or sell your company and move on with the new idea.

It's also critically important to invest in aspects of the organization beyond the product portfolio. A successful organization not only has great products, but also great people. Invest in developing leaders rather than followers. Invest in developing a culture of innovation – value-oriented, customer-centric collaborators. They will win every time.

Finally, successful people and organizations are ones with a strategic plan – a compass, a destination in mind, a sense of purpose, and a vision of what success looks like. Here, too, the collaborator has key advantages. The process of strategic planning and implementation is not for loners. Gone are the days when the role of a CEO was to climb down the mountain once a year to provide direction and vision for the masses. If the masses don't understand the strategy, they won't do it. They need to own it and live it. They need to engage in its formation and its ongoing evolution as the journey unfolds. It's a collaborative effort.

In summary, those of us who develop collaboration skills have a number of important advantages when it comes to innovation. Collaboration, especially externally, can be a struggle, but learning to do it provides a sustainable edge that will benefit us as individual leaders and innovators, and as organizations seeking to maximize ROI, stakeholder value, and make the world a better place. If you want to win, develop the collaborative edge.

Developing collaborative advantage requires bridging across the various strategic innovation agendas:

1. Partnering with shared strategic intent, so that purposes and goals are clear, well communicated, and synergistic, avoiding any misaligned expectations or hidden agendas.
2. Partnering intelligently, sharing vital knowledge, which is especially likely to be highly insightful when engaging in external collaborations.
3. Value driven, with clear win–win value for the collaborators.
4. Respectful and cognizant of all stakeholders involved on all sides of the collaboration.
5. Oriented toward improvement and shared change agency.
6. Leveraging complementary capabilities, and hopefully also strengthening the capabilities of the individual partners.
7. Action based, so that rather than just talking about partnering, the collaborators actually get on with it and achieve specific, desired results.

Engagement

Every enterprise is fundamentally nothing more or less than a collection of relationships – with customers, employees, partners, and other stakeholders. It's no accident that relationships and engagement sit at the heart of the problem, central among the psyche centers. Therefore, it's surely no surprise that the effectiveness or ineffectiveness of engagement within these relationships is often the most critical determinant of success or failure.

chapter 12

Frightfully Disempowered Followership

"No man will make a great leader who wants to do it all himself or get all the credit for doing it."

Andrew Carnegie (*c.* 1900)

The fifth sin

The condition of frightfully disempowered followership is the "fifth sin" blocking innovation and driving efforts toward unnovation.

Misconceptions about leadership

There are arguably more books on leadership than good leaders, and certainly more leadership "gurus" than well-led organizations. But considering all these books and gurus, I've found no real "science" of leadership, no clear definitions, and no framework or coherent guide on how to lead effectively. So, it's hardly surprising that ineffectual leadership is the rule rather than the exception.

Most "how to lead" guides are purely anecdotal: successful executives sharing hard-won snippets of wisdom, or academics or consultants who've closely watched successful and unsuccessful leaders. I'm not saying their wisdom lacks value, only that there's no coherent theory or practical guide on how to lead.

Given all the confusion, it's probably useful to start with some definitions. The term "leadership" is used to refer to the act, process, function, responsibility, or position of an individual person or group. We often think of leaders as the people authorized, empowered, and entrusted to set direction and make decisions. We say someone is a leader in relation to others, or to an organization, if they are in a position of formal authority to manage. And yet leadership can be informal as well as formally recognized. We sometimes refer to people with great influence as "leaders from behind." Such leaders often guide and shape events without being in a position of formal authority. The wizard Merlin was, if he existed, such a leader in relation to the formally recognized leadership of King Arthur.

We also differentiate between leaders and followers in fields of competitive activity. We refer to leaders in sport, music, or any field of human activity based on their degree of recognition and success. Their leadership is in relation to some specific notion of what's important. A golfer may be deemed to lead based on trophies won, prize monies earned, or general acclaim and fame. The definition of success is often subjective, and someone can rise or drop in our overall estimation based on perceived hygiene factors. Witness Tiger Woods' approval rating after revelations about his personal life.

Further, we refer to organizations and countries as leaders. The "leadership team" of Microsoft is an obvious group, while the organization Open Source Initiative (OSI; or its precedent, the free software movement) is arguably a much less obvious grouping that defines a subset of leadership within a broader community. We may say Microsoft is a leader because it dominates certain markets, is the market leader, or is more successful than its competitors. We may say OSI led major innovation within the field of software development and distribution globally. In other words, there are many different forms of leadership, and clearly they are not of equal value.

The important underlying point here is that any given concept of leadership is in relation to some measure of value, it is tied to definitions of success. Our notions of what makes a good or bad leader critically depend on what we focus on. Let's illustrate this with a well-known figure from history, who had the job title of "leader" in the not too distant past.

Adolf Hitler's role as führer made him the unquestioned person in charge – the formal leader. But was he a "good" one? Some have argued that he was a very strong leader, with great influence, charisma, and power over his fellow citizens. He is also sometimes credited with getting Germany back on its feet, in terms of national pride and industrial power, following the devastating effects of World War I and the Treaty of Versailles. But I have a simple notion of what's important in relation to the role of leaders that clearly and unequivocally exposes Hitler as a terribly "bad" leader. Value is the metric, and no one can argue that Hitler wasn't responsible (along with others, of course) for massive destruction of value during World War II. Humanity is still affected by the loss of life, and much more, that resulted.

Of course, war also stimulates innovative advances in communications, medicine, and physical sciences. But that doesn't take away from the fact that Hitler and his Nazis destroyed the lives of many millions of people, with countless knock-on effects to the current day. At the time, for a while, the Germans congratulated themselves as world leaders, the master race, and dominant force in Europe. Had they won the war, there would no doubt be countless books praising the leadership of Hitler and his cronies. None of that takes away from the fact that the value they gained as conquerors was at the expense of others. The ultimate barometer for deciding whether a group or an individual were "good" leaders is whether their existence and impact on history was positive or negative in terms of overall value – not just the bit they got to selfishly cling to, for a time.

Historical perspective

The overall impact or "net value" of any individual leader, or leading group (company, country, or civilization) is difficult, if not impossible to assess. We have to consider their impact on a planetary scale and over vast expanses of time. We might say, for example, that the Roman Empire was "good" in the long run, in terms of its legacy of laws, civilization, and other innovations. However, it is difficult to assess the costs, through the destruction of other civilizations or those that might have come into being, and the resulting loss of their potential contributions.

The same might be said of the British Empire, and indeed all the European empires, in terms of their disastrous impact on the peoples of the Americas, Africa and Asia. I recommend Diamond (1997) for an interesting summary of geopolitical history. But to close off the present discussion, let's face the fact that our assessment of whether someone or some group is a good leader is tied to our subjective notions of the value they created or destroyed (including lost opportunity costs), and the net balance of the two. My subjective assessment is that Hitler was a disaster, for the Germans, and for the world. I think we're still paying the price.

I also think Hitler was a product of his times. He didn't exist in a vacuum. He was, in a sense, created and shaped by his times – his upbringing as a poor, struggling artist in the Austro-Hungarian Empire, his personal experiences during World War I, and their aftermath. Humanity has long suffered from a sort of insanity, disguised as rational self-interest. Those afflicted with this condition think it's OK to increase their own net worth, regardless of the cost to others. Enlarge our empire by killing or subjugating our neighbors and stealing their land. Under this perspective, "all is fair in love and war." What matters is winning, not how one wins. The one with the biggest piece of pie wins, even if most of the pie gets destroyed in the fight. This is the model of leadership based on competition. The winner takes all, and is the recognized leader, and the author of the history books.

Traditional, top-down leadership

The competitive model of leadership, that the leader is the one who "wins," goes hand in glove with what I call the traditional, top-down leadership paradigm. In fact, the top-down, command-and-control leadership model has its origins in precisely the same insanity as the competitive model. Top-down leadership comes from the paradigm of command and control, militarism, and war.

In top-down leadership, the dictator (or equivalent: caesar, führer, emperor, king, queen or whatever) commands the generals to win battles and wars. The generals command the colonels, who command the majors, who command the captains, who command the lieutenants, who command the NCOs, who command the soldiers to march, kill, or die. The good soldier doesn't question authority and is willing to be sacrificed for the higher good. The "higher" good is, of course, that of the dictator and all those who greedily eat scraps from the dictator's table.

The dictator may be driven by vision rather than ego. At worst, their dictatorship is all about enriching themselves and their loyal lieutenants.

But many of the greatest dictators – the ones who had a massive impact on history, good or bad – were driven by a vision of greatness and glory. Alexander the Great, Julius Caesar, Genghis Khan, Napoleon, and Hitler were all such men. All left a powerful legacy, and we can argue until the end of days what the scales look like in balance, in terms of their net overall value impact on value (innovation) in the world they lived and died in. But that is not the point here. The important point is simply that there is such a scale – a mathematical reality – for each leader, although we as humans can never absolutely know it. We can intuit the reality. The majority of us can probably agree that Hitler was an overall negative and therefore a bad leader. On the other hand, we can probably, for the most part, agree that Roosevelt, Churchill, Gandhi, and Mandela were good leaders, leaving lasting legacies of positive net impact on humanity. This latter group of leaders were not dictators; but let's hold that thought for the moment.

In the traditional model, the dictator or supreme leader sits at the top of the heap, providing direction based on greater wisdom. The leader has a clear sense of direction and vision based on high altitude. Perhaps the leader even enjoys greater clarity of thought and foresight based on the cleaner air up there. Ideally, the godlike leader instructs the rest of us on what to do and how to do it for the greater good of the organization. But, in reality, the leader is often someone who has clawed their way up the heap of bodies, bruising (or worse) others along the way. Although they may try to surround themselves with loyal servants, the characteristics that allowed the leader to rise to authority are also to be found in these other would-be leaders. Therefore, at least some of the leader's precious time and focus is spent retaining the leadership position, and some of the attention of others is devoted to the opportunity to assassinate. This is what we refer to as "organizational politics," which seems to be the primary avocation in some organizations.

The traditional model evolved in early civilizations, as humans found ways of organizing that led to survival in a competitive, often brutal world. The roots of the model are militaristic – command and control. As the complexity of societies and organizations grew, the art form also grew, from simple militaristic chains of command to full-blown bureaucratic systems of governance. But the form and function remained the same – hierarchical, stratified, and top-down.

The traditional model is highly successful, but flawed. It has certainly stood the test of time, in that most businesses and other organizations still employ it, to varying degrees and with varying degrees of success. However, the main reason for continuing to employ the traditional model isn't that it's the most effective approach. One reason for not giving it up is that the individuals who have managed to claw their way to power are reluctant to bring in fundamental change. It's in their nature to preserve and protect their power. The traditional approach is the "easiest" approach – most tuned to our human psyche. As individual egos, some of us are driven to achieve recognition, glory, adulation, and all that goes with power, successfully applied. Those who are not so driven are often happiest when led – when provided with clear direction, sense of purpose, and occasional strokes or praise from the powerful leader figures they look up to.

Fundamental flaws

So what's the problem? The essential flaw has to do with the phenomenon of power itself. When power is concentrated and applied unidirectionally, the "system" lacks intelligence. To create intelligence in any system, power must be distributed. In the most adaptable, successful organisms and organizations, the ability to process information, to make decisions, and to react intelligently is distributed throughout. Through distributed computing, our bodies are infinitely better able to deal with and adapt to our ever-changing environment.

In organizations, people must be empowered to lead at every level if the organization is to maximize its overall chances for survival. The flow of information must become multidirectional, so that decisions can be made when and where needed. The intelligence of the system increases as the neural connectivity and flow of data increases. Data applied to analysis and decision making becomes information, information becomes knowledge, and knowledge becomes wisdom. When information is hoarded by the powerful few, wisdom seldom develops.

When a system becomes intelligent, it often also recognizes that a strictly hierarchical, stratified form is suboptimal. Therefore, costly layers are often removed with no loss of leadership; in fact, there are more likely gains in overall system leadership effectiveness based on the streamlining of communications and other key functions. Those who tend to horde information, because it is their power, may learn that others have valuable insights and perspectives. Even someone like Hitler can learn to respect expertise, intellect, and diversity, up to a point.

The reality of most traditional, top-down leaders is that although they may respect the value of experts, they are rarely able to fully empower distributed decision making. They are happy to allow the specialists to function within a confined space, wearing a leash. But they are not willing to allow anyone, even the experts, to question their ultimate judgment, authority, or direction. Why?

Fear and insecurity are at the roots of the personal weakness that prevents most top-down leaders from changing. This is egotism. There is an inherent egotism in the assumption that the top-down leader knows best, or at least better than those below (who are usually closer to the problems that need to be understood and solved). But the underlying reality of egotism is insecurity, given that the evolutionary function of ego is self-awareness for self-preservation. Deep inside every raving egotist there is pathetic insecurity. The more bloated the ego, the more shriveled the inner self-confidence. At the core of every supremely egotistical, outwardly powerful traditional leader is a small, weak, inner child who probably didn't get loved enough by mommy and daddy. The resulting adult is flawed – insecure, unable to trust others fully, unable to lead except through fear and force; in short, a bully.

Another flaw of traditional leadership is that the entire model is designed so that value flows to the top. Money flows from customers to sales and service representatives, and upward to the owner-managers. At the top, the rewards are greatest, for the CEO, the capitalist, the dictator, or the despot. The job titles may differ, but the model remains the same: top-down power, bottom-up glory and reward.

Of course, some value remains at each level. Paltry amounts get consumed by the slaves (food and water, for example), whereas buying the loyalty of guards and soldiers further up the hierarchy requires a greater share. But the overall system is designed to maximize the amount of value that floats upward to the top. In fact, the value pyramid is the opposite of the power pyramid, as illustrated in Figure 12.1. From the standpoint of capitalists, and other kinds of despots, there is no problem with this model. Things are as they should be. All is well. But there is a problem. There is yet another fundamental, fatal flaw.

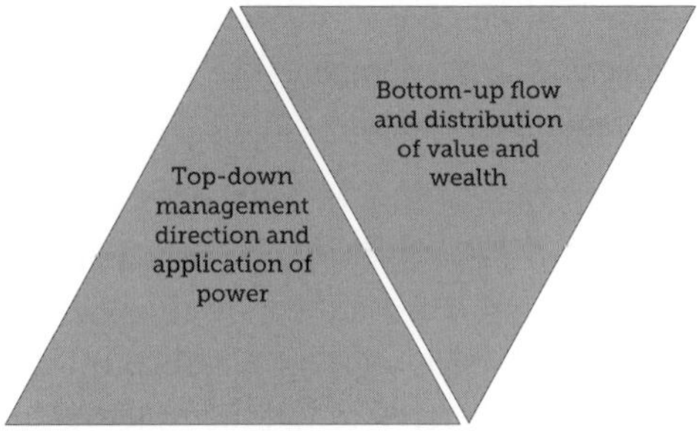

FIGURE 12.1 Traditional leadership model

The essential problem with the traditional leadership model is unsustainability. The degree of unsustainability is based on the degree of imbalance, and the underlying greed that creates and fuels this imbalance. The more extreme the imbalance, the quicker the model will perish. It's fundamentally unstable. There will be more revolutions, strikes, and palace revolts – the more unfair the model. A simple example; if the dictator doesn't share table scraps with the generals, it won't take long for the generals to replace the dictator. It will take longer for slaves to rise up and insist on becoming peasants, but that too will happen – eventually.

Dealing with the unsustainability is costly. Lots of effort is required to maintain a degree of stability. There's a word for this: bloat. Protecting the privileged positions and interests of dictator, generals, and the rest requires a lot of effort, supervision, eyeballs, and eyeballs watching other eyeballs. Think of the Gestapo, the KGB, or Saddam's Iraqi regime. Top-down leadership structures must employ many layers of management. When decision making is not distributed based on empowerment and when organizations are designed to filter value and information unequally upward and downward, the task of saying "No" can become quite complex. Expectations and perceptions must be managed. Fear must be managed and measured, and doled out in the proper doses. There's even a special word for it, invented by Max Weber (1922), German political economist and sociologist, to describe the leadership paradigm we all know and love as "bureaucracy." Believe it or not, Weber was a proponent of bureaucracy, and advocated it as a beautiful, efficient, and idealistic organizational form.

Although there is symmetry in the traditional model that some would see as beautiful, there is an essential instability and unsustainability based on the foregoing "fundamental flaws." The despot needs to sleep, eventually.

The most fundamental issue with the traditional leadership model is that it is not empowering. The word "empowerment" is typically used to refer to the leadership act of delegating authority to another leader – empowering them to lead on a specific issue or opportunity, or with a specific remit. But I'm using the word "empowerment" in a broader sense.

Empowering innovation is maximizing the ability of resources to get the desired job done. This is about empowering all the resources that must be marshaled, inspired, applied, and managed effectively for innovation to occur.

Disempowerment might happen when there is no leader or champion for an innovation, no visible leadership, when those in charge lack critical leadership skills or attributes such as the motivation and courage to lead, when there's bad strategy, when people are fearful, or when resources are simply insufficiently applied or mismanaged. If innovation is not "powered" by the right resources and levels thereof, then it will fail.

Working through fear

Let's label organizations that work through fear as WTF. The fundamental flaws of the traditional, WTF leadership paradigm are based on the centers of human and organizational psyche. Consider them, bottom up in relation to the sin of frightfully disempowered followership:

1. Fear is the main motivator, the underlying driver in the "engine room" of WTF organizations. In a climate of fear, it becomes the defining aspect of "culture" and psyche. Fear creates a "leadership no-go zone."
2. Fear also stifles creativity and ideation in WTF structures. Fear blocks trust, and without trust, people won't share ideas or engage in creative conflict. People won't experiment and risk making mistakes or failing if they fear punishment. Fear blocks the seeds for innovation.
3. The many layers of management bureaucracy and supervision required to manage a fear-based, inequitable WTF structure create baggage, bloat, and costs that weigh against value, and are therefore inherently unnovative, as well as performing the function of spreading fear, and

stamping out any ideas, or glimmerings of hope, or thoughts that there might be a better way. Bureaucracy also results in ineffectual decision making, lack of direction, and therefore lack of focus, which typically means underinvesting in or underempowering key initiatives.

4 The value management model is always, at least to some extent, unfair in a WTF organization, and therefore unsustainable in the long run. If value distribution is unfair, people won't remain motivated to engage and contribute. In extreme cases, insane levels of greed generate huge momentary value for the few, and a destructive, massive loss of value and long-term ability to create and enjoy it for the many. The collapse of Lehman Brothers, which precipitated the global economic crisis in 2008, is a perfect example, reported in depth from an inside perspective by McDonald and Robinson (2009).

5 People are not able to speak the truth in WTF environments. In such places, the emperors rarely know when they or their organizations are exposed. The organization might be about to be criticized, but for fear of speaking up, chances are no one wants to deliver the bad news.

6 The unequal flow and sharing of information and power (information = power) in a WTF organization, operating only top-down, essentially limits "system intelligence." As a result, the WTF organization is often blind, or nearly so. At the very least, it probably needs a thick pair of glasses, in the form of some expensive management consulting firms to give them the vision they require and are incapable of achieving on their own.

7 Last but not least, the WTF organizational model is disempowering, blocking the essential purpose of leadership, which is to empower everything. WTF leadership fails to empower leadership throughout the organization, with concentrated (rather than distributed) decision making. It fails to empower resources to achieve their full potential. And this loops around and connects with the performance layer.

In summary, the above aspects of psychology conspire to produce the fifth deadly sin of innovation – ineffectual leadership, disempowering the resources required for innovation success. On the other side of the coin, the responsible empowerment of people and other resources is the fifth entrepreneurial virtue, and an essential act of leadership. As Bill Gates said: "As we look ahead into the next century, leaders will be those who empower others" (Pritchard, 2012).

Responsible empowerment

There's a powerful new, and much more effective leadership paradigm emerging in leading-edge organizations worldwide, which counteracts the fifth sin, leading to the corresponding virtue – responsible empowerment. I call the new paradigm "upside-down, bottom-up leadership," illustrated in Figure 12.2.

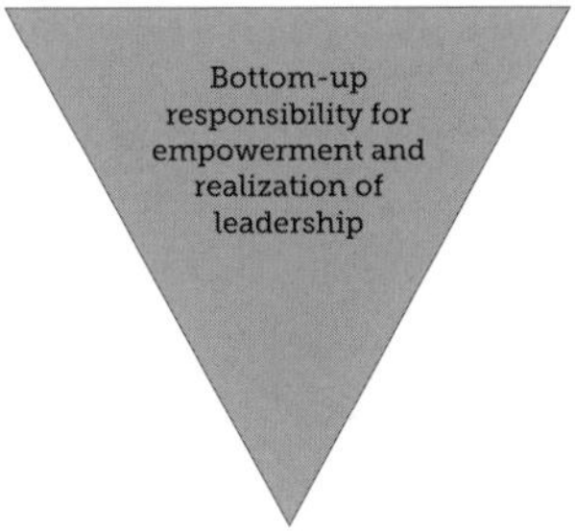

FIGURE 12.2 Upside-down, bottom-up leadership

As shown in Figure 12.2, the upside-down, bottom-up leader flips the organization on its head. How can this be done? It is no harder, or easier, than a mindset shift. It's a mental flip, easy to conceptualize, but initially difficult to practice. For a start, instead of thinking of the leader's position at the top of the organization, think of it at the bottom. Think of the leader as shouldering responsibility for the entire structure, supporting and serving it, rather than being supported and served. The new paradigm leader is at the bottom, leading bottom-up rather than top-down. I'm sure you can see this is simply a matter of perspective. A small but important mindset shift.

A further mindset shift happens when an organizational leadership model is flipped. In order not to be crushed under the weight of responsibility represented by the organizational pyramid, leaders seek to empower others. They seek to infuse the organization with leadership at all levels, to get others to "pick up the bags," assuming responsibility, and lightening the overall load. A flipped organization encourages empowerment.

In an overall sense, the entire purpose of an organization might be conceptualized as creating as wide a platform as possible to serve its customers. Conceptually, the flipped, flattened organization has a wider "coalface" at the top. In many ways, the most important empowerment provided by leadership is at the coalface, where the organization meets the customer. The people who interface with the customer must be empowered to lead the delivery or manifestation of value, empowered to solve problems as they emerge. This empowerment is what distinguishes between really excellent customer service and mediocrity. When organizations require service decisions (problem solving and so on) to be escalated up the management chain, they lose. They lose time, value, and customers.

When an organization achieves the "upside-down" mindset shift, it will naturally reconfigure itself to maximize value delivery. The pyramid will reshape itself, perhaps collapsing under its own weight, to be as broad as possible at the top – the coalface – while also eliminating bulk in the middle. An organization with an intelligent customer interface doesn't need bulky layers of middle management to process, digest, report, and monitor decisions. The first, initial shift is revolutionary, a mental flip from top-down to bottom-up. Then, something else tends to happen, an evolution toward a flatter, more distributed leadership model, as illustrated as the second step in Figure 12.3.

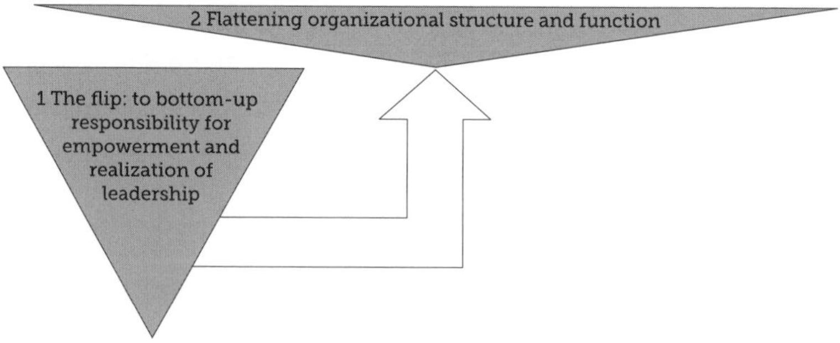

FIGURE 12.3 Evolutionary flattening of upside-down organizations

The reality is that people sometimes need top-down direction as well as bottom-up empowerment. It's a dance. It's about situational leadership boiled down to a simple truism – employees have different levels of competency and sometimes can handle being empowered, other times not.

Enlightened leaders will naturally adopt a bottom-up leadership style, employing top-down direction and control only when required, such as in an emergency where there might not be time to coach someone else in developing their ability to handle the issue. Most leaders and organizations reflect a mix of top-down and bottom-up management. Many leaders try to empower others because they know it's the right thing to do, but sometimes revert to top-down styles when feeling challenged or pressured. In some organizations, a top-down style from the most senior leaders is countered and corrected to an extent by more enlightened middle managers. In these cases, middle managers may empower themselves and those they manage, in spite of top-down autocracy. And many organizations are undergoing a journey of change from top-down autocracy to bottom-up democracy.

At any given point in time, within any organization, we may find some managers who can flip the leadership paradigm while others don't. In most organizations, we'll find a mix. The ones that lean toward the new paradigm – bottom-up, upside down – will be the more effective leaders. And by distributing leadership throughout the organization rather than focusing it in the hands of a few human beings, more intelligent, effective, and powerful leadership will be achieved overall. As Drucker (1939) said: "No institution can possibly survive if it needs geniuses or supermen to manage it. It must be organized in such a way as to be able to get along under a leadership composed of average human beings."

The ability to lead innovation effectively is crucially dependent on the ability to responsibly empower resources, in relation to each of the strategic innovation agendas:

1. Ensuring resources are clear on the strategic intent driving the innovation, because people who understand strategy can contribute to it, criticize it, improve it, and help it succeed.
2. Distributing knowledge and intelligence by engaging resources in owning, generating, and sharing it, because intelligent resources are more effective than stupid ones.
3. Properly and fairly valuing the contributions of resources, and ensuring they understand their role in the creation and provision of value, underlying values, and overall value delivery model of the organization, because poorly paid people in win–lose relationships with employers rarely give their best.

4 Empowering effective stakeholder engagement, because people who are able to say "yes" or even "no" to customers, when appropriate, are far superior to people who always have to escalate decisions to their superiors.
5 Encouraging change agency, because people who are encouraged to see the need for change and suggest specific improvements are far more valuable than people who are afraid to put ideas forward, or who resist change based on fear of the consequences.
6 Investing in the development of capabilities, through education, training, and other developmental opportunities for personal growth, skills, and abilities, because people appreciate being invested in and are likely to "give back" ROI, whereas people who simply feel used and abused tend to give no more than they feel they must.
7 Empowering action, enabling people to make decisions and take decisive action that can make the difference between winning and losing, instead of waiting for orders, like frightfully disempowered followers. The first task of any leader should be to consider their own psyche, as recognized by Zhuge Liang (181–234), once acknowledged as China's greatest strategist, who said: "First organize the inner, then organize the outer. First organize the great, then organize the small. First organize yourself, then organize others."

chapter 13

Painfully Boring Uncreativity

"The chief enemy of creativity is 'good' sense."

Pablo Picasso (*c.* 1920)

The sixth sin

All innovations begin with ideas and so do unnovations. Therefore, the sixth sin of innovation – painfully boring uncreativity – comes in a number of specific forms: lack of ideas, bad ideas, failure to adapt and develop ideas, failure to engage ideas that "aren't invented here," inadequate listening or engagement of potential sources of ideas, and failure to kill some ideas in a timely manner to enable focus on the ideas that most merit further development. Either way, the overall message is "innovate or die." As Gary Hamel said (quoted in TRIZ Journal, n.d.):

> Somewhere out there is a bullet with your company's name on it. Somewhere out there is a competitor, unborn and unknown, that will render your strategy obsolete. You can't dodge the bullet – you're going to have to shoot first. You're going to have to out-innovate the innovators.

Idea inadequacy

Ideas are often lacking or inadequate for the following main reasons:

- Creativity is simply lacking in some people and organizations. Psychologists are not entirely sure "where" creativity originates, or how it happens.
- Employees aren't engaged, properly incentivized, and actively encouraged to contribute ideas, to challenge each other's or management's ideas, to engage in creative conflict, and to actively scan their environments, in and out of work, for potential new ideas.
- Leadership stifles ideas, challenge, and creative conflict by creating and maintaining a culture of complacency or, worse, a climate of fear.
- People don't ask the right questions. As Jay (1967) said: "The uncreative mind can spot wrong answers, but it takes a very creative mind to spot wrong questions."
- Customers aren't properly listened to and engaged with through structured processes for capturing their ideas, such as focus groups or survey approaches such as NPS, or by effective sales, service and any other customer-interfacing staff.
- It's important to differentiate between choosers and users when considering "customer perspective" as a source of ideas. There's a tendency to focus sales efforts and research on decision makers – the choosers, such as business owners or procurement managers, or their key influencers. But the end users of a company's products will often be an even better source of innovation ideas (von Hippel, 1988, 2005) if appropriately engaged.
- Non-customers are often almost totally ignored, yet they can be a vital source of ideas for growth and innovation if appropriately engaged by sales ("why aren't you buying our products?") or structured research (such as NPS).
- Competitors can be a fantastic source of ideas, yet a surprising number of organizations fly blind, not really knowing, other than in a general sense, what their competitors are up to, what they're planning, or what specific innovations they are working on.
- According to the Global Benchmarking Network (2008), most organizations (61%) don't perform best practice benchmarking, another highly valuable source of ideas for innovation. Further, most benchmarking is only against leading organizations within the same sector, industry, or

geography. Benchmarking is far more useful when done against leaders in other industries or areas of enterprise. A perfect example is Lee's (2004) consideration of *If Disney Ran Your Hospital: 9½ Things You Would Do Differently*. Any service organization, such as lawyers, accountants, restaurants, or government agencies, would do well to benchmark against Disney, a global service best practice leader, rather than other organizations in their sectors. This could well lead to "breakthroughs" rather than less valuable ideas for incremental improvements.

- Suppliers, distributors, and other partners are often overlooked as sources of ideas; yet their relatively intimate knowledge of our organizations and "neutral external view" can help us spot deficiencies, inefficiencies, and other ideas for improvement. The problem, potentially, is that it's sometimes not in the best interest of our suppliers or partners to help us truly solve our problems, especially if their product is tied to them. For example, I've witnessed armies of consultants and software developers spending hundreds of person-years of effort to solve network management problems for telecom operators, seemingly intent on working ad infinitum, when a simpler approach may be to redesign from scratch rather than heaping complexity on top of the complexity and problems that already exist.
- The external world in general is an exciting and potentially invaluable source of ideas. In fact, most great ideas for innovation don't come from R&D departments, from within the four walls of organizations, or from the "four walls" of our own heads. The world can be an inspirational place, and most entrepreneurs and innovators should spend more time exploring it.
- Experimentation is a vital innovation process, and yet, according to Phillips (2012):

  > Most organizations do so much research, so much perfecting of one product or service, and so little experimentation that they too can claim not to know hundreds of ways to deliver value to their customers [referring to Edison's claim that he knew a thousand ways not to make a light bulb], but not because they experimented and failed, but because they never experimented at all.

- Most organizations aren't diverse enough to bring a sufficiently rich set of perspectives to debates about innovation. For example, a survey reported by Hewlett et al. (2013) found that 78% of companies lacked diversity within leadership teams, going on to say that:

> Without diverse leadership, women are 20% less likely than straight white men to win endorsement for their ideas; people of color are 24% less likely; and LGBTs are 21% less likely. This costs their companies crucial market opportunities, because inherently diverse contributors understand the unmet needs in under-leveraged markets.

- Hewlett et al. (2013) further pointed out that a lack of leadership diversity is only half the problem – a lack of diversity within wider workforce is another obstacle to innovation.
- Finally, many organizations simply don't get the process right. Brainstorming sessions where certain people dominate or where the discussion turns too quickly to all the reasons why ideas won't work are simply ineffective. Organizations that don't "establish a culture in which all employees feel free to contribute ideas" (Hewlett et al., 2013) are much less likely to innovate successfully.

The idea tornado

From the above, it should be apparent that one of the keys to innovation success is to capture as many ideas as possible and then mix them together to see what new ideas emerge or how ideas might combine or clash. Part of the process is to narrow down the ideas, creating focus. This is often portrayed as an ideas or innovation funnel, however, I think a more descriptive metaphor is an ideas or innovation tornado. The challenge is to build it wide at the top, in order to capture as many ideas as possible, mix them vigorously, and create focus, as illustrated in Figure 13.1.

In the world of innovation, there's no such thing as too many ideas or a bad idea. The innovation machine needs lots of ideas fodder. Ideas are the vital starting point for any innovation. Individually, they're almost worthless little specks of dust, but stuff that will ultimately form the gold bricks of the solid foundation for a highly successful business.

Great innovation companies build a wide "funnel" to maximize idea capture. The person or organization better able to connect with and listen to more sources of ideas will win, all other things being equal. Sure, it pays to be brilliant, creative, and full of bright ideas. But most of us don't get that way by accident. Innovative enterprises foster lots of internal creativity (see Kelley and Littman, 2001) encouraging people to find and share ideas. They get people talking, playing, listening, and challenging. Further, the really smart players think outside the box. They look outside their own four walls, their own culture and mindset, and seek ideas in strange places. Some even talk to their customers. In all seriousness, organizations that properly engage customers in ideation and as sources for innovation insight, carefully consider and understand their competition, but also benchmark against innovation leaders outside their own industries will enjoy an ideas advantage.

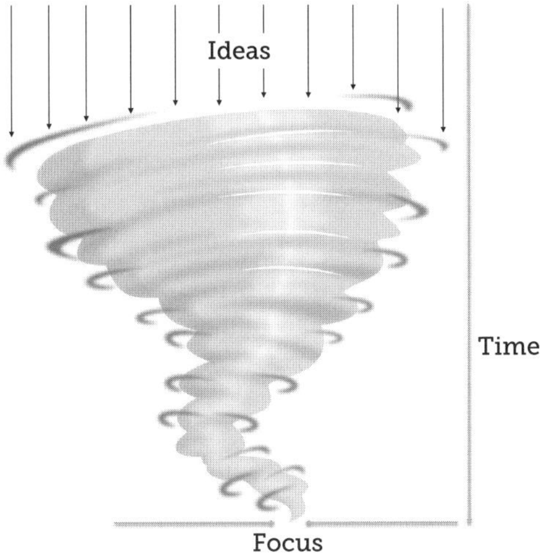

FIGURE 13.1 The ideas tornado
Source: http://pixabay.com

It's essential to get lots of good ideas into the "hopper" as the basic "fuel" and raw material for the innovation "machine." Without ideas, or with poor ideas, an enterprise cannot innovate. Of course, ideas require sources of ideas, but in many ways the key is to bridge between leadership and culture, so that leadership explicitly fosters and empowers a culture where people are willing and feel encouraged to share their ideas, where no idea is a "bad" idea even if it's half-baked. Fear stifles creative expression. Ask any musician how their performances are affected by anxiety. Similarly, the effective expression of ideas and even the basic willingness to share them are reduced by anxiety.

If leaders create a climate of fear, creativity suffers, the idea hopper will be empty, and the beginning point for the innovation process will dry up.

Ideas that are unexpressed are missed opportunities. Someone who doesn't share their half-baked cake, because they are fearful of rejection or worse, is failing to offer someone else the opportunity to finish baking it, icing it, and turning it into something fabulous. To ensure that lots of ideas are generated to feed the innovation machine, vanquish fear. Ferret out the bullies who intimidate others, creating fear, and eliminate them. Tell people it's OK to share half-baked cakes, and that any idea is potentially a good one, and mean it. Celebrate the sharing of ideas, and reward the best ones lavishly, publicly, and often. Ideas are the stuff of innovation.

Another key way in which leading innovators enjoy an advantage over rivals is they kill good ideas quickly, so that great ones can thrive. Good ideas can't be allowed to consume any more resource, airtime, or attention than is absolutely necessary to determine they're merely good. Only the great ideas should be nurtured and raised up through the innovation process. If an individual or organization tries to do too much, failure is inevitable. Better to do a few things well than many things poorly.

Most organizations don't kill ideas and their resultant projects off quickly enough, thus avoiding unnecessary expenditure of precious time and other resources on things that will never fully and successfully make it out the door anyway. Lacking focus, too many would-be innovators try to do too much with too little. Instead of doing one thing really well, they do more, but only with mediocre results or failing entirely. For example, a typical scenario when faced with the need to cut R&D budgets is to slash across the board, rather than killing entire programs to maintain sufficient resources on the most important ones. This is a failure of leadership – indecision, lack of clear priorities, and failure to focus – ultimately failing to empower resources and projects to succeed. But this particular failure of leadership is also a failure of ideas management.

Idea blockers

Failures and weaknesses within the individual and organizational psyche produce the sixth sin of innovation, painfully boring uncreativity, as follows:

1 Not having clear ideas regarding the purpose for an innovation, or innovation in general. Also not defining the overall purpose of the organization in terms that imply, foster, or demand innovation. For example, compare these mission statements that clearly embrace innovation:
- Merck: "To preserve and improve human life."
- 3M: "To solve unsolved problems innovatively."

with these:
- GM: "GM is a multinational corporation engaged in socially responsible operations, worldwide. It is dedicated to provide products and services of such quality that our customers will receive superior value while our employees and business partners will share in our success and our stock-holders will receive a sustained superior return on their investment."
- Xerox: "Xerox is a quality company. Quality is the basic principle for Xerox. Quality means providing our external and internal customers with innovative products and services that fully satisfy their requirements. Quality improvement is the job of every Xerox employee."

2 Ideas that are not inspired by or toward a strategic vision that is audacious as well as realistic, and ideas that are bland or banal are uninspiring, while ideas that are completely impossible, unfeasible, or perhaps just ahead of their time are equally unlikely to lead to innovation success.

3 Ideas that aren't spoken, shared, or expressed, that are untrue, false, based on falsehoods or incorrect information or assumptions, or that are not oriented toward value creation, including ideas that might be destructive, are all examples of blockages related to giving effective "voice" to innovation ideas.

4 Not effectively engaging in collaboration, including creative conflict and consideration of the diverse values, perspectives, and requirements of the various innovation stakeholders, will reduce the quantity and quality of innovation ideas, thinking, and planning.

5 If the ideation and idea development process isn't effectively encouraged, empowered, and led, then even great ides can be ignored, or can flounder, wither and die.

6 Ineffectual creativity, such as when ideas for innovation are not inspired by entrepreneurship, change agency, and a desire for improvement, or when the creative juices simply aren't flowing or the wellspring for creativity has somehow dried up, can mean there simply aren't enough good ideas for innovation to enable uncovering and developing great ones.

7 Lastly, if there is no underlying motivation for creativity, or hope and belief that it is possible, or foundation for effective ideation based on knowledge, then ideas can't possibly be generated and implemented.

In summary, any one of the seven aspects of psychology can reduce creativity or prevent the successful creative generation and development of ideas for innovation; or they can all conspire to produce the sixth sin – painfully boring uncreativity – arguably defeating innovation before it even gets started. In contrast, the sixth entrepreneurial virtue is creative ideation.

Creative ideation

Entrepreneurial, innovative enterprises maximize creative ideation in relation to their strategic innovation agendas, as follows:

1 While maintaining clear intent based on mission and vision, they are also open-minded and open to new ideas, including new missions and visions or improvements to existing ones. The paradox here is that creativity is, to an extent, dependent on a balance between intending to be creative and being open or receptive to it.

2 Knowledge breeds creative ideation. A rich collection of intelligence related to any specific domain is fertile soil for spawning ideas for innovation in that domain. A blank piece of paper can be a useful device for ideation, but more so when the brain connected to the hand holding the pen is filled with relevant knowledge, understanding, and insight.

3 A specific realm of understanding that is qualitative as well as quantitative, linking to intelligence, is the realm of value. When ideas are linked to the value agenda, focused on creating, maximizing, and delivering value, they are, by definition, drivers for innovation.

4 The best ideas often emerge in relationships, as a creative, collaborative effort to generate, refine, and develop them, so the most effective innovators will actively engage in creative ideation within all stakeholder relationships.

5 When creative ideation is motivated by change agency – the desire to improve – and the underlying restless discontentment with the status quo, then ideas are more likely to be positively transformational.

6 Ideas emerge from capabilities, such as platforms of expertise, technical tool sets, existing bases of intellectual property, frameworks of expertise, and libraries of knowledge. Organizations that develop and cultivate such capabilities will have a natural superiority for creative ideation relative to impoverished ones.

7 Last but not least, creative ideation is most effective when ideas are tied to actions. Ideas without action and follow-through are just "brain farts."

chapter 14

Comfortable Complacency

"Tolerance is the virtue of the man without convictions."

Gilbert Chesterton (1905)

The seventh sin

The seventh deadly sin of innovation is comfortable complacency. This is the realm of mindset and culture, potentiality and performance. It's also the realm of strategy implementation.

The roots of mediocrity

Complacency is the root cause of mediocrity. As Benjamin Mays (1895–1984), US educator, sociologist, and social activist, said:

> The tragedy of life is often not in our failure, but rather in our complacency; not in our doing too much, but rather in our doing too little; not in our living above our ability, but rather in our living below our capacities.

Complacency comes in many forms; in fact, for any given enterprise, there may be as many forms of complacency as there are stakeholders. Complacent managers and staff won't try to confront mediocre performance and results. Complacent owners won't invest in improvement. Complacent customers won't bother to complain, they'll simply take their business elsewhere or, if that's not possible, tolerate the state of affairs. Think of Russian customers tolerating the poor range of products and dreadful service provided by Soviet-era stores. Given a sense of hopelessness and zero choice, consumers would line up and even queue out the door and down the street in freezing Russian winters just to get a loaf of bread.

Less extreme examples of complacency, and the resulting tolerance of mediocrity, can be seen everywhere. People stand in queues at airports the world over, in effect tolerating slow, poor service. We do so because we accept queues as an inevitable reality of air travel. But does it have to be so? Can we imagine a world, perhaps with more advanced technology, that would enable much faster check-in, security handling, and passenger processing? Obviously, this would be physically possible, and one may argue that it will happen someday, if airports, airlines, and governments invest to enable it. The point of this little thought exercise is simply this: looking back, passengers experiencing a much more effective system would not tolerate the queues of today, any more than Russian consumers would tolerate a return to Soviet-style shopping.

Human beings tend to be incredibly tolerant of current reality. If we live in a police state, such as North Korea, the vast majority of us simply accept that. We accept living in societies where religious zealots persecute people for being human, treat females as second-rate humans, or worse. In many parts of the world, otherwise "normal" human beings accept living in societies dominated by leaders who are documented psychopathic murderers.

As civilized Westerners, we abhor such extreme examples of tolerating the intolerable. Yet, I can think of many ways in which we also tolerate mediocre performance and results in our day-to-day lives, simply accepting these as inevitable aspects of reality. Why do we accept multi-hour commutes to work? What about having to fiddle our way through multiple call options when we want to speak to a service representative? Why do we tolerate a tax burden that claims half our income (or more), especially when a large share of that tax is used simply to support the huge and ineffectual bureaucracy required to collect the tax? Why do we tolerate a healthcare system that, in spite of being massively expensive, often provides substandard care? How can we "live with" hospitals that reportedly kill patients by accident on a daily basis; for example, it's estimated that 100,000 patients per year are accidentally killed in US hospitals? Would we take a commercial flight for a holiday if, as airline passengers, we had the same chance of being killed?

Human beings are, in fact, amazingly tolerant creatures. We put up with loads of rubbish, especially from each other. In fact, we seem to expect other people to let us down, provide poor service, fail to keep promises, be poor leaders, and generally disappoint us at every turn. Sure, we get angry from time to time, and, less often, we find more constructive ways to confront each other. But one of the saddest aspects of the human condition is that we tend to accept our condition, with all its imperfections.

The roots of complacency

As discussed above, one of the roots of complacency is tolerance, a state of having very low expectations, or being unhappy but "used to it." For example, Jon Krakauer (1966), US writer and mountaineer, observed:

> So many people live within unhappy circumstances and yet will not take the initiative to change their situation because they are conditioned to a life of security, conformity, and conservatism, all of which may appear to give one peace of mind, but in reality nothing is more dangerous to the adventurous spirit within a man than a secure future.

So, complacency can result from tolerating discomfort, but also from a sense of comfort, security, and satisfaction. Indeed, it can even come from a sense of success. As William Pollard (1828–93), Quaker minister and author, said: "The arrogance of success is to think that what we did yesterday is good enough for tomorrow."

The roots of poor performance

Poor performance can reflect a lack of skills, expertise or other resources required to perform. But performance also requires motivation and the right mindset or attitude. With no motivation, no one shows up to perform. But if someone "shows up" to perform with the wrong mental attitude, the performance suffers. Lou Holtz, US football player, coach, and motivational speaker, captured this perfectly: "Ability is what you're capable of doing. Motivation determines what you do. Attitude determines how well you do it."

Peak performance flow can only happen when abilities, motivations, and positive attitudes resonate through all the psychological centers, as suggested in Table 14.1.

TABLE 14.1 Relating abilities, motivations, and attitudes to the psyche centers

Abilities and motivations	Centers	Attitudes of winners vs losers
To self-actualize, or help others actualize, fulfilling meaningful purpose	Purpose and mission	W says: "How can I help?" L says: "That's not my job"
To envision, intuit, insightfully define success, and develop an intelligent plan to achieve it	Goals and vision	W: Always has a plan, or works to develop one L: Always has an excuse
To influence, share your truths, sell and market, and deliver value	Influence and communication	W: Always part of the solution L: Always part of the problem
To love and be loved, belong, engage, partner and collaborate, to be appreciated, and manifest win–win value in all relationships	Partnership and engagement	W: Works for the success of others or the team L: Blames others when things go wrong
To lead, manage, be in charge, but also inspire, direct, motivate, and empower	Empowerment and leadership	W says: "It may be difficult, but it's possible" L says: "It may be possible, but it will be difficult"
To improve, create, learn and grow, move onward and upward	Ideation and creation	W: Sees an answer for every problem L: Sees a problem for every answer
To perform, manifest skills, expertise, and capabilities	Mindset and culture	W: Believes new heights can be achieved L: Just "shows up"

Tolerating poor performance

One of the principal ways in which complacency limits the success of organizations and their attempts to innovate is when people tolerate poor performance. They might simply look away, feeling: "I'm OK. You're not. But it's not my problem." Or they may decide it's easier to accept than confront the poor performance of a colleague. Even managers and supervisors often tolerate poor performance rather than confronting the ineffectual behavior, lack of motivation, or losing attitudes underlying it.

There are many problems with not confronting poor performance, beyond the fact that the performance itself is accepted and therefore continues to be poor. For one thing, tolerating poor performance sets a low benchmark and sends a signal that mediocrity is acceptable. Mediocrity becomes normal, expected, and acceptable. For example, Riley (1993) said:

> When a great team loses through complacency, it will constantly search for new and more intricate explanations to explain away defeat. After a while it becomes more innovative in thinking up how to lose than thinking up how to win.

Further, otherwise hard-working people can be demotivated and even driven away from organizations that tolerate mediocre or poor performance. There are few things more demotivating than seeing someone's poor performance tolerated, with the possible exception of seeing the poor performer promoted.

Culture of comfort

An organization that has developed a "comfort culture" will fail to confront mediocrity, poor performance, issues requiring resolution, and needed improvements. A tolerance of mediocrity, and the resulting state of mediocrity, stems from a lack of abilities, motivations, bad attitudes, and wrong or ineffectual behaviors. It could be that there's no pleasure taken from mastery and expertise. Or there may be no remaining sense of hope and resulting drive. Underneath it all, there may be a state of contentment with the status quo, however unpleasant it might be. Ignoring it makes it go away. The inconvenient truths are not spoken. The writing on the wall is papered over, and the sorry state of affairs is simply tolerated. This is ineffectual psychology, and when applied to groups or organizations, ineffectual culture.

Complacency

Success can also lead to complacency. People can be forgiven for thinking that great results must mean we're doing something right: "If it ain't broke, don't fix it." Success sustained over long periods can lead management and entire organizations to feel that "business as usual" is a good thing. But there's an underlying arrogance at play here and a dangerous assumption – that good is "good enough." However, this assumption and the resulting lack of drive for change and improvement limits investment in innovation, performance, and results.

Comfortable complacency

As with the other sins, the seventh sin of comfortable complacency results from blockages or a lack of resonance through the various individual and organizational psyche centers:

1. When an individual's motivation, abilities, beliefs, or attitudes don't relate to or connect with a personal sense of purpose, or when the purpose of an organization or intended innovation doesn't motivate and resonate with people and their passions. Complacent people have no passion and are just "showing up" to work out of habit, or for the money. People who are working for money rather than love aren't in the right jobs. Work should be fun.
2. When people aren't focused on goals and visions for success, with the right mental attitude toward achieving it, including the fundamental belief, intuition, and insight of what's possible. Comfort cultures tend to have weak goals, poor goal definition, and low accountability – weak linkages to goal achievement. This also becomes a breeding ground for "goal drift" (goals evolving over time with no communication or agreement) and goal/vision misalignment.
3. When there's no expression of the desire to innovate, compete, win, or provide value – no attempt to influence anyone to engage with or adopt the intended innovation – or no enthusiasm, compassion or integrity behind the expression.
4. When relationships are nonexistent or ineffectual, perhaps based on no desire to engage or collaborate, or an inability to do so due to lack of empathy, or poor collaborative relationship skills.
5. When individuals or organizations lack the confidence, courage, empowerment, disposition, or abilities to lead, or to take on personal responsibility, make decisions, or direct and empower themselves and other resources.

6 When there's a poverty of ideas and creativity, due to closed minds, unreceptivity, "not invented here" syndrome, "we've always done it like this," and other blocks to considering or being open to potential ideas for improvement or development. As Fromm (1959) said: "Creativity requires the courage to let go of certainties."
7 And last, and most fundamentally, when there's no hope or drive to *do* anything. When people just show up. When the organizational lights are on, but nobody's really home.

In summary, the seventh deadly sin of comfortable complacency is based on mindsets and cultures where innovation is impossible. The seventh entrepreneurial virtue, driven mindset, is the other side of the coin.

Driven mindset

Enterprises can encourage entrepreneurship and cultivate winning cultures through effective engagement in the various strategic innovation agendas:

1 By encouraging people to dream, find their passions, and do what they love, and when some people in the organization aren't passionate and "loving it," helping them regain that, or leave.
2 A vital part of the enterprise's knowledge agenda should be to understand its culture and the psychological makeup of the individual people within it. One example that can be useful for resource development and succession planning is a database of aptitudes, skills, and interests. Less obvious, but equally useful data can include psychometric profiles on attitudes, satisfaction or dissatisfaction with employment, personality profiles, intelligences, and motivations. For example, motivational maps, invented by James Sale (see motivationalmaps.com), can yield powerful insights regarding levels and patterns of motivation, and, even more importantly, the actions that can be taken to improve motivation and performance.
3 Cultivating a culture and individual mindsets focused on maximizing value should be part of the enterprise's value agenda, as should ensuring that the enterprise's values are "lived."
4 The people within the enterprise are key stakeholders within the SRM agenda, but, equally, are going to be engaged in the various relationships with other stakeholders. Attending to how these relationships play out,

in part based on the qualities of empathy, appreciation, and attention brought to the relationships, as well the behavior, attitudes, and motivations of staff, is an important consideration for SRM.

5 Change agency, attitudes toward change, the motivation or lack of motivation to change, and individual behavior in relation to the enterprise's change agenda will be major determinants of the success or failure of change initiatives.

6 The enterprise's capability agenda, what it's capable of now and what capabilities it can develop in the future, will depend on the overall culture and individual psychologies. It should always consider questions such as: Are we diverse enough? What fresh new perspectives should we recruit? Have we achieved a healthy balance between youth and experience?

7 Last but not least, what's happening in terms of performance and results? Are we fundamentally discontented, uncomfortable, and doing something about it?

Embracing adversity

Culture can be a tremendous advantage for any organization. Innovation winners such as Google, 3M, and others have carefully cultivated great cultures. It's instructive to read accounts of how innovation leaders create the right physical environments, organizational climates, space, and time for innovation (for example, see google.com/about/company/facts/culture). Most organizations would do well to look at the positive things that can be done to incubate, nurture, and ultimately strengthen a winning culture. But it's also informative to focus on how leading cultures deal with adversity. A perfect example is the All Blacks 2014 victory over Ireland, snatching victory from the jaws of defeat and winning only after the clock stopped – evidence of a winning mindset shared by the whole team and organization, therefore a "culture" that is simply unbeatable.

Periods of extreme challenge represent a huge opportunity. "When the going gets tough, the tough get going" (Leahy, 1954), and the weak perish. There's more food, space, and other resources for the survivors. When faced with problems, we can ignore them, hoping they'll go away. They won't, but we might. We can worry and work to mitigate risks. But from this negative mindset, the best we might manage is survival. The smartest among us, future success stories, see problems as opportunities. Winners see challenges as fun.

Adversity breeds discontentment, a root condition for entrepreneurial innovation. Faced with adversity, real leaders rise to the challenge and deliver special results. Adversity creates the conditions for breakthrough innovation, stuff no one can predict. Adversity can arise from many sources, such as the economy, competitors, demanding customers, diversity, and conflict. Indeed, clever leaders work to foster creative conflict and always provide a healthy degree of impedance to ensure that ideas are fully developed before being progressed or killed.

Successful leaders aren't fools. They're not starry-eyed optimists who dream their way to success, following a supposedly "secret" formula. Yes, negativity will attract negative results. Optimism and hope are essential early ingredients for success. But there's more to it than wishful thinking. Creating success is hard work. As you do it, the law of attraction kicks in. Success attracts more success. It builds on itself, often in unexpected ways that smart leaders embrace and exploit.

Let's consider Walt Disney, whose company has grown to become the largest and most successful global entertainment conglomerate in history. Disney was born out of and evolved through adversity. In 1928, Walt traveled across America to request a small pay rise for creating Oswald the Lucky Rabbit. The request was refused and his backers pointed out that they owned all the rights to Oswald. On the train back to California, Walt came up with a new idea. When he told his wife about Mortimer Mouse, she responded: "Great idea, but you need a friendlier name" – thus, a famous mouse was born. Gold is smelted in the hottest flames.

Years later, Walt was sitting on a park bench as his grandchildren played. He was bored. Wouldn't it be nice if there were parks where adults as well as children, indeed whole families, could enjoy themselves? Disneyland opened in 1955, further fulfilling Walt's life mission of "making people happy." It was an unmitigated disaster. Over 28,000 people showed up, most holding counterfeit tickets to an invitation-only event planned for 11,000. Almost every aspect of the infrastructure was inadequate – from parking to plumbing. Within hours, the park ran out of food. Freshly laid asphalt was still soft and sticky under an unseasonably hot California sun. Rides broke down and tempers flared. There was inadequate security, crowd control, and first aid – in short, utter bedlam. Most businessmen would've run for the Mexican border, cash in hand. Not Walt. He again embraced adversity, and set about solving the problems experienced on "Black Sunday." He had lost money, but now invested more. In spite of bad opening publicity, Walt reinvited his guests to come and experience the park as he had intended. On reopening, Disneyland was a much slicker operation. And Walt continued to drive innovation until the day he died.

Walt perfectly illustrates the entrepreneur's paradox. Is the glass half-empty or half-full? For a remarkable person like Walt, the answer is both. It's half-empty, never quite good enough. The park can be better. The mousetrap or mouse can be improved. More people can be made happier. In short, great leaders and entrepreneurs are great change agents. They don't get that way being complacent, thinking things are good enough. But here's the paradox. The great entrepreneur's glass is also only ever half-full. Entrepreneurs are and must be optimists. Pessimists cannot lead innovation: "We can't do that. Tried it before … it will never work." This is useful for pointing out all aspects of problems, but not for leading to solutions.

Disney was a great optimist, a lover of life, and a merchant of hope. But he was also constantly dissatisfied, looking for better ways, trying new things, failing and trying again. He created the foundations for one of the world's most successful companies out of the adversity that shaped him and his plans.

Like Walt, tomorrow's successful entrepreneurs and companies are, right this very minute, investing time, effort, and other scarce resources to make the world a better place. They're dissatisfied with current reality and want to change it. They're optimistic that with the right people, backing, and a bit of luck, they can do it. And they will, through resolve, determination, and relentless focus. They will create their own "luck."

So let's wrap up. A key point is that adversity breeds discontentment, a root condition for entrepreneurial innovation. Faced with adversity, winning cultures and teams rise to the challenge and deliver amazing results. Rather than seeking comfort, they seek discomfort and challenge. Adversity creates the conditions for breakthrough innovation, stuff no one can predict. Adversity can arise from many sources, including the economy, competitors, demanding customers, diversity, and conflict. Indeed, clever leaders work to foster creative conflict and a healthy degree of impedance for innovation, so that only the strongest ideas survive and make it through the birthing process into reality. As the economist Paul Romer said: "A crisis is a terrible thing to waste" (cited in Rosenthal, 2009).

part III

Prescriptions

"I always pass on good advice. It is the only thing to do with it. It is never of any use to oneself."

Oscar Wilde (1895)

In this part of the book, I offer a number of specific prescriptions related to the real-world challenges of entrepreneurship and innovation. I've tried to write each of the prescriptions in a way that hopefully makes them interesting and applicable for all readers, even if you don't face the specific challenge in question: revitalizing a business, starting a business, running a family business, selling a business, or running service, social, or public enterprises.

The prescriptions draw on the foregoing model and observations about innovation sins, entrepreneurial virtues, and the need to bridge various psychological and organizational factors in driving innovative results. Hopefully, the packaging in Part III will help you with further insights on how to apply these thoughts, and possibly trigger an idea or two that will be of value for you. If so, my objective will have been met.

chapter 15

Revitalizing Enterprise

"When we look at living creatures from an outward point of view, one of the first things that strikes us is that they are bundles of habits."

William James (1890)

Stuck in a rut

Human nature is such that as we mature, we tend to get into ruts. Organizations consist of people, so it comes as no surprise that they also develop bad habits, become stagnant, stop behaving strategically, and fail to innovate.

Organizations may choose to revitalize for many specific reasons, including the realization that they've developed an ineffectual culture, their products or brands have lost sizzle, they're losing the competitive war, or they must improve outmoded business processes and practices. Whatever the drivers, you won't be surprised to read that my suggestion is that a strategic, entrepreneurial approach to innovation is the best way to revitalize any enterprise. I've participated in lots of approaches that generally fail to deliver. Consider a few:

- Rebranding is all too often an exercise in renaming that does little to change the underlying fundamentals. Unless rebranding is done as part of a wider revitalization plan, it's a costly but ineffectual way to attempt real change. Rebranding alone doesn't achieve revitalization, any more than simply renaming the problem makes it go away.

- Replacing leaders is another favored way chosen by boards to revitalize enterprises. The core assumption is that leaders are responsible for success or failure. In most cases, the reality is that while leaders might be held responsible, they're only ever partly responsible for anything. If things aren't working out due to underlying fundamentals within the enterprise, putting someone else in charge is only going to help if they can rapidly spot the problems others have missed, and then quickly identify and drive solutions. Usually the opposite is true. It can take a new leader many months to get their feet under the desk, learn what's going on, and begin to appreciate what needs to change. Usually, the outgoing leaders could have told them, if they'd been allowed to stick around long enough for an effective transition.
- Reorganizing the management team is also a popular approach, particularly if the top leader or leaders are surviving and most likely focusing "blame" on the next layer down. Shuffling the team, repartitioning or reassigning roles and responsibilities is intended to "shake things up." But giving people a good shake is rarely an effective way to improve focus, motivation, resolve, or creativity. Reorganizing problems doesn't make them go away.
- Rightsizing was a highly favored approach through the 1980s and 90s. The theory, still practiced by many, is that if the organization gets rid of the bottom ten (or whatever) percent of performers and replaces them with "new blood," the remaining people will sit up and take notice, work harder and smarter, and achieve more. However, the reality is that when organizations work in this mode, they rarely manage to retain and develop the best people. I advocate chopping away dead wood, and clearing out poor performers as and when they emerge. But attempting to revitalize an organization by shrinking it simply doesn't work. It creates a climate of fear (a WTF culture), where people don't enjoy working, spend unnecessary time around the water cooler, and the best people tend to be the first to leave.
- Restructuring the business model goes deeper than shuffling management chairs, and if it's done right can achieve revitalization. Focusing on core businesses, streamlining operations, eliminating waste, creating simplicity from complexity can all improve value delivery; however, simply moving elements of the business around, shedding

perfectly viable business elements that might be underperforming because of inattention or underinvestment will not.

- Resigning oneself to the situation is arguably the most common and least effective of approaches. However, the sad fact (as discussed in Chapter 14) is that complacency is all too common. Even when mounting displeasure drives a leader to feel that a situation is intolerable, leading to a momentary drive toward action, the path of resignation will always be the path of least resistance.

So what does work? Let's consider the seven elements of strategy that need to be revitalized, along with the innovation agenda underlying each element and connecting it to the next.

Revitalizing mission

The enterprise's mission should, at the very least, be carefully reconsidered if revitalization is required. It may be that the mission is "fit for purpose," but equally, it may be that a spark of change is needed here to kick-start the whole revitalization effort. This isn't just about putting some "highfalutin" words on paper. The right words can inspire and engage passion within and outside the enterprise, and new-found passion can be a massively important energy for any revitalization effort. People need to get excited. They need "a sense of urgency" (Kotter, 2008).

You can excite people by shouting at them, throwing fancy rebranding parties with loud music and flashy slideshows, and maybe even by holding hands and chanting the company mantra. But for me, the most basic and most powerful way to meaningfully engage people is through their sense of purpose, feelings and thoughts about what is meaningful about their work and the enterprise they're part of, and their personal passions.

The best way to develop a "revitalized" mission is to involve everyone in creating it. Start by asking each person to define their personal working purpose, as passionately as possible, in terms they might use to describe to a friend what they do. Ask them to try to work in a sense of "why" their job function exists, and indeed why the enterprise exists, what it exists to do, and what it represents in the world. For example, a nurse should express their mission in terms of saving lives, or at least improving health – things that matter.

Ask every person in the enterprise to write and then rewrite (making it more succinct) a one or two sentence statement of purpose. It might look something like this: "I'm the head pediatric nurse at Southampton General Hospital, and my purpose as a member of the leadership team is to save lives and improve health outcomes for our patients and community, and contribute to continuous improvement in the hospital's ability to do so."

Get people to share their missions and give each other feedback on how to bring out greater passion, make them more succinct, and more powerful. Encourage people to continue working on and refining their individual missions, as an ongoing process of tuning, adjusting, and continually improving. But it's also time to take the next step – to develop an overall mission for the organization.

Ask everyone to write a one or two sentence description of the more general purpose of the overarching enterprise, still in terms they feel passionate about. For example: "Southampton General Hospital saves and improves lives, as a leading contributor to the health, safety, and wellbeing of our community." Now break the entire group into pairs, assigning anyone extra to a three-person team. Get them to merge their individual mission statements into a shared statement they're all happy with. Don't rush this process, as some important things are happening through the communication – relationship building, healthy debate, but most especially people are engaging their passions. Then, merge groups of 2 into 4, into 8, into 16, and so on until you arrive at the mission of the entire enterprise, something everyone has discussed, debated, argued, and engaged in.

This prescribed process is time-consuming and messy, but well worth it. The alternative approach is the "well-trodden path" of hiring a consultant or agency, going on an "awayday," or even just spending a few minutes as the boss, writing a new mission to "hand down" to the troops.

The interesting thing, and I always say this to my clients before facilitating a mission rollup exercise, is that the boss's mission and the whole team's rolled up mission is likely to be more or less the same. But there are a number of important differences, apart from the fact that the rollup process takes more time and effort. The rolled up mission has been passionately debated, such that every word is laden with meaning, and the team feels a strong sense of ownership. Try finding a team that feels any degree of passion about a "handed-down" mission statement crafted by a boss, the leadership team awayday, or a consulting agency.

Once you have the new, revitalized mission – use it. Post it on your websites, tweet it, blog it, embed it in your marketing material and communications. Shout about it.

Another aspect of "mission" is nesting and nested missions. Get each individual to relook at their personal mission to see how it supports the overall mission of the enterprise. Discuss how the missions either do or do not support the overall mission. This process is useful for understanding individual roles, and potentially identifying areas of weakness or disconnection.

The final step in the process is to look at the missions of any distinct functions, departments, or subgroups within the enterprise. Get them to hold breakout sessions to discuss and agree their distinct missions and how these support the overall enterprise.

In the case of SMEs, everyone might be present and the unit of analysis is the SME. However, the mission exercise might be conducted with a group of people representing a subsidiary, product line, brand, or operating entity. In such cases, I still advocate starting with individual missions, jumping all the way to the top level – the overarching enterprise – and then considering the mission of the sub-enterprise or entity represented by the people present.

The point is that many organizations consist of lots of sub-entities, and it's important to develop specific missions for each and then discuss how these missions either align, fail to align, or potentially conflict. Note that conflict or misalignment might be acceptable, even expected; for example, if a parent company has two competing subsidiaries. The point is to understand, analyze, discuss, and ultimately agree on this all-important aspect of strategy – purpose and mission.

Revitalizing championship and intent

Successful revitalization will require an effective champion or group of champions. It's not enough to just "put someone in charge." The revitalization effort must be seen as receiving the full support, if not direct championship from all leadership. But equally, someone needs to serve as the key driver, with the underlying beliefs and insights into what needs to be done, and with the overarching spirited purpose and drive to make things happen without settling for a mediocre result. Of course, the defining purpose of championship is driving the "success agenda" based on strategic intent – the combination of mission and vision.

Revitalizing vision

If an enterprise requires revitalization, then a vision with a rich, well-defined constellation of strategic goals is required. In many ways, this aspect of the prescription is key to the revitalization effort. The first thing you need to do is to define the problem. What needs to be revitalized? What's the problem?

I recommend breaking people into small discussion groups of three–six, and then having each group present the three ideas that most excite them. List all the ideas, combining or merging the same, similar or highly related ideas. Then, prioritize the list based on discussion. I sometimes find it useful to ask people to identify their first three choices and rank the list based on averaging.

What should emerge is a prioritized list of revitalization objectives or goals (some may even be big, hairy and audacious). Carefully consider and seek the right balance between aspiration and realism. Real business intelligence is required here, to know what is possible in terms of investment, focus, and achievement. Don't try to do too much, but equally, if you attempt too little, revitalization will not be achieved.

Once the revitalization goals have been defined, it should be possible to state what the overall vision for the revitalization is. Articulate it and give it a name. For example, a company might decide it has languished, lost market share, and slipped into third place in terms of competitive position. The team may decide that the goals for revitalization are to refresh the design of an existing product, launch a new, lower cost version of the product and also a new, higher cost, higher functioning product, launch a new website and social media strategy, hire some new salespeople and retrain the entire sales force, and launch a revitalization marketing campaign aimed at winning back previously loyal customers, offering specific incentives including free trials of the new products. Giving the plan an aspirational name, such as "Regaining the High Ground" will help to galvanize people, creating resolve and impetus.

Revitalizing learning and intelligence

In going through the visioning exercise, chances are it became apparent that the organization lacks the vital knowledge required to ensure that the vision and goals are achievable or correctly targeted. If an enterprise requires revitalization, there's a distinct possibility that it has underinvested in learning and building the necessary understanding of customers, markets, competitors, and other aspects of the external environment, as well as clarity about the enterprise's internal strengths and weaknesses.

Investing in greater learning and understanding can take many forms – focusing time and resources to develop a learning organization (see Senge, 1990; Wheatley, 1992), or acquiring externally (outside experts, new hires, acquisitions), but generally should include a strong focus on building a solid understanding of value (as per Chapter 3).

Revitalizing the unifying message

A great starting point for revitalizing an enterprise's sales and marketing efforts is to ask everyone to develop an "elevator pitch" – a passionate, powerful overview of the enterprise, describing its USP in terms that will excite potential customers, investors, employees, or partners. Ideally, this is done in the context of training everyone to deliver an effective pitch, which is useful whether they will subsequently sell, network externally, or simply hone their presentation and communication skills. Guidelines should be given, explaining that the pitches should take 30 seconds or less, avoid jargon that ordinary people wouldn't understand, and, most important, must strongly convey personal passion for the enterprise, as well as serving as a personal introduction.

Everyone should first write their pitch and then deliver it to one other person, giving and receiving feedback. Get everyone to really listen and change their pitches so that they're designed to be spoken from the heart, not read off the page. Get people to wander around and practice their pitches. Ultimately, everyone should pitch to an audience and receive feedback.

There's never going to be one best way to pitch an enterprise, because, ideally, every pitch is uniquely personalized to the individual pitching it. The pitches need to be owned, and to roll off the tongue as the deliverer's personal truth and passion for the enterprise. However, as individuals pitch to each other, they should be encouraged to borrow or steal anything they like – a word, a turn of phrase, or a way of structuring. A few very similar pitches will emerge and they can and should become the basis for marketing, sales, and other enterprise communications. This process can take weeks, but it can also be done in a day with proper focus and facilitation.

Revitalizing the value agenda

The compelling value proposition emerging from the above should now form the heart of the organization's value agenda. The value proposition is the central message or "battle cry" for persuading key stakeholders to engage with the organization's value delivery model. The entire model needs to be defined, along with the strategies for influencing the intended recipients of value to engage, through the right marketing mix and approach to selling.

The next aspect of the value agenda to consider is customer value. Naturally, the elevator pitches should reflect customer value, as should the core values of the team. But it's vitally important for any enterprise to clearly and fully understand customer experience, perceptions, and loyalty. Insights from customers, arising from the knowledge agenda, should directly shape the value agenda.

Additionally, an exercise to reconsider core values is often highly useful when seeking to revitalize an enterprise. Brainstorm a list of values, but invite people to debate whether specific values are currently manifested in the behavior and character of people in the enterprise, or if they are, to an extent, "aspirational" – desirable but not yet fully realized. Put an asterisk beside any values that one or more people feel are aspirational, thus requiring further work to manifest within the organizational culture. As the debate continues, place one, two or three marks beside each aspirational value, roughly indicating the amount of work required to develop and manifest each value.

It's also useful to brainstorm specific ideas for what can be done to realize or strengthen the various aspirational values, and then to ask who will champion each initiative. At this stage, it's often interesting to see that specific values may lack championship, in which case I would either rectify this or cross them off the list ("brain farts").

Next, the list should be "boiled down" by developing clusters of connected values. It's also helpful to pick one word as a label for each cluster. For example, consider these three clusters of values, and the selected label:

- **Integrity:** loyalty, authenticity, sincerity, caring, honesty, selflessness, openness, and trust
- **Professionalism:** courtesy, politeness, empathy, engaged, appreciative, leading by example
- **Responsibility:** hard-working, determined, proud, motivated, empowered, accountable.

Once the enterprise's core values have been distilled to a reasonable number (probably between five and ten), the final list should be communicated as an ongoing visible reminder to everyone, and used for performance reviews or appraisals, discussions of individual and team development needs, and continuous improvement. This exercise is useful for revitalizing a sense of shared values within an enterprise, among the leadership, other teams, and employees.

Revitalizing engagement

Disengagement is often the heart of the revitalization problem, unsurprising given its central position among the psychological centers. If participants don't have the fundamental desire and attraction to partner and collaborate toward win–win value creation, optimizing outcomes, then they're unlikely to achieve any greater level of vitality. This is where leadership and communication must meet to respectively empower and influence people as active drivers and participants in the revitalization effort. This is all about achieving a state of inspiration.

Revitalizing key relationships

All stakeholders are important, but when revitalization is required, a key question to ask is: Which relationships have become stagnant, stale, or boring? Where does "the love" have to be rekindled? The answer might be "in all stakeholder relationships," but even so, it should be possible to prioritize and create initial focus in the areas most needing repair. Then, it's time to come up with specific ideas to "get the love back." These might include visits to customers who've been neglected, employee team-building activities, or a comprehensive review with a key supplier or partner.

Revitalizing leadership

If employees, customers, or other stakeholders have "lost the love," the root cause usually lies with leaders. If the business owners or leaders no longer love the enterprise, how can they expect others to? Love is infectious – it spreads. But so is the opposite, hatred, and the neutral state, ambivalence. If employees sense ambivalence from leaders, they become ambivalent. If customers sense ambivalence from employees, they too will become ambivalent or negative toward the enterprise. When I speak to groups of business leaders, I often say: "If you don't love your business, pack it in. Sell, retire, or just walk away and find something you do love."

If you're like most people, you have good and bad days, or months, or years. If you're in a down patch, try reminding yourself why you got into the particular enterprise in the first place. What did you love in the beginning? And ask yourself what might make you love it more.

Another key question to ask is whether you're showing the love enough. Are you "out there" infecting others? Many leaders care passionately, but just don't know how to show it. I heard a story of one such leader who used to arrive at the office, go up the elevator, turn left and go into his office, and close the door, there to work hard all day on a company he founded and dearly loved. One day, he started turning right as he got off the elevator and wandering around talking to people. The effect was transformative, and his love spread like wildfire.

Some specific things to consider are:

- Do you walk about the office enough, and do you talk to people and also really listen?
- Do you get out of the office enough, for example to meet key customers?
- Do you show your feelings, or are you stoic and steely-faced?

- Do you express your appreciation for people? Are you passionate in doing so, or measured?
- Do you say "thanks" enough? Are there more creative ways you could express thanks, such as rewards or public displays of affection?
- Do you empower others to have and champion ideas and to lead, making decisions and applying resources to make ideas happen?
- Do you encourage others to engage in the above behaviors, such that it becomes the norm, the modus operandi, the prevailing leadership culture?

Revitalizing change agency

A key aspect, in a sense underpinning effective leadership, is change agency. It's one thing to love a business, but another to see when tough love may be required. Seeing what needs to change, who needs to change or go, and how the organization must be transformed to win the love back from all key stakeholders are all vital aspects of the change agenda to drive revitalization.

Revitalizing creation

Change requires ideas, and therefore a climate and culture that encourages and supports ideation, providing the foundation below. Another equally important role is to bridge between the love and value that exists in relationships (the psyche center above ideation/creation), bringing vital passion to the realm of ideas.

One key is to be open to new ideas, recognizing that most will be half-baked cakes. Someone else may have the other half of the recipe, a few critically important ingredients, the oven to bake it in, or the icing to make it pretty. For example, 3M might have the wherewithal to turn an idea for a new cleaning product into reality, but it may well be a hotel maid who has the idea in the first place. As von Hippel (1988, 2005) has demonstrated, the sources of innovation can be surprising. But a key lesson from many years of cutting (bleeding) edge innovation experience is that many ideas are simply insufficient on their own. The product designer may have the beginning of an idea for improvement, but can't quite bring it to fruition without a key piece of information in a customer's, supplier's, or competitor's head.

In relation to enterprise revitalization, here are some key considerations for effective ideation:

- Create a culture of creativity and collaboration, where no idea is a bad one. Eliminate fear, including fear of rejection.
- Start with value in mind – what value must be manifested to revitalize the business? Then, working back, what needs to be done to deliver that value?
- Think out of the box. Look for ideas in unexpected places, especially in relationships, at the edges, in the cracks – diversity, messiness, creative tensions.
- Get into the customer's head to see your world differently. Get a friendly customer to hold up a mirror for you and have a good, hard look. Is your offering getting a little gray, or frayed around the edges? Is it time for a refresh? Have you become a one-trick pony? Is it time to add something new and exciting to your portfolio of offerings? Do you have a portfolio? Even multinationals with extensive product portfolios have "gone bust," in part by becoming too tied to a particular niche. Stand too close to something like the Internet when it's about to implode and you might lose, big time. Ask Nortel. Oh, sorry, they're not around to ask anymore.
- Create focus. Once you get lots of ideas into the hopper, the next task is to decide which ones to focus on. Don't underresource, and if you have to cut back, kill something rather than underresourcing everything.
- Move quickly on great ideas, as delay is costly. Delay will kill ROI, and if you have the idea, so do at least two other people who will beat you to market, given half a chance.
- Fully realize passionate championship of ideas to ensure persistence, drive, and ability to make them happen. Individual championship isn't enough, instead build a coalition – be multidisciplined. Within large organizations, executive sponsorship can be a key requirement for success, to marshal resource commitments, break down barriers, or break the rules.
- Be disciplined about process, but also prepared to break all the rules. Be multidisciplined – collaborative. Look for ways to accelerate the path to market, such as alliances, OEM deals, channels, and lead customers.
- Create a culture of effective ideation by celebrating great ideas, encouraging creative conflict, and rewarding creativity.

Revitalizing capabilities

New capabilities are often required to underpin the change agenda and enable the successful implementation of ideas. Bridging between the capability agenda and value agenda, there are four key questions that should be explored, as shown in Figure 15.1.

Capabilities / Value model	Current	New
Current	How can we enhance the value of our existing offerings to our existing customers by better leveraging our existing capabilities?	How can we expand our value delivery portfolio, through new products or markets served, by creatively using or recombining our current capablities?
New	What new capabilities can we develop or acquire to add value to what we do now?	What new capabilities do we need to develop to address future opportunities to expand our portfolio of value delivery, through new products or markets served?

FIGURE 15.1 Defining the capability agenda

Revitalizing culture

If an enterprise is languishing, I dare say the culture and individual mindsets are a root cause. As already pointed out above, a lack of passion and love, a lack of focus and commitment, and an unwillingness to share and debate ideas are all manifestations of individual and group psychology.

There are only two ways to change a culture, which after all is simply the "group soup" comprising all the ingredients of individual psyches. You can change people, or you can change *the* people – by which I mean get rid of, replace, or bring in new people. If an enterprise requires revitalization, both options should be considered.

Changing people can be a slow and sometimes painful process. However, when you consider the vital information, skills, or other attributes that exist within people, it usually becomes clear that they are worth the investment of time, effort, or money to turn them around. Even the most negative people might be highly valuable, and in fact their negativity often stems from strong motivations and unaddressed concerns about the enterprise. They can become valuable champions or supporters for change, if nurtured in the right way.

On the other hand, getting rid of a highly negative person or a poor performer can work wonders, perhaps sending a needed shock wave through the organization, or at least showing that leaders notice and care. Getting rid of people can be a destructive process if badly managed, but can also be a starting point for breathing new life into a dying enterprise.

Bringing in new people with fresh perspectives, new skills and ideas can be a constructive approach to revitalization. The key is to ensure that they infect the enterprise with their fresh enthusiasm before the prevailing culture infects them with complacency. You might also consider this when recruiting, as some people are, by nature, more positive and more impervious to negativity than others.

When recruiting, organizations should profile the psychological makeup of the existing team and identify gaps. For example, if you look at personality types (there are many models, but I tend to like the Myers-Briggs Type Indicator, based on Carl Jung's theories), you might consider the implications of not having some particular types represented. What if the entire team consists of extroverts, who hired each other because they like extroverts – given the advantages of introverts (see Olsen Laney, 2002)? If teams tend to coalesce on factors such as information processing and decision preferences, there's likely to be a greater tendency to "groupthink." The overall point is that diversity is good for healthy cultures. If a culture needs revitalization, it's probably time to bring some new blood and DNA into the gene pool.

Revitalizing action and performance

Having a plan for revitalizing the enterprise is one thing, but doing it is another. With the plan emerging from the above in place or at least forming, the key is to take action, monitor results, and tune the plan accordingly.

Revitalizing innovation agendas

In summary, if your organization requires revitalization, chances are you need to reconsider and breathe new life into the various strategic innovation agendas:

1. Ensure strategic intent is up to date and clearly focused on achieving success.
2. Invest to build current knowledge, especially a powerful SWOT analysis, focusing on how to address the opportunities and threats facing the enterprise.
3. Clarify your central value proposition, values, value model, marketing strategy, and sales messages.
4. Be clear on who the key stakeholders are, their priorities, and their relative importance to the enterprise – and balance accordingly.
5. Know what changes must be made to succeed and overwhelmingly achieve them.
6. Identify mission-critical capabilities and invest in developing or acquiring them.
7. Ensure that the revitalization strategy reflects strongly in what people are actually doing, their day-to-day commitments and actions, and hold them accountable for the required results. As Walt Disney said: "The way to get started is to quit talking and begin doing."

chapter 16 Startup Enterprise

"The reason a lot of people do not recognize opportunity is because it usually goes around wearing overalls looking like hard work."

Thomas Edison (1921)

Early missteps

One of the great things about creating a new enterprise is the "blank sheet of paper," although starting from scratch also typically involves unique challenges. A new startup enterprise or venture isn't necessarily started from scratch. Existing enterprises frequently launch new ventures, which may, in the early stages, be a strategic initiative, later evolving into a new subsidiary or spinoff. A new venture may have its own budget, leadership, and resource base, although tied to the "mother ship." Further, a "startup from scratch" may employ capital, skills, IP, and other resources of the founders, derived from previous enterprises. To what extent an enterprise is truly a "new venture" is arguably a gray area.

In any event, the principles for success – the elements of the prescription for success – are arguably the same for all startups, whether newly founded enterprises, new ventures, or strategic initiatives of existing enterprises:

1 Clear, compelling purpose

2 Powerful vision for success
3 A compelling offering and plans to market and sell it
4 Stakeholder identification and engagement plan
5 Inspiring business case and plan for employing and leading all the resources required to develop and implement the enterprise
6 A great idea for a solution to a problem, needed benefit, or unmet value requirement
7 Ability to manifest the skills, capabilities, and drive required to deliver the idea in reality.

The first problem with most startups is they approach the above list sequentially, starting at the bottom. Most startups begin with "who we are." As startup entrepreneurs or managers of new initiatives, "who" is typically based on some sort of domain expertise, such as an understanding of an industry or a problem, and based on having the right mindset – discontentment, motivation, and drive, in other words, the entrepreneurial "bug."

Next, and perhaps only a "blink of the eye" later, there's an idea. In some sense, the idea is usually the conceptual starting point for the new enterprise. It's an idea for a product, a solution, or a way of creating value.

Then, we begin thinking about the resources required to bring the idea into reality, and at this point we start to formulate a business plan. Most business plans fail to articulate, at least in early iterations, higher elements of strategy such as vision and mission. The plan is usually an expression of the product idea and a gross underestimation of the resources required to take it forward.

Stakeholder engagement usually begins at the point an initial business plan is conceived, often commencing with a few potential business partners and early stage investors (or requests for budget from the mother ship). The people who get involved at this point usually do so more on faith than the quality of the plan, which at this point typically still lacks the higher elements of strategy.

At this point, customers are still often an afterthought, as are sales and marketing. This is classic "technology push" – solutions looking for problems. Products seeking customers, rather than products designed to solve problems, address needs, and deliver value. The sales forecasts and specific marketing plans to make them happen are typically among the weakest aspects of the emerging business plan, full of wishful thinking rather than science, and often lacking any real understanding of customer needs, market dynamics, competitive alternatives, and other factors that will ultimately affect customer adoption decisions.

Developing a vision for success tends to happen late in the startup process. Many startups are pushed into defining vision, such as exit strategies, only when they seek investment backing. Investors will rarely commit funds for a venture with a half-baked concept of "success." To many entrepreneurs, the idea of defining an exit strategy before they've even created their enterprise may seem strange, possibly even unpalatable. But how can an overall strategic plan be complete without some notion of what it means to "win"?

Finally, defining a mission statement or sense of purpose for something that doesn't exist may also seem strange. A common misconception about new ventures is that they must start with the idea for a new product. However, the starting point for a new enterprise should answer the question why it exists rather than simply indicating what it will provide.

Spirited purpose

Spirited purpose is arguably the beginning point for successful innovation and entrepreneurship. Personal passions and love are the essential fuel to power entrepreneurial innovation. As Steve Jobs said: "If you haven't found it yet, keep looking. Don't settle. As with all matters of the heart, you'll know when you find it."

Why should the new venture exist? This includes answering questions such as what the venture is meant to do, for whom, and why they should care. Is the entrepreneur passionate about the potential value delivery and how it might make the world a better place? The mission or purpose of the new venture should, in a sentence or two, convey answers to all these questions, but it's fundamentally about the "why."

Of course, the why is connected to the how and the what. The purpose, at the top, is supported by but also supports and feeds all the other elements of entrepreneurial and organizational psyche. Recognizing this, it's especially important for the founders of any new venture to keep revisiting their sense of purpose, ensuring that it remains true and vital, and adjusting it when required; but also ensuring that other decisions and directions remain consistent with the core mission, and otherwise revising or discarding them accordingly.

Given that the founders have a sense of their innovation, their personal passion for it, who it's for, and the value to be created, they should be able to define why the new venture should exist. If they take this step, the mission statement will provide a powerful, overarching sense of purpose that can be used to help motivate stakeholders and keep everything else in focus, as inevitable "drift" takes place. Schedules may slip, products may not be developed exactly as originally envisioned, and the environment may change, with new competitive options changing the enterprise value model. A well-formed, crystalized sense of purpose will ensure that the emerging enterprise stays true to its core purpose, and/or the purpose is revisited to ensure that it is still valid and vital in the face of the underlying changes.

The psychological starting point for spirited purpose and a motivational mission is passion and love, another of the many two-sided "yin/yang coins" of the human psyche. The entrepreneur's love and passion for the intended innovation idea are the essential fuel that will drive the idea all the way to successful reality. Another psychological coin at play here is, on one side, the restless discontentment of the entrepreneurial spirit and, on the other, championship.

Championship

Championship combines spirited purpose with an audacious goal to form strategic intent and the drive toward success. Effective championing is required to survive the idea-to-reality process, ultimately becoming a successful innovation. Many excellent ideas are rejected outright, or developed and later fail, simply because they lack a champion. On the other hand, mediocre ideas can progress too far as a result of powerful championing, in many cases all the way to market introduction. To champion an idea effectively, the proponent must believe the idea is great. In many instances, champions make personal sacrifices (working long hours, losing sleep, and so on) and take personal risks (such as alienating colleagues, bosses, and spouses) to progress their idea. Effective champions are in love with their idea, often believing it to be superior to all others, in spite of possible evidence to the contrary. An effective champion is required, but doesn't ensure success.

The starting point for championship is spirited purpose and the underlying restless discontentment of the entrepreneurial psyche. And beyond a sense of why a new venture should exist, the first requirement for it to move forward is championship. In the case of startup enterprises, typically the founders are, by default, the champions. In the case of new ventures spawned by existing enterprises, the selection of an appropriate champion is vitally important. A champion may have "presented," pitching the idea for a new venture. But enterprise leadership must consider whether the presenting champion has what it takes to deliver or can be developed and supported to do so.

The audacious goal

The passion or love for an idea must be grounded in the audacious goal, a vision for how and why the idea is great, offering a huge opportunity for value creation and making the world a better place. Another aspect of the audacious goal or vision that is often overlooked is that all new ventures should have an exit plan.

If a country, fearing war, decides to raise an army, there should be a plan to eradicate the threats, to achieve peace, and to end the requirement for the new military venture. Similarly, a pharmaceutical or medical technology venture may envision the elimination of a diseased state, ending the requirement for their drug or device. The entire healthcare industry should, arguably, be focused on creating wellness, not managing diseases. And at a smaller but equally important level, any new business should, from the inception, try to define how the founders will exit within a reasonable time frame, say, two to ten years. A "lifestyle" business built around the founders and their special talents or desires to earn a living may not require an exit strategy, but then the business has no sustainable long-term value for ownership. This isn't a business, it's a job.

Knowledge

Good vision is based on knowledge – built on intelligence – and new ventures need vital knowledge every bit as much as existing enterprises. However, by its nature, a new venture may lack key sources of data, such as track record, and a customer base. Nonetheless, founders should invest to research potential customers, competitors, markets, partners, regulatory conditions, and so on. Of course, time is limited, and I would argue that a founder's time may not be best spent on research. But again, a key challenge for startups is limited resources, and possibly no ability to hire a researcher. The problem is that without such research, new ventures are frequently blindsided by competitors they didn't know about, regulations they run foul of, or patents they infringe.

Marketing and sales

Effective entrepreneurship requires persuasiveness. It's not enough to believe and be passionate yourself, at least not in a large organization with lots of competing demands for scarce resources. One must also be able to infect others with the same enthusiasm for the idea. The most successful entrepreneurial champions are those who convincingly sell their ideas on their merits to others – investors, bosses, colleagues, staff, and boards of directors.

Beyond persuasion, the new venture requires specific plans to market and sell, identifying target customers, channels to market, distribution plans, and sensible sales targets. These feed upward into the intelligence that underlies the vision and goals, and downward into the next aspect of the innovation agenda – driving value. Indeed, persuasive salesmanship requires something to sell – a compelling value proposition.

Value and worth

Many startups lack a coherent, let alone compelling, value proposition. I frequently meet entrepreneurs who struggle to tell me, in a sentence or two, about their new product idea. Of course, the product is only one of many parts of the marketing mix. But if you can't explain what the product offers, what problem it solves, or what benefits I might derive from using it, then you'll be lucky to ever sell it.

With an incoherent or nonexistent expression of value, a venture will probably fail to attract the required investors, partners, channels, or suppliers, and will also probably fail to engage and motivate employees. The USP is the central element of an effective business (value) model, also linking customers' values and the enterprise.

Partnering and engagement

A key question that the leaders of any new venture should ask is who they should consider partnering with. The broader question is how the entire new model should be operationalized and, on that basis, who needs to do what. This may include manufacturing, distribution logistics, or after-sales service. What are all the operational elements required to effectively implement the value delivery model (above) in relation to all key stakeholders (below)?

Let me address a common mistake made by founder entrepreneurs, that of giving equity or too much equity to key people along the way. Being a business founder entrepreneur can be a lonely place and one way to make it seem a little less lonely is to have partners. Unfortunately, they don't always turn out to be the partners you thought they were or might become. I've seen numerous cases where partners had stakes they were granted or allowed to purchase, which were no longer justified or fair based on business contribution.

In one case, a friend had been taken into an existing business and rapidly made an equal partner, on the basis that his skills neatly complemented the founder. The new partner was expected to run the business so the founder could continue focusing on innovation. However, the partner turned out to have poor people management skills, and was ultimately far more interested in golf than managing and growing the business. By the time they recognized the issue and began to discuss how to address it, the business hit difficult times and rapidly went under.

In a similar case, a founder had taken in a close friend with a clear value to bring to the business. Before long, this partner married one of the administrative staff, and when they divorced a few years later, the staff member now owned a quarter stake, and the original partner moved away, leaving a huge hole in the business. Let's consider one more quick example, and then what should have been done differently. A founder brought in a former friend as a partner to take on the day-to-day running of the business, incentivized with a great salary, a profit share, and an equity stake. It turned out the partner wasn't a very good manager and had to be bought out. This was an expensive mistake, as were the other examples.

So, what should they have done differently? Five things are key:

1 Try to think dispassionately about your motives and needs for bringing in or elevating someone to the status of partner. Why do you want a partner

and what specific new skills or abilities are needed in the business? Why are you attracted to bringing in this particular partner? Is it based on their talents and attributes, or are you motivated by friendship, wanting to give them something or seeking their approval? Having a friend in the business can seem like a good idea, but friendships and businesses both tend to evolve. What if you drift apart or your friendship becomes strained or nonexistent? Would you still want this person as a partner? I'm not saying that friends or family members should never be considered as potential employees or partners in a business, only that when a hiring or equity decision is made, it should be done with careful, rational consideration and not based on emotions or egos – yours or theirs.

2. Take independent advice regarding the person you're considering and the package you're planning to offer before you do so. I suggest talking to an executive recruiter, showing them your friend's CV and asking for their thoughts. For no fee, they'll probably give you something to think about, in terms of other potential candidates, questioning whether your friend's skills and experience are adequate, and some ideas about what remuneration would be fair. I also suggest talking to a business lawyer, although this will cost you. However, an appropriate contract with performance and get-out clauses could save you the fee many times over.
3. Perform proper due diligence on the partner you're considering. If the partner is a friend, it might seem strange to check them out. However, it's estimated that over half of all CVs contain falsehoods (see Olson, 2013), such as exaggerating accomplishments, omitting employment gaps, and fabricating degrees. It's human nature to trust your friends, but it's common sense to perform due diligence. One way is to have an independent person, perhaps someone already in the business or a business consultant, do this for you – interviewing and checking out the proposed partner.
4. Consider alternative partners. If you think there are no alternatives, think again. No one is so unique, special, talented, or all-round great that they're irreplaceable or indispensable. You should try to consider at least two or three alternative potential partners for anyone you may be considering bringing into or elevating within your business. If considering alternatives feels inappropriate, or seems to "defeat" the whole point of the partnership, then I suggest you go back to the first point above and reconsider your motives. Unless you can honestly say you looked at several options and decided the proposed partnership is the best one, you may well be committing an error you'll regret one day.

5 Consider alternative approaches. Suppose you know you want a particular person "locked in" to a particular role. A specific equity stake may feel like the best way to achieve "lock in," motivating them to stay and grow within the business. However, you should consider alternatives, such as various levels of equity, using options versus equity, granting or purchasing equity, earning equity in lieu of bonuses, earning equity over time based on specific contributions to the business, and scenarios whereby equity might revert or be bought back. Is equity really required to motivate the partner, or might alternatives such as remuneration, bonuses, or perquisites be equally effective? The bottom line recommendation here is simply this – consider the alternatives rather than just implementing based on a knee-jerk reaction to a request, or an impulsive desire to do something to attract or lock in a partner.

Once the partners and operational participants in the new venture have been identified and engaged, the next consideration is how to achieve overall balance among key stakeholders.

Stakeholder map

You don't need to, and quite possible can't, engage all stakeholders from the inception of a new enterprise. However, you need to have identified all relevant stakeholders and developed a plan for "proactively" managing them well in advance of when a particular stakeholder's money, purchase decision, time, or other resources may be required. A new venture founder would therefore do well to make and keep an up-to-date list of stakeholders, and a Gantt chart indicating when stakeholder engagement will occur. This should include identifying when customers will be delivered to, even identifying specific customers if possible (especially for a B2B businesses). Other potential stakeholders to consider include investors, government agencies, regulators, suppliers, distributors, other partners, employees, communities, neighbors, and friends and families of the founders.

Founders ignore or overlook stakeholders at their peril. Even something as simple as letting your spouse know you'll be away on a road trip for several months, well in advance, can avoid all kinds of unwanted complications and issues (he said from experience). Ensure there's a complete list of stakeholders, with a regularly updated view of when and how they should be engaged to benefit the new venture.

For any new venture, there are arguably two stakeholders who are more important than others: the customer and the investor. First, let's consider the potential customer. Be as specific as you possibly can. A business or product that will try to be all things to all people is much less likely to succeed than one with a strong focus on a small niche. Therefore, if your definition of customers is essentially anyone, think again. Try to narrow it down to a specific subset of potential customers. Also, try to define the customers in terms of their need, problem, or value requirement. The resulting statement should be something like: "People who need XYZ." Or better still: "Young females beginning to experience the pain associated with menstruation need relief." You get the idea. Define the intended customers as specifically as possible, in terms of who they are, where they live, what they do, what they need or will need, what problem they have or will have, or what they do or will value.

New ventures typically require investment, but sometimes not as much as founders think. In planning the resources required (next) for the venture, the tendency to overestimate can be just as costly as the tendency to underestimate. Ideally, the venture should have resources available, including investment, but take as little as possible – just what's necessary and sufficient to get the job done. By minimizing investment, the venture will maximize ROI, as any given level of return will achieve a higher ROI if the creation costs have been limited. Further, by minimizing investment, founder entrepreneurs will have retained greater equity (as discussed above). Aside from minimizing resource utilization, other ways to limit the investment required include securing government grants, utilizing partner resources (which can be less costly than replicating them within the new venture), and the highly underrated acts of "begging, borrowing and stealing."

Matthew Cain (2014) points out the fact that many social entrepreneurs aspire to overly high levels of investment, although I feel the problem is also true of many commercial entrepreneurs:

> The peculiarity of social enterprises are the number of entrepreneurs that pursue ideas that only work at a large scale. Businesses that would solve mammoth problems – but only if millions could be thrown at the problem. Some succeed, others never make it off the spreadsheet. Successful start-ups are built to scale.

Empowering and leading resources

Founders should give special consideration to how the venture will secure, manage, and empower the various resources required for successful development and implementation. What leadership is required and, looking at the founders in particular, what are the gaps? Does the leadership team have the ability to attract, engage, and inspire all the resources required, including investment, employees, or other stakeholders identified above?

A venture with inadequate resources will fail, so a key requirement for any new venture is to proactively and carefully identify all key resource needs, and a plan to secure them.

Investment needs are often pivotal to new ventures. Many potential new ventures languish either because the founders don't manage to connect with potential investors, or they connect but fail to convince and inspire the potential investors of the opportunity. Founders must themselves invest adequate time to develop a compelling business case for investment – to convey the "wow factor" to investors. This is true whether the founders are startup entrepreneurs, or intrapreneurs within a larger, existing organization. Someone, somewhere will hold the purse strings that will enable or fail to enable the new venture to commence with adequate resources.

Beyond financial resources, the right people – leadership and others – are vital to success. The new venture must define the skills and numbers of employees, whether direct or contracted. Similarly, suppliers, channels, or other partners should be identified, including when and what they are expected to deliver and the "business case" (value proposition) for their involvement.

Whether a venture requires tanks and planes, warehouses and retail outlets, or factories and offices, or all those and more, the point is that the enterprise leaders must identify all the required resources over a reasonable planning horizon. Failure to do so can mean losing the war, race or game, by falling short or tripping over your own shoelaces, even as you approach the finish line.

In summary, the new venture needs a complete "shopping list" of all the required resources, including leadership team, other staff, technology, facilities and everything else, plus budgets, needed to successfully develop and implement the strategy.

Transformation

It might seem strange to think of a change agenda in relation to a new startup. However, what is a new startup if not a change, a birthing of something new and transformative. In many ways, the startup agenda is a change agenda, but the important point here is that the new enterprise will need a road map for its own development – a plan on how it will grow, what new resources and relationships it will need (above), and what new capabilities and ideas it will need (below) to fuel that growth and development. This transformational process will require careful leadership, nurturing, and a constant eye for how things might be improved.

What's the big idea?

A new venture needs at least one big idea for innovation and it must be compelling enough to be worth launching, investing resources in, and so on. But as an idea moves forward into development and fruition, through whatever R&D process may be required to bring it into being, it's important for the founders and others involved in a new enterprise to remain open and receptive to the creative process. Ideas for improving the original idea, ideas that complement it and help propel it forward, and refinements and additions are all possible ways the creative process might continue.

But there's also an essential lesson here, based on the ideas tornado discussed in Chapter 13 – focus. While being open to new and improved ideas, it's important to maintain relentless focus on the central "big" idea. The key prescription for many startup entrepreneurs is to be wary of their essential makeup. The restless desire to come up with new ideas can take their focus away from implementing and succeeding. Follow-through is required in addition to creativity.

Another key consideration in relation to ideas is IP protection. Seeking the right expert advice in terms of patents, copyrights, and trademarks can save and secure a great deal of value.

Capability

The core capability for any new venture is its potential to create and deliver value, and arguably this is the soul of the big idea discussed above. This should be driven by core competencies, world-class domain expertise, and mastery second to none.

The "existing" capability at any particular moment in time will be a moving, changing snapshot, or more to the point, a frame in an emerging "movie." This is true of all organizations, but perhaps most true of startups. Startups often need to develop new capabilities or die trying. Of course, capability is the connection point, or bridge between the ideation/creation center and the lower, mindset/culture center, and also between the transformation agenda and the realm of action and performance/results.

Mindset and culture

The mindset/culture layer is all about implementation, where capabilities meet performance in the real world of people and all their funny, terrible, and lovely little quirks. This "root" layer reflects the ability or inability to put the strategic plan for the new venture into action – to implement it and measure and monitor its success.

Everything required in the present moment, including skills, mindsets, ideas, leadership, and appropriately communicated value messages, vision, and mission, tie together and manifest "where the rubber meets to road," at each and every point of implementation. We've already discussed the need for a great idea, well-led resources, stakeholder engagement, communication, vision, and mission. So, presupposing these exist, the fundamental issue that remains is whether the people in the new venture possess the right skills, perspectives, attitudes, beliefs, motivations, and other aspects of psychological makeup, and the further, related question of whether they chemically "gel" together into an effective culture.

Stated another way, the potential of any venture to innovate, lead, engage, deliver value, achieve success, and fulfill purpose is fundamentally underpinned by human nature, frailties, chemistry, and capabilities. Potentiality is rooted in individual psychology and culture.

Consider a "think tank" meeting designed to launch a new venture. If the wrong people are in the room – wrong-minded, wrongly motivated, lacking vital perspective, overly egotistical, or in whatever other ways flawed and unable to work with the others present – then the right ideas won't emerge, the right decisions won't be made, and the right actions won't be agreed. This is true at every level, in every aspect of the enterprise from leading resources, through stakeholder engagement, and ultimate fulfillment. So, what can be done about this?

At one level, the answer is simple. As Jack Welch and others have said, it's about getting the right people in and the wrong people out, as quickly as possible. Easy to say, but how about doing it?

Action, performance, and results

In my opinion, judgments about people should be based on their performance and the results they contribute. This means ensuring that people in a new venture are committed to action, accept ownership of their initiatives, and are willing to be held accountable for the results. If not, they must be replaced.

My prescription for getting the right people, at the right time, in the right roles is as follows:

1 Discuss the venture's purpose with potential people to be involved. If you don't sense an alignment of passion and purpose, that they "get it" and truly want to be involved, then pass on their involvement. No one can be successful contributing to something they can't feel passionate about. If you're not getting a sense of passion from someone, ask them what they do feel passionate about. If they light up talking about something like skiing, but not talking about the enterprise, pass. If they don't light up at all, pass.
2 Share your vision for success, and again try to assess (using head, heart, and gut) whether others share your excitement about the potential. What are they trying to achieve, in terms of personal success. Is there a healthy degree of alignment, or a potentially unhealthy mismatch?
3 Communicate your values, including core values and USP. Do potential participants "get it"? If not, is it you or them? If you honestly feel you've expressed yourself well and they really don't seem to understand, do you really want to work with them?
4 Explain who your key stakeholders are, and especially how the potential participants might be involved in that engagement. If they glaze over, don't seem to understand what a stakeholder is, or otherwise fail to impress and engage, then pass, pass, and pass.

5 Outline your leadership philosophies, the resources required for strategic success, and how you plan to inspire and empower those resources. Not every potential participant will be expected to serve in a leadership role, but they should at least demonstrate, conversationally, an understanding of your philosophies, your aims, your expectations of them, and what "responsible empowerment" means to them. Better still, it will help if they have some leadership qualities, bearing in mind that a new venture will need leadership, empowerment, and independent thought at all levels.

6 Articulate the new venture's "big idea" and make special note of whether the potential participant seems to resonate with it, perhaps even offering suggestions or asking penetrating questions. Again, if there's no apparent spark of interest or excitement, you must ask yourself why. Have you failed to convey the big idea, or is it simply "not for them"?

7 All the above suggestions rely on your powers of communication and observation. I'm not going to suggest you go and buy a book on neurolinguistic programming or any other form of self-help, "pop psychology" text. Frankly, I know of no evidence for the efficacy of such amateur approaches. What I will suggest, as a professional psychologist, is the help of a professional psychologist, especially one with relevant business experience. Avoid clinical psychologists, who will tend to see clinical problems wherever they look. Avoid armchair psychologists and the temptation to be one. Find a psychologist with the ability to perform the relevant analyses of the psychological makeup of the potential participants in your new venture. Have the same analyses done for existing participants, including yourself, and be sure to check the compatibility or "chemistry" within the existing team as well as with potential new team members. And when I say "look for chemistry," I don't mean looking for people who you'll easily get along with unchallenged. Look for diversity, the ability to engage in creative conflict, courage, and honesty. Powerful relevant tests may include emotional, verbal, mathematical, and other forms of intelligence, personality traits, motivations, attitudes toward change, leadership potential, and aptitudes. Note that any psychologist who offers to perform such analyses based on tests without meeting and interviewing someone is a charlatan, who should be avoided at all costs. Tests provide data, which are no substitute for direct observation.

Startup innovation agendas

In summary, startups require careful focus on the strategic innovation agendas:

1. Clear strategic intent.
2. Solid intelligence-based knowledge.
3. Compelling value proposition and USP.
4. Engaged stakeholders, most especially early investors, customers and partners.
5. Change agency – fire in the belly, with the clear desire to improve the world as we know it – to make a difference; to matter.
6. The capability to do something interesting.
7. The right people, with the right mindsets, most especially the drive of the founders.

chapter 17

Family Enterprise

"To put the world in order, we must first put the nation in order; to put the nation in order, we must first put the family in order; to put the family in order, we must first cultivate our personal life; we must first set our hearts right."

Confucius (5th century BC)

All in the family

I recently met Anthony Woodhouse, the managing director of Hall & Woodhouse, a UK-based family brewery and pub operator established in 1777. Anthony had agreed to speak at an Institute of Directors event I was hosting titled An Evening with Entrepreneurs. When we met, he said he didn't view himself as an entrepreneur but as a custodian. His great-great-great-great-grandfather, the founder of the company, was a man of vision who risked all to achieve greatness. Now Anthony feels his task is to hand on the company, in better condition than he found it, to the next generation of stakeholders. He views himself as a steward of the business, seeking to find the right balance between improving and preserving the business for future generations of shareholders. In my view, he is an entrepreneur, and I'm glad to say I've convinced him of that fact, and also that all chief executives are simultaneously stewards and change agents – seeking the right balance between preservation via risk management and improvement via entrepreneurship and innovation.

However, I believe family enterprises have some unique challenges, while having much in common with other forms of enterprise. Let me offer the following observations and prescriptions for success, again following the form from top to bottom centers of entrepreneurial psyche and associated innovation agendas.

Pathways to purpose

A key challenge many family businesses tend to face is "moving ahead with the times." What I mean by this, specifically, is that family businesses in a particular niche or specialism tend to rigidly define themselves in terms of that niche. A shoemaker wants his sons or daughters to learn the art of making shoes. A brewer wants to cultivate future generations of brewers to pass down the family recipes.

And yet Hall & Woodhouse is an example of a brewer that has moved with the times. Seeing a clear and continuing decline in the "old boozer" style of pubs, it opted to invest in acquiring and developing family-friendly "pub-restaurants," now a familiar model throughout Britain. These pubs feature the family's famous brews, some of which (especially the flagship brand of Badger beer) are exclusively available in its pubs. We discovered Hall & Woodhouse pubs shortly after relocating to the UK in 2007, and they remain a family favorite based on their healthy yet appealing and innovative menu, their child-friendly atmosphere, and the fact that "daddy" loves excellent "real ales."

But for every Hall & Woodhouse that moves with the times, there are many more family enterprises that fail to do so. I know of many examples of enterprises that failed to survive the cross-generation transition, and the primary factor I blame is inflexibility of purpose and the related emotion – passion. This inflexibility works both ways. On the one hand, many older generation business owners are rigid in their sense of what the family business exists to do. "We have always been home builders and will always remain home builders," said one crusty old chairman and majority shareholder of a company that no longer exists. Equally, the younger generation may be "to blame" for failing to be inspired by the company's mission or failing to be flexible enough in thinking about the future possibilities.

Let's consider a few examples:

- What if the daughter of the above builder, who had already become a lawyer specialized in property conveyance, had seen the possibility of keeping the home building business going, bringing in someone with a passion for the building craft to manage it? Could the building company, with its long-established brand and market niche as a quality builder, have survived and served as a "cash cow" to support other related ventures? Might the daughter have thereby funded her dream of creating her own law firm?
- What if the son of a carpenter, who owned a highly successful manufacturer of replica antique furnishings, had seen the wider possibilities? He didn't enjoy woodwork, and was instead eager to seek his fortune working in the city, where he worked managing a clothing store, hoping some day to own it or some other retail business. He enjoyed selling, and yet he and his father both failed to see the possibility of establishing a furniture store (or chain of stores), and the synergies with the furniture manufacturing business.
- What if the CEO of an international philanthropic organization had early on recognized the potential for his inclinations toward social entrepreneurship to be supported by the family business, a highly successful jeweler, which in turn might have benefited from promoting their philanthropy? Perhaps his grandfather wouldn't have died, brokenhearted, knowing his business would be sold to the highest bidder.
- What if the owner of several hotels, who is reluctant to take partners on board to invest in much-needed business improvement, because he doesn't want to dilute equity in the hotels before passing the business on to his daughter, could see as clearly as I do that his daughter is completely disinterested in the hotel business, and will probably sell it as soon as it's her decision to do so?

What's clear from the above is that older generations need to help their children or other potential heirs to the business to find *their* passions. Passions can't be passed along or inherited. As Harry Truman said: "I have found the best way to give advice to your children is to find out what they want and then advise them to do it." Older generations can hope to "infect" the younger generations with their passion and sense of purpose. But they must also be open to the possibility that the younger people may initially develop passions that seem unrelated to the family business. When this happens, a degree of flexibility of thought may benefit both the older and younger generations.

Hall & Woodhouse explicitly encourages younger generation shareholders to get involved in the business, but only if they have true passion to do so. They aren't hired into elevated roles specially designed for them, but instead start at the bottom, demonstrating the ability to learn the brewing craft, to serve in a pub, or work in other roles in the business. But Hall & Woodhouse is unusual in having many younger generation shareholders to choose from. As per the examples above, there may be only one potential heir to choose from, who may or may not have found that their passion in any way relates to the family enterprise. In such instances, my prescription is to talk. The generations need to talk about their personal passions, what they love or don't love about the family business, what they love about other areas of human enterprise, and what they hope to achieve in life – their personal sense of purpose.

Talking won't always avert tragedy. It won't necessarily bring the generations together in their thinking – a meeting of the minds. But I guarantee that *not* talking will not help. Through talking and open-minded exploration of ideas on both sides, and perhaps a little thinking outside the box, older and younger generations may come to a meeting of the minds and a potential convergence of interests. Perhaps paths will diverge for a while, but eventually come back together, particularly if there's a degree of flexibility.

Intentionality

A problem with family enterprises can be that intentions become lost or forgotten. Early intentions can get lost in translation or simply not be passed on. A founding entrepreneur such as Henry Ford may have an intention, such as transforming the world as he knew it by providing a car to every family, which possibly never gets expressed to subsequent generations in a way that makes them feel the same sense of purpose or dedication to the original strategic intent.

Vision quests

Further to the above points about engaging passion, meaning, and purpose, a key problem for younger and older generations in family enterprises is an inability to envision professional life differently. The older generation can be resistant to, or seemingly incapable of, envisioning a different pathway for the business – a different game – a different articulation of success. And the younger generation can fail to envision how the business might actually serve their strategic interests. The young can be just as intractable as the elderly in their views of what constitutes success.

Again, a key aspect of my prescription is talking. However, another is what I refer to as a "vision quest." In Native American traditions, when young warriors came of age, they would be sent into the wilderness to find themselves. Unarmed, cold, alone, hungry, and afraid, they were expected to have "a vision" that would inform them and their tribe of their path.

In family businesses, I recommend encouraging the youthful family members to seek their vision in the wilderness, in the outer world of education, business, and life. Stated another way, young people who are brought into the business at too early an age, especially if pressured to demonstrate leadership or entrepreneurial qualities, will tend to fail. On the other hand, those allowed and actively encouraged to find themselves through education or other work experience are more likely, in my view, to return to the tribe as effective warriors. They will have the skills, perspectives, and experience that will be invaluable to the family enterprise.

In fact, Anthony Woodhouse returned to Hall & Woodhouse in 1999, following a career in the City, where, in his words, he had became "disillusioned with the nature of business and culture of greed." For a decade, he worked full time in the voluntary sector as well as supporting the family business, but in 2009, he agreed to become managing director. In Anthony's view, one of his key challenges is to develop a culture of entrepreneurship in a 236-year-old family business. In his words:

> We want to be a growing, independent family company for many centuries to come. Who knows what businesses we will be involved with in the future? We have survived and prospered by reacting and adapting to change – and we must keep and promote that culture of entrepreneurship if we are to continue to do so.

Intelligence

Intelligence isn't entirely hereditary. As with any enterprise, a family business must invest in current knowledge and understanding of competitors and customers, or face the consequences. Family enterprises need to look beyond the family for vital knowledge and avoid groupthink, which is quite likely to occur. While a degree of diversity exists within any family, arguably it is less than the diversity among humans in general. The prescription is to spice things up with outside perspectives.

Finding your voices

Psychologically, a family enterprise has much in common with any enterprise, plus the additional emotional "charge" that comes with familial territory. If at age 3, little Johnny stole little Sally's favorite toy, then at age 43 there is probably still a residual emotional charge that can manifest itself within the family business. Similarly, it's hard enough for people from different age generations to see eye to eye, but when one is a father and the other a son – or any parent–child relationship – the differences are magnified. Further complications can arise due to positional difference among family members. For example, if the CEO happens to have a daughter and a niece in key roles, there may be jealousies involved, perceptions that one is favored over the other, based on position rather than merit.

The prescription of keeping emotions in check is applicable to family businesses, but also to enterprises of all kinds. It is always and only a question of degree. Here are some specific ideas for keeping emotions in check and hopefully preventing them from creating irrational divides, conflicts, decisions (or indecisions), or affecting the behavior or performance of individuals or organizations:

1 The rational recognition that ego is the root of all emotion is a good starting point. If we can all individually accept that our ego is rooted in survival instinct, a conscious mechanism based on self-awareness and preservation, then we can recognize that emotions such as anger, fear, attachment, and so on are simply expressions of ego, and not something empowered with greater authority, morality, or rightness. In other words, get off your high horse.

2 Get out of your own box. Get over the idea that your perspective is the only one that matters. Realize that there are three sides to every story: his, hers, and the truth. If you will attempt, for even a single moment, to empathize with "the other" side of the story, you will quickly (unless you're an emotional idiot; sorry, there are caveats to everything) take the emotional energy out of your "righteous" perspective, realizing that the other perspective also has elements of truth, and that there is likely a higher perspective – the truth – somewhere in the middle.

3 Tune in to your inner power. By reminding yourself that you're not three years old and incapable of tying your own shoes, you may find that you're able to see a perceived threat or conflict differently. In particular, if you remember that there's nothing to fear except fear itself, what do you have to lose by simply allowing someone else's anger, or other emotional outburst, to simply wash over you? It can't hurt you. You don't need to be afraid of it, its effect on you, or its consequences. In fact, it's much less likely to have any consequences if your reaction is more like "water off a duck's back" than a nuclear holocaust. Your nuclear reaction is going to be far more powerful if used sparingly, based on strategic choice, rather than in a reactive, emotional way.

4 Remind yourself, at least for a moment, why the person you're having issues with is dear to you. What's good about them? How do they serve you? In what ways do you value your relationship? Do you love them, or at least like something about them? Connecting with such ideas, even for an instant, can help your rational, higher mind overcome the irrational ego mind and its knee-jerk reactions.

5 Take time to find your voice – your truth – so that you may speak it. This isn't literally about speech, it's about behavior in the broadest sense. Silence, action, inaction, speech – these are all forms of communication that can escalate or de-escalate a conflict. The key here is to engage the gap. Even if it may not seem so to the conscious ego mind, there is a gap between any stimulus and our ego's response. Especially immature egos may have infinitesimally small gaps – instant anger, sadness, or other ineffectual emotion in response to the same old stimuli, all in a moment. But the reality is that there is a gap, tiny though it may be, between any stimulus and any response. In this gap lies freedom. Freedom to choose the response, or even a non-response.

6 Analyze. Engage your intellect, your rational mind. Also engage your intuition, not to be confused with ego and emotion. For intuition is also based on rational mind. It's rational mind that we can't quite explain. We know what we know, without knowing why. That's OK. Engage it and see what it has to offer as a balance or a foil to ego's emotion. In your analyses, try looking at your own motivations, attitudes, beliefs, or other psychological states or conditions that might affect how you feel, think, or act. Do the same for the other "side." If this doesn't help, you're not trying hard enough.

7 Engage your sense of purpose, your underlying sense of passion for what's true, right, and worthwhile. In this light, does the conflict, decision, or argument in question matter? Is this the right fight or the right time to fight? Is there another way? If fight is the only option now, you should be filled with the inspiration to win. If not, look again.

Common values

Common values bind together families, cultures, and nations. If an enterprise lacks some commonality of values and shared psyche or culture, it will wither and die. In one sense, this can be a source of strength for family enterprises. The sharing of roots, ancestry, and strong cultural elements can mean that family members tend to be more in synch, with more shared values than, say, a random sample of people. On the other hand, generational differences can divide families, as can experiences of conflict. The strengths that can come from shared values can be offset by the psychological baggage and emotional charge that may come into play, based on differences among family members.

Vulnerability

Much of what I've said so far about communication and values also relates to engagement. Fundamentally, the point of engaging in relation to purpose, vision, and values – and engaging rationally as a balance to emotion – is all about how to create and sustain effective engagement within key relationships, achieving win–win value.

One problem here for families is the tendency to take each other for granted. "I'm your father, and always will be" is a form of taking a relationship as a "given." No relationship is given; it is precious and something to be nurtured and cultivated. Put another way, all relationships are vulnerable, at risk of being lost. And here's a paradox. The best starting point for the preservation and strengthening of any relationship is from a position of vulnerability.

As Lencioni (2002) points out, if we begin by showing up with vulnerability, we can cultivate trust. By being vulnerable, showing our humanity and our imperfections, we establish a baseline on which trust can be built. Vulnerability is key to effective leadership (also see Staub, 1996, 2002).

If fathers, mothers, daughters, sons, and other relatives can remember to be vulnerable – stop pretending to be perfect, stop pretending to know, or to be right, or in some way superior – then true engagement and relationship, with less "ego charging," becomes possible.

If we can be vulnerable and enable trust, then we can engage in creative conflict – the essential ingredient for all sorts of good things in any enterprise: effective decision making, leadership, strategy, and innovation. So get with the program. Be vulnerable.

Stakeholder complexities

All enterprises face challenges in balancing across various stakeholder needs and wants, but there are some special challenges for family enterprises:

- Nepotism may be expected by some family members, who think they can expect gainful employment, perhaps in spite of lacking the necessary skills and abilities.
- Nepotism may also be perceived by non-family-member employees, even when it doesn't exist, thereby damaging morale.
- It can be difficult for board directors who are also business owners to clearly separate their responsibilities for governance from their accountability to shareholders. These challenges become even more complex when the same people also work in the business as executive managers or in other roles.
- Family get-togethers can become forums for business discussion and decisions, sometimes competing with or circumventing board meetings and the formal governance process.

Letting go

Quite possibly the greatest act of courage for any leader of a family business is to truly empower another family member to lead, to decide, to take action, to implement, and to suffer whatever consequences may arise.

Delegation is a first step, putting someone in charge of something, along with the implied threat of holding them accountable. True empowerment involves the further step of giving them the resources necessary to win, to succeed. These resources may include time, money, people or tools, even your support. Only through empowerment can leaders grow. An effective boss knows when to "let go," to allow others to learn and grow, to overcome their mistakes, and to thrive.

Empowering change agency

Again, the core psychological challenge revolves around ego. The "boss ego" must decide it's OK to let go, to let someone else drive change or the chance for improvement. This means realizing that the business can survive whatever "learning experiences" may arise from the delegation experiment. It means deciding it's OK to be the boss and to be imperfect (vulnerable), having made the (obviously, in hindsight) incorrect decision of empowering a "junior" to "fail." And it means standing back and allowing the "junior" the limelight, the glory of succeeding.

Letting go is as much about letting go of personal ego as anything else.

Quieting the mind

We've talked about creative conflict, letting go, empowerment and allowing "juniors" to creatively explore their own ability to solve problems, generate solutions, drive growth or other opportunities. Now we'll cover a deeper aspect of creativity, particularly the fact that powerful creativity also requires transcending ego, or at least getting it to "shut up" for a while.

Have you ever noticed that the most powerfully creative ideas rarely come from making a massive effort? How often have you gone to bed wondering how to handle a problem and then woken with a solution? The wellspring for creativity within the human mind is not the conscious, ego mind. Rather, it comes from the part of our mind that we are not conscious of, that remains a mystery, even to modern psychological science.

Various philosophers, psychologists, and others have speculated about the elements and processes that may exist and interact within the unconscious creative process. Some, and I include myself here, believe we simply aren't aware of everything that occurs within our amazingly complex brains. So, the creative process that may occur while we sleep or engage in other activities may involve neural interactions or connections made without conscious effort or awareness. Others believe that creative ideas may come from sources outside us, such as higher forces or a collective unconscious. Whatever the answer may be, exactly how it works is still a mystery. What is clear, however, is that the conscious ego mind can stifle the mysterious, unconscious creative processes.

Writer's block and similar blockages seen in artists, composers, designers, and various other "creatives" don't happen by accident. Similarly, other creative pursuits such as business problem solving, decision making, strategizing, and coming up with good ideas for innovation are also "blocked" for specific psychological reasons. It has to do with creative flow, which is constricted and reduced, or even entirely stopped and blocked, by ego.

Consider the ego elements that can block creative flow:

1. Ego trying to force, through willpower, creativity in an area that's fundamentally out of alignment with true purpose and passions.
2. Not having a clear concept, visualization, or understanding of what one is trying to create, or the problem to be solved, or the requirement for creativity – or having a false or "off target" conception that the ego clings to, perhaps in spite of creative "impulses" to the contrary.
3. Trying to create something that is out of alignment with personal values and truths can result in an inability to articulate or express creativity, or failing to have any core values, or not having found one's voice or truth.
4. An inability to engage in collaborative idea generation and development will stifle creative potential.
5. Failure to empower oneself to create, or failing to feel empowered by anyone regarded as a leader, manager, boss or owner.
6. The ego can block or reject ideas for change agency based on limited conceptions of what's "good enough," what's "desirable" or indeed

what's creative. Thinking out of the box means thinking outside the ego's self-limiting structures.

7 The underlying potentiality to create requires belief, attitude, and motivation, and can therefore be blocked as follows:
- If one lacks the belief in one's ability to create, which can be affected by the beliefs of others.
- If one lacks a positive mental attitude toward the creative process.
- If one lacks the intrinsic motivation to create, or is extrinsically demotivated.

In summary, there are many ways for ego to get in the way of creativity, but they all relate to the seven psyche centers. A healthy, balanced ego is therefore a requirement for creatives of all kinds. And hopefully it's clear that the leaders, managers, and participants in family enterprises – just like participants in enterprises of all kinds – will create more value and be more innovative if they cultivate their creative capabilities. Creativity isn't just about art, music, the entertainment industry, and advertising. Creativity is arguably the fundamental underlying energy to drive all innovation, improvement, and fulfillment of human potential.

Capability

Skills and expertise (capabilities) are essential ingredients for effective ideation, and driving ideas to reality requires capability to develop and deliver. The key message here for family enterprises is simply to look at the needs of the organization for winning capabilities, and either develop, buy, recruit or partner with them. Don't do it the other way around – building the enterprise based on what you've got, the capabilities that exist within the family.

The culture within

Family enterprises must, like any enterprise, invest in developing capabilities to enable ongoing value delivery and innovation. These investments may include tangible assets such as facilities and ICT infrastructure, as well as intangibles, the most important of which is organizational culture. The special challenge for family enterprises in this regard is managing a culture within a culture. Remember, the concept of "culture" is simply the shared psychological characteristics of any group of people. Therefore, families, companies, and countries all tend to have distinctive cultures.

Let's consider two examples of managing a culture within cultures.

The first example can be applicable to any organization that works in more than one country or areas with distinct cultures (often found within single towns, either "side of the tracks"). This challenge arises because the organization's culture usually has a starting point based on geography and the associated culture of the founders. Oracle Corporation is an example of a company that started in Silicon Valley and now operates throughout the world. There are many such examples, and each one has an original "inner" culture based on where it began, as well as a broader culture. Multinationals also have distinctive cultures within specific operating geographies. Further, any organization with distinct divisions, operating units, or functions – arguably all organizations of any size – will likely have distinct cultures within the wider culture.

The second example of cultures within cultures is unique to family enterprises, and has to do with the fact that a family is a group and may therefore share a family psyche – a culture. If a family group has a strong culture – distinctive, possibly even somewhat unique traits, attitudes, and so on – then it will stand out within a wider organizational culture that includes non-family members. The result can be problematic, for family and non-family participants in the family enterprise. For non-family, the family can look and feel like a clique, an exclusive club they are excluded from. This creates problems for the family and the enterprise:

1. Lower motivation, poor working attitudes, and the belief that one can never really succeed unless one is a family member can all conspire to undermine performance.
2. Non-family become uncreative for reasons outlined in the prior section, but also may not want to engage in entrepreneurial creativity within a business they feel (or know) they can never own a stake in. Many family businesses, including Hall & Woodhouse, do not dilute family ownership as a matter of principle.
3. Non-family may not feel truly empowered as leaders, even if they are directors or key executives, perhaps feeling that they would be replaced if the "right" family member emerged to take their place.

4 Relationships between family members and non-family members will always be qualitatively different, unless of course there's a marriage, as happened when Anthony Woodhouse's great-great-grandfather married a member of the Hall family.
5 Families can have strong and distinctive core values or "truths" that may seem exclusive to non-family.
6 If a family's vision for success of the family enterprise doesn't manifest success for non-family, there's an inherent problem.
7 Last but not least, if the purpose or mission of a family business is more about supporting the family than anything else, it's highly unlikely that non-family will find a sense of spirited purpose in participating.

These potential problems are expressed as they might be experienced by non-family participants in family enterprises. However, there's another side to the coin – the problems as experienced by the family. Clearly, the problem for the family is to create and lead a business that is as successful as possible for the family, and so the problem is to manage all the potential cultural disconnects that might undermine success.

As Anthony Woodhouse said to me: "You simply can't attract and retain seriously talented people if they somehow feel like 'second-class' citizens. We try and create a sense of belonging to the Hall & Woodhouse family, with the Woodhouse family serving as the stewards of that shared culture."

Performance and results

As alluded to above, challenging poor performance by a family member can be even more difficult than challenging it in general – and it's hard. The prescription here is simple. Ensure that targets and key performance indicators are in place, clearly define accountability and the consequences of falling short of the defined goals, rigorously measure results, and then objectively implement consequences for underachievement.

Conclusion on family business

Family enterprises tend to share the same sort of challenges, strengths, and weaknesses as other types of enterprise. The differences are psychological. They're based on our beliefs and attitudes about the nature of families, which is of course cultural. Human factors such as loyalties, obligations, and expectations are at play in all spheres of enterprise, but certainly to no lesser extent than one might find when blood is involved.

Family businesses require careful focus on the strategic innovation agendas, as follows:

1. Strategic intent that will likely have a degree of built-in legacy and stewardship, but must also look to the future with an open mind and an eye for innovation.
2. A knowledge agenda that embraces the need to look beyond the family to engage diverse perspectives.
3. Build on the strength that naturally comes from common values, and avoid the ego-based pitfalls that can lead to unnecessary emotional baggage in family relationships.
4. Explicitly recognize and address the special complexities that can exist in stakeholder relationships in family enterprises, avoiding real or perceived nepotism, or undermining good governance.
5. Empower change agency to continually develop the entrepreneurial, innovation drive within the younger generation, the family, and the enterprise in general.
6. Ensure that the family enterprise has winning capabilities, even if that means looking beyond the capabilities of family members.
7. Hold all people, including family members, accountable for their performance and results.

chapter 18

Getting Ready to Sell

"Every one lives by selling something, whatever be his right to it."

Robert Louis Stevenson (*c.* 1880)

The need for an exit plan

If you don't plan to sell your business, you should. If it's a "lifestyle business," it's really a job and everyone should plan to retire from their job someday. And why not plan to maximize your retirement benefits by building something of value? All business owners should have an exit strategy from the beginning. Even if you don't presently want to sell your business, the strategic consideration of selling will ensure that you focus on maximizing the performance and value of the business and decreasing its dependence on you, the business owner. Whether you're a sole founder and owner, a primary shareholder, or a partner in a business, this chapter is designed to help you consider and plan for your inevitable exit and maximize the business's valuation and therefore the gains you'll derive from selling your stake.

Why?

Planning for exit is a good starting point, but you should also be clear about your personal objectives in relation to exit, including an amount you'd like to derive from sale, a time frame for your personal exit, and any preferences you may have in terms of future ownership of the business.

There can be many specific reasons for exiting a business, and one main reason for planning for it is the fact that exit is inevitable. However, being clear about your personal reason or reasons for planning an exit is vitally important to getting it right – to exiting in the most beneficial and graceful manner possible. How and when you exit might be different depending on whether your goals are to start another enterprise, retire, spend more time with loved ones, or engage in philanthropic initiatives.

Strategic intent

Beyond your personal objectives and building on them, maximizing the value of the present business requires a compelling strategy, starting with the key elements of a powerful purpose and audacious vision. If these are absent or stale, start by revitalizing them (see Chapter 15). But on top of that, be clear about what your business is worth now, and establish a reasonable but fairly audacious goal for the valuation by the time you want to exit, or if that may be a long way off, set a three-year goal.

Goals and requirements

The point is to be as specific as possible in what you want to achieve within a specific time horizon. Simply having a vague intention to eventually sell for as much as possible is not going to achieve the same level of value as setting specific targets based on your requirements and then working and engaging others in working to achieve them. Of course, the overall goal should be to maximize the valuation of the business.

Financial, estate, and tax planning

It's one thing to maximize business valuation but another to maximize the value you are able to retain. This requires expertise and intelligence. Before you started or got involved in your business, you should have obtained expert advice to help you legally maximize your retained gains. Perhaps you didn't, and even if you did, you may benefit from seeking up-to-date advice applicable to your citizenship, residency, and business. This should include tax, estate, and financial planning with the appropriate experts. Unless you obtained excellent advice at the start and along your business journey, you'll probably find you've created unintended problems that will have a negative effect on your potential exit.

The right expert advice can help you identify the best purchasers for your business, maximize the value that purchasers will see in the business, identify contracts that need to be renegotiated that would otherwise reduce the value of your business, and spot ways to tune the business model and structure to maximize financial performance and valuation. It is not my intention to impart such advice here, because the advice you receive must be specific to you and your business. My intention is only to provide an overview of what you should consider.

Communication

When, how and to whom you communicate your intention to sell are questions that must be addressed with care and consideration. Employees can become demoralized or worried about insecurity. Customers and suppliers can start looking at other options. Competitors can sense and attempt to exploit weaknesses. Conversely, a competitor may become a good purchaser. Employees may also become key to a management buyout. The overall point is that if you never put the message out that you may wish to sell – if it remains a well-kept secret until the last minute – you may well lose out on some value and opportunities in relation to your exit plan. This is about finding the right balance, getting the right message out in the right way, at the right time, to the right people. Again, expert advice may well be highly valuable in this process.

Valuation

Once you've established your intel-based strategic intent to drive valuation, you need to develop a value agenda to drive the worth of your business to the desired levels. The value agenda is defined by your marketing mix and sales growth strategy, your value delivery model, the values you and the business operate by, and a detailed understanding of how customers experience value and specific plans to improve customer value.

Your target valuation and estimates of the multiples that might apply will establish market growth targets, so now the questions are: What is the strategy going to deliver? Is your marketing mix up to the challenge, or do you need additional product lines, additional or more effective salespeople, or improved ways to connect with potential customers? Is your online strategy up to date and working to deliver new business growth? Do you have the required marketing expertise in your organization, and are you achieving acceptable ROI on marketing investments? Is this an area of innovation or unnovation within your business?

A key way to drive sales growth is to improve customers' value experience. That can translate into invaluable marketing help in the form of referrals and recommendations, more repeat business, upselling, and the ability to command higher value-based prices. Customer experience is tied to your product solutions, but also your sales and service, and the values that customers perceive you and others in your business operate by. Getting a solid handle on these perceptions and how to improve them, for example via Net Promoter or similar methods, becomes the backbone of a value agenda, to drive toward your valuation goals.

Placing the right value on your business and establishing strategic intent to drive existing value upward requires careful thought. Especially relevant here is a consideration of potential purchasers. This might include management, competitors, partners, or other businesses with interests in expanding into the domain of your business. Thinking out of the box here can make a huge difference to your business valuation.

The worth of your business will always be tied to aspects of financial performance such as profits and growth, but the multiples used to compute value can vary widely. To a competitor, the value of your business may simply be increased market share, but to a company wishing to enter the market, your company might be much more valuable and include domain expertise, know-how, and other intellectual capital that may not be valued as greatly by a competitor with their own way of doing things. Further, the strategic value of your business will be even greater if a purchaser enjoys business model synergies in production, products, or delivery mechanisms. Looking for companies with such synergies is an art and science that few practice, so again, the right expert advice should be well worth the cost.

Engagement

The aspect of engagement that is most important to consider here is collaborative partnering in relation to the enterprise's operational business model. The main reason is that the enterprise's value may be much greater to a complementary enterprise than to a competitor, the management team, or purchasers simply investing in the business. A supplier may value the enterprise as a channel to market. A channel may value your production capabilities. Or a business that's into complementary business areas may value the IP that exists within your enterprise in ways that others wouldn't. As stated above, industry know-how, business processes, knowledge of and connections to key customers, and so on can be valuable, but probably less so to a competitor with their own IP.

Stakeholders

You should be well aware of all the stakeholders involved with your business, but it's important to give special consideration to how they may be affected by a potential business sale. Let's consider a few key examples of categories of relationships and how they are typically affected.

Customer value management (Gale, 1994) and effective CRM are vital to business valuation. But a further consideration is how to ensure that the most important customer relationships can survive a sale. Business is all about relationships, so part of an exit strategy is to ensure that key customer relationships can survive the owner's departure through careful transitioning or establishing multiple points of contact.

Employees are the lifeblood of any business, and when they get wind of a potential sale, various problems can arise. One way to avoid problems is to keep the potential sale quiet, but you'll be amazed at how the rumor mill can "spill the beans." I believe a better approach is honesty and being open about eventual plans to sell. However, when transactions are in play, secrecy is sometimes required. Again, your advisers should be helpful here. Aside from whether or not employees may know about a potential sale, a key consideration is to maximize their effectiveness and loyalty to the business. Appropriate remuneration packages are essential, but the right environment, training opportunities, feedback, and other factors can be equally motivating or demotivating within a business (see Sale, 2014). The level of motivation in your business will affect performance and value, as will the ability to attract and retain the best people. Most of us are intensely aware of the "vibe" when we walk into a business and a potential purchaser will be no exception.

It's important to consider all other stakeholders, including any suppliers who might be affected by a business's sale, but let's consider for a moment any additional owners of the business. In Chapter 16, I pointed out that many business owners have inappropriately given away or sold equity in their business, often by taking in or establishing partners within the business. If you already have a partner or partners, you should consider whether they're really the right ones to have in the business. The "acid test question" is whether their presence in the business adds at least as much equity value as they own. If the answer is no, then one of the keys steps to consider on the path to business exit is whether you might buy them out. Why keep them if you're going to invest to drive valuation growth, and they're only "baggage" along for the ride? A related question is whether you should establish new partners in the business, such as important leaders, innovators, and contributors in the business. If any employee is vitally important to the ongoing success of the business, having them participate in owning the business can be a highly effective way of increasing their sense of ownership, their motivation, and their loyalty to the business and its ongoing success.

Leadership

Ensuring effective leadership in preparation for a sale and through the transition process is vitally important. Thinking ahead toward exit, you must ensure that you develop leaders who can replace you. If no one in the existing organization has the potential for such development, it's time to think about recruiting someone who does have that potential and will be able to develop it within your exit horizon. As you think ahead to exit, it's time for you as a leader to give thought to how you empower others within the organization to lead, without your direction and guidance. The valuation will be greater if you've developed a leadership culture that can survive your departure.

Improvements

A change agenda to identify and drive specific improvements in the business will complement the above and serve as a tangible way of supporting your growth strategies, ensuring that the business is scalable, can assure quality as it grows, and therefore sustainably grow in value. You should have and manage a continual change agenda, but it deserves special consideration when thought of in the context of a potential business sale.

Ideas

What specific improvements might enhance the value of the business in the short and longer term? Ideas for improvement and value creation are always needed, but even more so when your aim is to create a business with a demonstrable track record of innovation.

Capabilities

Maximizing your exit valuation is about being able to convince purchasers of the organization's sustainable ability to create and deliver value. This encompasses everything from your people, through your business processes, to your products, and your relationships. Arguably the most important organizational capability is the capability for innovation.

Entrepreneurial culture and mindset

Your organization's capability to innovate is largely determined by culture and individual mindsets. Are there other entrepreneurial individuals within the business or are you alone? If you are the strongest entrepreneur in the business, what will happen when you leave? Will the business still have an entrepreneurial spirit and a driver for innovation without you? If not, the value of the business will drop like a stone as you walk out the door.

Hopefully, your strategy already includes succession planning to minimize the risk of, and damages resulting from, losing key people. However, in thinking ahead toward exit, you need to be especially cognizant of the entrepreneurial succession. At a minimum, you need a replacement for yourself. Better still, you need to cultivate and develop entrepreneurial leaders in your business. Best of all, you can create an entrepreneurial culture, where people are actively engaged in innovating. The bottom line is that the value of your business will be greater and more sustainable if you develop entrepreneurship in others.

In too many businesses, the prevailing culture is non-entrepreneurial, although there's often a legendary, almost mystical entrepreneur leader at the helm. These leaders are great and deserve our admiration and respect. But the companies they've created would be even more valuable if they could cultivate greater entrepreneurship within the rank and file.

Taking action

The bottom line is that if you're an owner or partner in any business, you should have thought about exiting. Even if you passionately love your business and your role in it, you should think about and plan for your eventual departure. By preparing your business to function with or without you, it will become a better, stronger, and more valuable business. And if you aren't still "in love" with the business, what are you doing there? Is it time to move on?

Moving on

Stated another way, and in summary, what are you going to do about your exit in relation to the innovation agendas?

1 Define exit "success" in terms of your specific aspirations and needs.
2 Employ the right experts to ensure that your exit and the sale are conducted intelligently, thus maximizing the value of the enterprise.
3 Clearly understand the existing and potential value of your business so that you don't leave money on the table, or fail to invest appropriately in the business as you prepare for exit.

4. Appropriately manage all stakeholder relationships leading up to and through the exit process.
5. Proactively invest in improving your business and its resulting value well in advance of an intended sale.
6. Develop demonstrable, sustainable capabilities, including competitive advantage and the ability to innovate.
7. Do it now. Avoid the more common "head in the sand" approach of not thinking about the inevitability of your departure from your business.

chapter 19

Service Enterprise

"If we do not lay out ourselves in the service of mankind whom should we serve?"

Abigail Adams (*c.* 1770)

Servants

What feelings or thoughts arise when you see the word "servant"? When I ask service providers, I frequently get negative reactions based on concepts of servitude and demeaning work. Yet, the definition of "servant" is someone who provides a service or serves in the employment of a person or enterprise. The president of the US and other world leaders are servants. What's demeaning about that?

Yet the quality of service we experience as customers is clearly and strongly affected by the attitude of service providers toward their roles. It's easy to tell when a waiter would rather be doing something other than serving us – they tend to provide poor service. Things are getting better, but Britain and the rest of Europe are still behind North America in the quality of service provided and experienced in restaurants. Some argue that the difference is all about tips. American waiters are accused of superficial, insincere friendliness, a perception reinforced by staff trained to paste on a smile and say "have a nice day." And no doubt the fact that their pay is unaffected by customer experience, European waiters may lack motivation relative to tip-hungry Americans. But the friendlier, more attentive approach we see in North American eateries is not insincere in the majority of cases. Money is not the only motivator of service excellence, just as it is not the only motivator for human work and play in general.

The overall point is that the quality of service is directly driven by the servant's attitudes toward the role, as much or more than as a function of training, processes, and leadership.

Ivory towers

Professional service providers such as medical doctors, lawyers, and accountants arguably struggle to see themselves as servants more than most. In fact, the biggest obstacle to innovation in professional service enterprises is arguably the ivory tower phenomenon. The core of the issue is that the service provider views the mission or purpose of service provision as one of providing expert advice or expertise-based service to the recipient. It's more about the provision than the receipt. It's more about the qualities of expertise than the quality of the recipient's service experience.

Purposeful service

In one sense, the ivory tower syndrome is a mindset and cultural issue, but that directly leads to the wrong "mental model" in terms of the purpose of the service.

Professional service providers would do well to consider that their role, their essential purpose is first and foremost the provision of a service, not just the provision of their expertise. Their expertise is, naturally, the enabler for the provision of service and is highly valuable. To the personal ego of the expert, the expertise may feel like the defining quality of "who I am." But to the recipient, the essential quality and value of the service is an experience of relationship, not one of gratitude for or worship of the enabling expertise.

In all fields of human enterprise, servants would do well to keep in mind that their purpose is to serve the customer. Even in cases where the customer is the non-paying recipient of charity or government service, the provider's purpose is not to do the recipient a favor. That mental model leads to bad attitudes and bad service. The purpose of servants is to serve. If the servants in your enterprise don't get it, get rid of them, and recruit people who do get it.

Civil servants should be in their roles because they love to serve, not because they want better job security or pensions than they can find in the private sector. Waiters should be recruited because they love to serve people food and drink, not because they love big tips. Charity workers should be, and hopefully are, mostly in their roles because they genuinely love helping people, not because they want to be seen as "good" people. And doctors, nurses, lawyers, accountants, and sales representatives should also all be in their roles because they too love helping people through their expertise and technologies, not because they are driven by money or status.

Intentionality and human error

What are you aiming for, OK or excellence? Teams and organizations that aim to provide "good" service generally don't. They only provide good service at best. Service, just like any other human activity or product of human activity, can never be perfect. Therefore, whatever "level" of service provision an enterprise aims for defines the upper limits on service quality, but due to human error, there will inevitably be instances of lower quality service. Enterprises that set their sights on imperfect service are typically regarded and experienced by customers as providing poor service. There's only one reasonable target to aim for and that's perfection or excellence. Then, when the inevitable errors occur, the enterprise's extraordinary responses will further differentiate them from competitors and impress their customers.

Service excellence

The vision for any service-based enterprise should embrace the concept of service excellence. Service excellence can mean many things, including outstanding quality, superior merit, service that is remarkably good or extraordinary, being best or better than most, being a fantastic value compared to alternatives, and being great rather than merely good.

Service intelligence

Achieving service excellence doesn't happen by accident. It's a process of continuous improvement, and sometimes breakthrough innovations based on key insights into how to achieve step changes in service quality. It starts with a vision for what "excellence" means, underpinned by intelligence on how the enterprise is doing (and is perceived) currently. Lee (2004) points out the deficiencies of many approaches to measuring patient satisfaction with healthcare provision. What's needed instead of a focus on trying to manage the numbers (driving statistically significant but unimportant incremental improvements) is a vision for step change.

Breakthrough innovations in service paradigms often result from benchmarking against leaders from other industries rather than leaders from within a given industry. This is Lee's (2004) point; if you want to become a world-class healthcare service provider, don't benchmark against other healthcare service providers. Instead, look at how you might emulate Disney, a global leader in providing excellent customer service experiences.

Another example of benchmarking against other industries to improve service includes the airline industry (Nance, 2008):

1. improving asset utilization and performance by applying observations of how pit crews turn around race cars to aircraft maintenance
2. improving passenger safety by implementing more disciplined approaches to cockpit communication drawn from the nuclear industry.

Nance advocates healthcare benchmarking with the airline industry to achieve a step change in patient safety, an elusive goal for health innovation. Arguably, a bag traveling around the world is much safer than a patient in a typical modern, well-equipped hospital.

Service excellence starts with the right strategic intent, including sense of purpose and vision underpinned by intelligence, enabling continuous improvement and breakthrough innovations. But it goes nowhere unless the aim and drive to achieve service excellence is communicated.

Communication

Internal communication of intent, including specific goals and targets, is important, together with communication of "how we're doing" – customer feedback and other forms of intelligence that can enable insights for improvement. But the bigger communication issue blocking service excellence is often that the service providers don't speak the same language as their customers. There's a tendency for service professionals to employ technical or professional jargon even when talking to normal people, which is not only unimpressive, but also unhelpful.

A key opportunity to improve starts with caring and compassion, and then extends to a genuine, enthusiastic, and integrous desire to influence the behavior or mindset of the customer or patient. For a start, it might help if the recipients of services are thought of first and foremost as customers, and only secondarily as patients, cases, or sets of accounts.

Communication can also be especially challenging for service providers when the recipients of the service are stressed. In the healthcare setting, patients and their families are typically distressed, as are the recipients of legal service. Even if the legal service is for something happy, such as the purchase of a first home, the fact is this is a stressful life event.

Another communication obstacle worth emphasizing in this context has to do, again, with ivory towers. Within service provision environs, there are typically degrees of specialization related to real or perceived ranks among providers. For example, a surgeon is often perceived as "godlike" compared to others in the operating theatre. Problems arise when nurses or others in that situation don't feel empowered to confront what they see as a potential error. The same issue preceded the fatal crash of two Boeing 747s in Tenerife in 1977, which then served as the wakeup call for the airline industry to improve safety (Nance, 2008; wikipedia.org/wiki/Tenerife_airport_disaster).

A final aspect of communication worth mentioning is marketing and sales. Many service providers seem to feel that promoting their service is somehow beneath them, it's unprofessional. Again, a subtle but important mindset shift is required. It's about connecting with the people you want to, and can, help. And then it's about influencing them to use your service and follow your advice or prescriptions to maximize the benefits they derive. Salespeople are all servants, and the best ones really focus on serving, not just selling. Most professional service providers would do well to embrace the fact that they need to sell, not only their service, but the solutions they're trying to provide their customers with. For example, we would achieve greater compliance among patients if doctors could and did take the time to "sell" the patients on the need for the drugs or other treatments being prescribed.

Value experience and values

Ultimately, the service solutions being provided by any servant need to manifest as customers' experience of value. As discussed in Chapter 3, value will be experienced only if (and the extent to which) the customer understands and perceives benefits and the fulfillment of needs or wants. To an extent this is driven by service provider communication and also engagement. Value experience connects or bridges between communication and engagement. But a customer's experience of value also requires a foundation underpinned by service provider values. Integrity, honesty, authenticity, humaneness, caring, empathy, dedication, and a genuine drive to achieve service excellence are key among the values required.

Engagement

Communicating benefits and value is one thing, but inspiring optimal service outcomes is another. Telling someone with compassion and enthusiasm what they should do is a first step, but inspiring them to lose weight, reduce their spending, or take a more collaborative approach on a legal issue are very different. Inspiring requires a collaborative, partnering approach with the customer, based on real empathy.

Stakeholders

The first stakeholder in service provision is the servant, who has hopefully been recruited based on the right attributes and attitude toward serving, and who has also developed the required skills, knowledge, and expertise to deliver. The second key stakeholder is the recipient of service, whose experience determines whether the service is excellent or not. But a direct provider–recipient relationship rarely exists in a vacuum. There are typically other stakeholders and requirements that must be considered in any service scenario. The demands of multiple customers, partners, suppliers, shareholders, and other organizational functions are just a few considerations. For example, medical doctors are typically required to limit their time with individual patients to minutes, driven by time/money constraints, insurance companies or government policies. Yet, key medical insights often come from intuitively taking the time to question a patient about things they didn't come to see the doctor about.

Leadership

Leading service excellence requires "servant leadership." According to Greenleaf (1982):

> The servant-leader is servant first ... It begins with the natural feeling that one wants to serve, to serve first. Then conscious choice brings one to aspire to lead. That person is sharply different from one who is leader first, perhaps because of the need to assuage an unusual power drive or to acquire material possessions ... The leader-first and the servant-first are two extreme types. Between them there are shadings and blends that are part of the infinite variety of human nature.

Servant leadership is a mindset, but also specifically requires courageous personal accountability, the ability to responsibly empower others, and the underlying confidence and change agency that all leaders require.

The drive for improvement

Leadership drives change agency, which must also be underpinned by creativity in the service organization. Improvement doesn't often happen by accident, but instead requires change agency and an agenda – a desire and a plan for improvements, whether breakthrough, incremental, or both.

Creativity

Continuous improvement and breakthroughs in service excellence both require creative ideas for improvement. These can be stifled for precisely the same reasons that surgeons, lawyers or other masters of their trade are sometimes not confronted even when support staff feel they're seeing errors committed. This also extends downward to the service organization's culture.

Capability

Service provision is a capability, and in most cases requires a range of supporting capabilities that might include specialist aspects of the service. For example, an accountancy firm might provide tax advice, bookkeeping, and advice on financial strategy in addition to basic accounting. All these require specialist expertise, education, and experience. All service providers require some training and development, and enterprises that wish to achieve service excellence must invest in their people accordingly.

Culture

Service excellence is about the behavior, mindsets, motivations, and attitudes of people. This brings us full circle, in that culture connects to purpose. If the service organization thinks mainly in terms of provision and not receipt of service, there will be an imbalance in how the service is delivered and experienced by the customer.

Results

The bottom line is that service excellence is a psychological phenomenon, an experience and the resulting perception. Enterprises can only know if they achieve it based on monitoring customer experience and service evaluation. But the results of service excellence, or indeed poor service, go far beyond customer experience, affecting repeat business, customer advocacy, growth, profitability, valuations, and survival.

Service innovation agendas

In summary, service organizations are more likely to achieve service excellence if they focus on the strategic innovation agendas, as follows:

1. Ensure strategic intent includes achieving service excellence.
2. Build knowledge and intelligence on exactly how your service is experienced and can be improved from the customer's viewpoint.
3. Understand the core value proposition, values, and value model that define your service, and learn that marketing and selling the service are not dirty commercial activities beneath service providers, but a central aspect of influencing the customer to do what's right.
4. Identify and find the right balance among all stakeholder priorities, never losing sight of the fact that service excellence within the core provider–recipient relationship is the primary objective.
5. Relentlessly focus on service improvement, embracing every failure as an opportunity to learn. Always remember that customer experience

and loyalty are shaped more powerfully by what you do when an error is made than by simply avoiding errors in the first place.

6 Think out of the box in terms of defining the service provision capabilities that your customers of today and tomorrow will derive value from.

7 Ensure that there's no gap between what you aspire to and what people are actually doing. Aspire to become a culture of servant leadership and excellence, and ensure that this is manifested in the actions, performance, and results achieved.

chapter 20

Social Enterprise

"Charity begins at home, but should not end there."

Thomas Fuller (*c.* 1650)

The hope gap

It's great to see more social entrepreneurship, especially among youth, encouraged by organizations such as the International Youth Foundation (IYF: iyfnet.org). Queen Rania of Jordan, on the IYF board, coined the term "hope gap" to refer to the growing problem of youth unemployment and the fact that many young people in developing countries can't realistically hope for a better future.

The solution to the problem, however, isn't just social entrepreneurship but rather entrepreneurship in general. As my friend Bill Reese (2013) stated:

> Over the past few years, it has become clear that the private sector simply cannot create enough jobs to keep pace with the vast numbers of young people entering into the job market every year. That's why there is a growing chorus in support of teaching them the basics of building and growing their own start-ups. If you can't find a job, the saying goes, create your own.

Social entrepreneurship is but one form of job creation, and yet the activities of the IYF, supported by its patrons and board, are also a form of social entrepreneurship, to solve a global societal problem. We can only hope that more leaders from across all spectrums of industry, commerce, and life will be inspired to look for ways to make the world a better place, beyond simply enriching themselves and their shareholders.

Purposeful giving

Similarly, any social entrepreneur, whether an 18-year-old in a developing country or a 70-year-old in a developed one, should approach social entrepreneurship in exactly the same way that any entrepreneur should approach a startup (see Chapter 16). Don't start a social enterprise simply based on a sense of charity or seeing a particular problem or need that should be addressed. Instead, base it on what you're personally passionate about. What problem would you love to solve?

Unfortunately, when organizations decide to engage in corporate social responsibility (CSR), the focus is usually purely philanthropic or purely motivated by public relations (Fleming and Jones, 2013). In contract, effective corporate charity and CSR should be tied to core purpose, just as it must in the case of individual entrepreneurship.

Here is an example of CSR – social entrepreneurship supported by private enterprise. At one time, the focus of Oracle Corporation's giving was to provide PCs to needy schools. No doubt this was greatly appreciated, but when you stop to consider that Oracle is a software company that doesn't manufacture PCs, you might not be surprised to learn that it shifted its focus to providing value related to its mainstream competencies and values. When the Oracle Education Foundation, an independent, philanthropic organization funded by Oracle, provided the programs Think.com and later ThinkQuest (which Think.com was merged into), it was giving free access to online collaborative capabilities, which represented the stuff that Oracle's leadership is based on, to the global primary and secondary school community. This is a perfect example of giving the best of what you have to offer, rather than just giving for the sake of giving. When an organization gives of the heart of itself, rather than just splashing cash in an effort to gain publicity or goodwill, it is more truly and powerfully giving of itself.

Any organization that wants to give or engage in CSR should ensure that the specific purposes of the social enterprise are aligned with the overriding purpose of the organization. Stick to your knitting and figure out how to use your knitting to benefit mankind, nature, or some other worthwhile endeavors that relate to your core business.

Strategic intent

With the right intentions, giving and engaging in CSR should be good business. They should synergize with the core business model, and there's no reason why they shouldn't benefit the business. Why shouldn't Oracle want future generations of leaders to grow up thinking that Oracle is a good business to work for, invest in, buy from, or partner with?

Yet, according to Crane and Matten (2013), the move toward aligning CSR with core value creation might be motivated by fatigue:

> CSR fatigue is spreading far and wide. Not only has CSR been totally "incorporated" and has become a mainstream practice for most large businesses, it has also not prevented the scandals we had the opportunity of talking about. After all, most of the culprits in those incidents, including the major banks at the heart of the financial crisis, all have very much to tell us on their websites about the wonderful things they are doing in the CSR, sustainability or corporate citizenship area.

In fact, one wonders whether Oracle's decision to discontinue ThinkQuest may be a case of CSR fatigue, or whether and when it might revitalize its efforts and launch something new and exciting.

Visionary impact

A social enterprise needs a vision for how it will make the world a better place, which must be every bit as realistic and yet audacious as any enterprise vision. The problem many social entrepreneurs have is being overly grandiose in their thinking, and coming up with ideas that require far too much funding, or try to solve problems that are beyond their means to address – a prime example being "world hunger."

Intelligence

To avoid the trap of simply giving for the sake of giving, social enterprises need to do research to understand the problems they want to try to solve, and to take account of what other government or NGO initiatives they may compete with, and perhaps should partner with. For example, it's just as important for the success of CSR initiatives as for core business to understand the intended recipients of value provided through the CSR initiative – customers – as well as competitors, legal and regulatory considerations, and everything else that might affect success.

Communication

Social enterprises and charities might tend to think they don't need or shouldn't squander precious funds on marketing and sales. However, any enterprise that wishes to deliver value to anyone needs a way of making that value apparent to the intended recipient, and influencing them to engage. This communication process involves marketing and selling. Underinvestment or misguided, ineffectual investment of resources in this aspect of a social enterprise will have the same negative consequences as it does in business.

Value

Thus, a compelling core value proposition is vitally important, underpinned by values that will guide its delivery. One would like to think that CSR and all forms of charity are motivated by an authentic desire to solve problems and improve the world. But one would be naive to ignore the fact that many CSR initiatives are motivated only by the desire for positive publicity, often to counteract negative publicity that the supporting business attracts through its normal operations or business style.

Engagement

The collaborative engagement of partners is arguably nowhere more important than in social enterprises. Why replicate resources others have already invested in creating? Why duplicate what someone else is already doing? The challenge is to figure out the simplest, easiest, and most effective way to implement an operational value model that will engage all key stakeholders from customers through to everyone involved in producing and delivering value to the customers. However, business competitors are rarely if ever willing to pool CSR resources and efforts.

Of course, the broad engagement of partners, stakeholders, and all the resources involved defines the enterprise's value delivery model. Social enterprises need to be clear on their business model, and how to innovate it.

Stakeholders

For optimal value to be delivered by a social enterprise, the primary recipients of value must be considered first and foremost. Other stakeholder interests must be considered, but again, if shareholders are more interested in profits than CSR, or executive management is more concerned about publicity than real impact, one must question whether the commitment to CSR is sufficient to sustain the initiative long enough and strongly enough to be worthwhile.

Leadership

The leaders of social enterprises arguably require even greater abilities to motivate and in other ways empower resources than their counterparts in the private and public sectors. There's typically less money and more volunteerism and other forms of sacrifice required in delivering CSR or charity, on average, than in other arenas of enterprise.

Change

The landscape around the various global problems that social enterprises attempt to address is every bit as changeable as the marketplaces and technologies affecting businesses. Therefore, leaders of social enterprises must continually respond to change, as well as attempting to drive change in the problem space they're working in. But, as with private and public enterprises, change efforts in social enterprises also tend to fail, usually for the same reasons, a lack of effective strategies or leadership, lacking ideas, or ineffectual cultures (see Figure 7.3 for the full list).

Creativity

Ideas for improvement and breakthroughs in CSR and philanthropy are every bit as important as in any other enterprise, although special challenges might include difficulty connecting with customers who aren't articulate about their needs or wishes, or a relative poverty of ideas for charity from within a mainstream business that is primarily focused on profits.

Capability

Good intentions can't substitute for the skills or expertise required to effectively deliver what's needed from a social enterprise. However, the perennial problem in the realm of social enterprises is a lack of funds and therefore general inadequacy of resources and organizational capability. The prescription is to focus capabilities where they can have the greatest impact, delivering the greatest value, and to be realistic about what challenges can be addressed effectively. Is it better to prolong ten lives by a few months, or save one life?

Culture

Social enterprises require effective organizational psyche or spirit, connected to purpose. As with any enterprise, the ability to attract, retain, and develop the right people, in the right place and time, and doing the right things will determine success or failure.

Performance and results

The bottom line is that social enterprises are also accountable for what they do or don't achieve. Their performance and results should fulfill their purpose for existing, or they should pack it in.

Social innovation agendas

In summary, social enterprises will successfully achieve innovation by focusing on the strategic agendas, as follows:

1. Ensure that strategic intent combines spirited purpose with insightful goals for how to make the world a better place.
2. Develop knowledge and intelligence on exactly why the enterprise is needed and who can help make it happen.
3. Develop a clear business model for the provision of customer value, just as you would for any for-profit business.
4. Identify all key stakeholders, understand their needs, and manage their expectations. It is especially important to ensure that those providing funds clearly understand what ROI may look like, as this value is not likely to be financial in nature.
5. Embrace the fact that the social enterprise is all about achieving change, responding to change, and embracing change in the form of continual improvement and innovation.
6. Be creative in finding and engaging ideas for improvement, value delivery, cost control, risk mitigation, cash management, and all the other factors and functions important to any enterprise.
7. Ensure that everyone involved with the enterprise is fully committed, motivated, and engaged for the right reasons. Take care to understand what motivates and drives people, and don't simply assume that their drivers are the same as yours.

chapter 21

Public Enterprise

"Government, even in its best state, is but a necessary evil; in its worst state, an intolerable one."

Thomas Paine (1776)

Why governments must change

Today, we need governments that recognize the unacceptability of business as usual. We need leaders willing to make tough decisions. We can't survive by tweaking and trimming. We need true value model innovation on a national and global scale. We need new approaches to delivering essential services and a tough re-examination of which services are dinosaurs or sacred cows. Why do we need so much duplication? Why do we need so many levels of government, or levels of management within government? Why do we need so many people to "represent us" in an age where, with the click of a mouse, we can express our views? These are just a few of the tough questions we must now ask and answer.

My main thesis in the case of governmental or "pubic" sector enterprises is that we would benefit from considerably more, and more effective, entrepreneurship. The role of government leaders isn't just to encourage greater entrepreneurship and job creation within society, more innovation, national competitiveness, and wealth creation. It is also to embrace entrepreneurship and innovation within the institutions of government. This can be the subject of a whole book (see Link and Link, 2009), but my purpose here is simply to provide a quick prescription for it, based on the model for entrepreneurial psychology, and bridging the various agendas of innovation.

Purpose

I think many public servants, both elected and employed, have forgotten, or perhaps never understood, the purpose of government. It is not for them to have a job, to be adored, or to lead. Instead, it is for them to serve, as in being "public servants." I won't repeat the points here, but in case you (the reader) are a public servant who opened the book here, look at Chapter 19 and particularly the concept of "servant leadership."

Public servants tend to enjoy levels of income, perquisites, and privileges they find justifiable, but most of the rest of society does not. Why should public sector pensions be indexed to inflation when most pensions are not? Why should elected officials have expense accounts that aren't even scrutinized? Why should politicians decide on their own pay rises? The issue is, at least in part, that the purposes that draw some people to politics and public service are not those of social entrepreneurship or trying to make the world a better place, but rather ego and an easy route to a good life.

I would prefer to see more public servants express their entrepreneurial passions for how they want to improve the world or their part of it. I'm not saying none do, just that we'd all benefit if there were more of this spirited purpose in government. Whole countries and governments seem to suffer from a "can't do" mentality. But some leaders clearly see that major change is required. Their political challenge is to gain enough buy-in and support for their plans – to create hope.

The spirited purposes of people in public service are one thing. The missions of government institutions are quite another. The problem with some institutions is they are not clear on what they do in terms of providing value. They can tell you *what* they do, but not *why*. Some missions are absolutely clear and vital, such as defense, police, education, and healthcare. But sometimes it's good to reconsider even the most basic missions.

Strategic intent and choices

Given the need for governments to do more with less, public enterprises need to begin making more strategic choices among potential directions, informed by mission and vision. For example, should the focus of the Department of Health (or NHS) be on wellbeing or care? What's the right balance between spending to educate children to do more exercise and avoid obesity versus spending on amputations for people with type 2 diabetes, a disease brought on by lifestyle choices?

The need for vision

Many public enterprises lack visions for success. Their vision is simply to keep on doing what they've always done, collecting taxes, processing applications for welfare, or fighting crime. There are noteworthy examples, such as the recent transformation of New York City from a crime capital to a tourist- and people-friendly place, based on visionary leadership (Zimring, 2012). But we need far more visionary leaders within the public sector to drive the fundamental and growing problem – the need to do more with less – to deliver greater value with less consumption of public resources.

Intel

New York's transformation is a great example (see www.youtube.com/watch?v=xJD-NcLEoYM) of how intelligence should be applied toward problem resolution. Neighborhood crime statistics were used to focus police resources, get the right leaders on and the wrong ones off the job, and ultimately to conquer the problem. While governments have whole departments and agencies focused on intelligence, the core argument here is that all government functions require intelligence. Otherwise, what they do is purely tactical rather than strategic, and sometimes their operations and use of resources are just plain dumb.

Communications

Public enterprises also tend to suffer from the inability to understand the importance of marketing and sales. Most have websites and spend money on brochures, and some also actively engage in marketing, usually tied to specific purposes such as recruiting soldiers or getting people to meet tax deadlines. But many more public enterprises would benefit from improved communication with and influence of the public they engage with. Further, my experience suggests that many public servants would benefit from training on how to improve their communications, particularly with the customer. They could start by learning how to spell "customer."

Values and value

Beyond learning to spell customer, really understanding what customers need and value is the key. Another remarkable police force transformation illustrates how a shift in values and focus regarding value delivery can lead to important change. In the early 1980s, on a visit to LA, I spent an evening hanging out with senior police officers. While "hopping" between bars, in a black and white police cruiser, it became apparent through conversation that the two cowboys riding in the front were racist, and saw their primary role as protecting fellow officers, rather than the public. For me, the whole Rodney King incident (he was beaten by LAPD officers following a high speed car chase in 1991) was a natural consequence of the impoverished and dangerously misdirected sense of values. In subsequent years, the LAPD has managed to embrace a lot more diversity, and shift the mindset of officers toward protecting and serving the public, dramatically reducing violence and other undesirable outcomes of police action.

Engagement

Collaboration is a rare skill in the public sector. Most agencies seem to think they must reinvent anything and everything "not invented here," and directly control resources rather than sharing or utilizing the resources controlled by others. A glimmer of hope is the public sector call for more public–private partnerships, based on the realization that there are skills, perspectives, and capabilities "out there" that are easier to engage with than duplicate.

Stakeholders

Civil servants face a number of challenges in serving us. While they may try to see "the public" – all of us – as their primary stakeholder, the reality is that their political masters are more commonly the most influential stakeholder. Of course, political masters supposedly represent the public, but in reality, rarely represent the views of more than their direct supporters. Further, the fact that political incumbents change from time to time often causes waste when programs are cancelled or redirected, and significant and prolonged periods of uncertainty within parts of our governments.

Leadership

The public sector has arguably produced some of the best, most exemplary leaders of all time, and some of the worst. As stated above, many current leaders would benefit from embracing servant leadership and rethinking their motives for wanting to lead.

A much broader problem is the need for greater empowerment of public resources. Within the public sector, there are still far too many disempowered servants, unable or unwilling to make decisions, solve problems, or champion change. There is still too much bloat, too many layers of bureaucracy, and middle management "buck passers." Many parts of government need the leadership paradigm shift discussed in Chapter 12 – a revolutionary flip to upside-down leadership, followed by the evolutionary flattening that will occur in an empowered organization. Some areas of the public sector, such as Special Forces, already do this brilliantly. They should go in and clean up other parts of government.

Another problem of public sector leadership is the lack of focus. I recently addressed a group of UK local authority chief executives. After my talk, some "big five" consultants gave a presentation on "business model innovation." I was surprised to hear them misusing the term, actually referring to "business process improvements." The latter is about tweaks, whereas the former is about fundamental transformation. We also looked at some budgets. I was struck by the fact that every local authority had much the same structure, with their own HR, IT, and marketing departments. Can anyone spell "outsourcing," "collaboration" or "sharing"?

A common tendency when faced with the need to cut costs is to ask every function in an organization to shrink by the same amount, more or less. This is a recipe for disaster. Governments, just like businesses, need to figure out how to deliver more, better, quicker, and cheaper. The global business community went through that in the 1980s and 90s. Some companies tried the "cut 10% from every department" approach; and then another 10%, and another. Now they're out of business. Smart leaders and companies focus and invest to win. Rather than cutting 10%, they kill major initiatives and overresource the remaining ones – a tough call, requiring guts and true leadership.

Change

Nowhere is change more needed and yet more difficult than in government. Part of the problem is the political process, the fickle wishes of voters, and the need for politicians to work for our votes rather than implementing tough medicine that we won't like. But the problem extends to the bureaucracies of government as well, which although supposedly apolitical, are far from it. People working there are every bit as human as elsewhere, and therefore self-serving, empire building, wasteful, and tolerant of mediocrity. It's difficult to inspire change agency within bureaucracies and among leaders trying to coast to comfortable retirement. Why should they stick their necks out?

A further issue is that when governments want to change, they typically hire consultancies who are happy to consume vast quantities of public funds not solving the problems they are hired to solve. An insider in one of the major consultancies working to reengineer the massive information systems of the US Internal Revenue Service once told me in no uncertain terms that the reengineering program was making the problems worse, by design, and the whole system could be rebuilt from scratch for a fraction of the cost.

Creativity

Out-of-the-box ideas for improvement in public service are unlikely to come from within. Governments should look to the private sector, and benchmark against industry leaders rather than other governments to find new models. They should listen to their public, their customers for ideas for improvement. But, all too often, this "listening" is in the form of box-ticking surveys or mind-numbing focus groups, rather than truly democratizing innovation (von Hippel, 2005). Perhaps nowhere is democratic innovation more needed than in government, and arguably even the methods of democracy could do with some innovation. Why, with present technology, do we need to pay people to live in capitols, on fat salaries and expense accounts, to represent our opinions?

Capability

Nations need the capabilities to defend themselves from external and internal threats, enforce laws and regulations, collect taxes, provide education and health services, and so on. These capabilities rest on a combination of people with their skills, expertise, and abilities, and supporting technologies. As illustrated in Table 15.1, capabilities are key to providing value – in fulfillment of the reason for organizational existence. To face the crisis of government funding and expansion, we need a strategic focus on how to better leverage existing capabilities to provide value in existing and new ways, and to identify and develop innovative new capabilities that will be essential to address new opportunities and threats.

Culture

The root problem in many public enterprises is culture – a culture of comfortable complacency and business as usual. "There may be a problem but it's not me." People hanging on for retirement, not wishing to rock the boat, not willing to put their heads above the parapet.

In contrast, within some areas of public enterprise, we see examples of innovative leadership cultures that we can all be proud of, such as the Navy Seals and the SAS.

For the most part, what I see in the realm of pubic service is people who care but struggle to make a difference within the prevailing "system." Arguably, what we most need is stronger leadership, both from our elected leaders and non-elected senior public servants. Cultural change starts at the top, with the driven, entrepreneurial mindsets of leaders.

Performance and results

Comfortable complacency leads to mediocrity. The bottom line is that to achieve better public sector performance and results, we need entrepreneurial leaders focused on driving the seven innovation agendas.

Public innovation agendas

In summary, public enterprises would do well to focus more explicitly on innovation, employing the following strategic agendas:

1. Ensure strategic intent includes a vision for success, and that it connects with a purpose that is vital and meaningful in today's world.
2. Develop intelligence on exactly what value the enterprise is producing, for whom, what they think of it, and how it might improve. Consider alternatives, such as allowing the private sector to do the job, outsourcing, partnerships, or sharing resources.
3. Focus on improving your business model, just as you would for any for-profit business. Cut out unnecessary elements and costs. In looking to do more with less, consider the lessons learned in the private sector decades ago, such as:
   - middle managers slow things down and consume massive budgets without adding value
   - some resources can be shared across departments, such that every little town government does not need an HR department
   - if some part of the operation isn't directly contributing to the value model, you can probably chop it off without losing any value.
4. Focus on key stakeholders other than other public servants. Politicians are typically treated as the primary stakeholders by public servants. They aren't. They are also public servants, but only temporary ones. Instead, learn to spell "customer" – that's the person your part of government should be designed to serve.
5. Consider the fact that "change" should happen within your lifetime. If you won't embrace change, why should the next person?
6. Democratize public sector innovation. Find those "customers" and engage them in helping you define your improvement priorities. Use NPS and other techniques to focus on what matters.
7. Get rid of the dead wood, and then jump on the pile if you know you should. Change recruitment so that you stop seeking the sort of people who will get along with the sort of people you already employ. Bring in fresh perspectives, talent, and, above all, the driven mindset of true entrepreneurs.

Bibliography

3M (2014) Mission statement (accessed September 2014, 3m.com)

A. Adams (*c.* 1770) in J.P. Kaminski (2009) *The Quotable Abigail Adams* (Belknap Press)

K. Albrecht (2005) *Social Intelligence: The New Science of Success* (Pfeiffer)

H.I. Ansoff (1957) "Strategies for diversification", *Harvard Business Review,* 35(5): 113–24

M. Arndt (2006) "3M's seven pillars of innovation", *Innovation & Design, Bloomberg Businessweek* (accessed September 2014, www.businessweek.com/stories/2006-05-09/3ms-seven-pillars-of-innovation)

Arthur D. Little (2013) *Global Innovation Excellence Survey: Getting a Better Return on Your Innovation Investment* (Arthur D. Little)

W.G. Bennis (1989) *On Becoming a Leader* (Perseus)

J. Bolte Taylor (2008) A Powerful Stroke of Insight (accessed September 2014, Ted.com)

J.L. Bower and C.M. Christensen (1995) "Disruptive technologies: catching the wave", *Harvard Business Review,* 73(1): 43–53

Brainyquotes.com is the source of unattributed quotes in the text

P.B. Brown (2013) "Hate risk? You could be the perfect entrepreneur", *Forbes,* 1 September (accessed May 2014, www.forbes.com/sites/actiontrumpseverything/2013/09/01/hate-risk-you-could-be-the-perfect-entrepreneur)

T. Brown (2009) *Change by Design: How Design Thinking Transforms Organizations and Inspires Innovation* (HarperCollins)

R. Byrne (2006) *The Secret* (Atria Books)

M. Cain (2014) *Made to Fail: 13 Secrets of Successful Startups* (CreateSpace)

R. Cantillon (1755) *Essay on the Nature of Trade in General,* trans. Chantal Saucier, ed. Mark Thornton (accessed September 2014, mises.org)

A. Carnegie (*c.* 1900) quoted by Neal Whitten (1995) *Managing Software Development Projects: Formula for Success* (John Wiley & Sons)

M.C. Casson (1982) *The Entrepreneur: An Economic Theory* (Edward Elgar)

H.W. Chesbrough (2003) *Open Innovation: The New Imperative for Creating and Profiting from Technology* (Harvard Business School Press)

G.K. Chesterton (1905) *Heretics* (Books for Libraries Press)

C.M. Christensen and M.E. Raynor (2003) *The Innovator's Solution: Creating and Sustaining Successful Growth* (Harvard Business Review Press)

CIPD (2013) "PESTEL Analysis", *Factsheet* (accessed September 2014, www.cipd.co.uk/hr-resources/factsheets/pestle-analysis.aspx)

J. Collins (2001) *Good to Great: Why Some Companies Make the Leap … and Others Don't* (HarperBusiness)

Confucius (5th century BC) *The Teachings of Confucius,* trans. J.H. Ford, S. Conners and J. Legge (2005) (El Paso Norte Press)

D. Cooper (2014) Are you aiming high enough in your business? (accessed September 2014, www.donaldcooper.com/index.php?option=com_content&view=article&id=319:artaimhighenough&catid=31:how-to-manage-more-effectively&Itemid=62)

S. Covey (1989) *The Seven Habits of Highly Effective People* (Simon & Schuster)

S. Covey (2004) *The 8th Habit: From Effectiveness to Greatness* (Free Press)

Crane and Matten (2013) "The top 5 CSR trends for 2013", Crane and Matten blog (accessed September 2014, http://craneandmatten.blogspot.co.uk/2013/01/the-top-5-csr-trends-for-2013.html)

M. Csikszentmihalyi (1990) *Flow: The Psychology of Optimal Experience* (Harper & Row)

M. Csikszentmihalyi (1996) *Creativity: Flow and the Psychology of Discovery and Invention* (HarperCollins)

M. Csikszentmihalyi (2004) *Good Business: Leadership, Flow, and the Making of Meaning* (Penguin Books)

T. Davila, M.J. Epstein and R. Shelton (2006) *Making Innovation Work: How to Manage It, Measure It, and Profit from It* (Wharton School Publishing)

J. Diamond (1997) *Guns, Germs, and Steel: The Fates of Human Societies* (Norton & Company)

Doblin Group (2005, 2012) *Innovation Success Rates* (reported in BusinessWeek Special Report, *Get Creative,* August 2005 and M. Lindsay in FastCompany, April 2012)

P.F. Drucker (1939) *The End of Economic Man* (John Day Company)

P.F. Drucker (1967) *The Effective Executive* (Harper & Row)

P.F. Drucker (1985) *Innovation and Entrepreneurship: Practice and Principles* (Butterworth-Heinemann)

J. Dyer, H. Gregersen and C.M. Christensen (2011) *The Innovator's DNA: Mastering the Five Skills of Disruptive Innovators* (Harvard Business Review Press)

T.A. Edison (*c.* 1920) quoted in an ad for GPU Nuclear Corporation, *Black Enterprise* (1986) 16(11): 79

T.A. Edison (1921) quoted by J.L. Mason (1990) *An Enemy Called Average* (Insight International)

T.A. Edison (*c.* 1930) in D.D. Runes (ed.) (1968) *The Diary and Sundry Observations of Thomas Alva Edison* (Abbey Publishing)

A. Einstein (1931) *Cosmic Religion: With Other Opinions and Aphorisms* (Covici-Friede)

K. Evans (2009) *Learning, Work and Social Responsibility: Challenges for Lifelong Learning in a Global Age.* Lifelong Learning Book Series, vol. 13 (Springer)

P. Fleming and M.T. Jones (2013) *The End of Corporate Social Responsibility: Crisis and Critique* (Sage)

S. Flowers, E. von Hippel, J. de Jong and T. Siozic (2010) *Measuring User Innovation in the UK: The Importance of Product Creation by Users* (NESTA)

V. Frankl (2006) *Man's Search for Meaning: An Introduction to Logotherapy* (Beacon Press)

E. Fromm (1959) *The Sane Society* (Rinehart)

T. Fuller ([c. 1650] 2010) *Wise Words and Quaint Counsels of Thomas Fuller* (Kimball Press)

B.T. Gale (1994) *Managing Customer Value: Creating Quality and Service That Customers Can See* (Free Press)

C. Gallo (2010) *The Innovation Secrets of Steve Jobs* (McGraw-Hill)

H. Gardner (1983) *Frames of Mind: The Theory of Multiple Intelligences* (Basic Books)

B. Gates and C. Hemingway (1999) *Business @ the Speed of Thought: Succeeding in the Digital Economy* (Business Plus)

F. Gault (2012) "User innovation and the market", *Science and Public Policy,* 39(1): 118–28

L.V. Gerstner (2002) *Who Says Elephants Can't Dance?* (HarperCollins)

G. Gifford and E. Pinchot (1978) Intra-Corporate Entrepreneurship, unpublished manuscript referred to by Macrae, 1982

D. Gilmore (2010) "The Top 10 Supply Chain Innovations of All-Time", *Supply Chain Digest* (accessed September 2014, scdigest.com/assets/firstthoughts)

M. Gladwell (2010) "The sure thing: How entrepreneurs really succeed", *The New Yorker* (accessed September 2014, www.newyorker.com/magazine/2010/01/18/the-sure-thing)

Global Benchmarking Network (2008) *Centre for Organisational Excellence Research Report* (accessed September 2014, benchmarkingpartnerships.com.au)

D. Goleman (1996) *Emotional Intelligence: Why It Can Matter More Than IQ* (Bantam Books)

D. Goleman (2006) *Social Intelligence: The New Science of Social Relationships* (Bantam Books)

R.K. Greenleaf (1982) *Servant as Leader* (Robert K. Greenleaf Center)

V. Hannon, S. Gillinson and L. Shanks (2013) *Learning a Living: Radical Innovation in Education for Work* (Bloomsbury Academic)

U. Haque (2009) "The worst business model in the world (and what you can learn from it)", HBR Blog Network (http://blogs.hbr.org/2009/06/wonga/)

B.E. Hayes (2009) *Beyond the Ultimate Question: A Systematic Approach to Improve Customer Loyalty* (ASQ Quality Press)

S.A. Hewlett, M. Marshall and L. Sherbin (2013) "How diversity can drive innovation", *Harvard Business Review* (accessed September 2014, http://hbr.org/2013/12/how-diversity-can-drive-innovation/ar/1)

E. Hubbard ([1906] 1998) *Love, Life & Work: Being a Book of Opinions Reasonably Good-natured Concerning How to Attain the Highest Happiness for One's Self with the Least Possible Harm to Others* (Kessinger)

IBM (2006) *Expanding the Innovation Horizon: The Global CEO Study* (IBM Global Business Services)

ICMR (2005) *Xerox PARC: Innovation without Profit?* (IBIS Center for Management Research, accessed September 2014, www.icmrindia.org/casestudies/catalogue/Business%20Strategy2/BSTR150.htm)

Y. Ijuri and R.L. Kuhn (1988) *New Directions in Creative and Innovative Management: Bridging Theory and Practice* (Ballinger)

W. Isaacson (2011) *Steve Jobs* (Simon & Schuster)

ISO (2009) "ISO 31000 – Risk management" (accessed September 2014, www.iso.org/iso/home/standards/iso31000.htm)

W. James (1890) *Principles of Psychology* (Dover)

A. Jay (1967) *Management & Machiavelli: A Prescription for Success in Your Business* (Prentice Hall)

S. Jobs (2003) Steve Jobs: "I'm an optimist", *Bloomberg Businessweek* (accessed September 2014, www.businessweek.com/stories/2003-08-12/steve-jobs-im-an-optimist)

C.G. Jung (1933) *Modern Man in Search of a Soul* (Harvest/Harcourt)

C.G. Jung (1963) *Memories, Dreams, Reflections* (Pantheon Books)

R.W.Y. Kao, K.R. Kao and R.R. Kao (2002) *Entrepreneurism: A Philosophy and Sensible Alternative for the Market Economy* (Imperial College Press)

R.S. Kaplan and D.P. Norton (1992) "The balanced scorecard: measures that drive performance", *Harvard Business Review*, 70(1): 71–80

R.S. Kaplan and D.P. Norton (1996) *Balanced Scorecard: Translating Strategy into Action* (Harvard Business School Press)

T.L. Keiningham, L. Aksoy, B. Cooil and T. Wallin Andreassen (2008) "Linking customer loyalty to growth", *MIT Sloan Management Review*, 49(4): 51–7

L. Keeley, R. Pikkel, B. Quinn and H. Walters (2013) *Ten Types of Innovation: The Discipline of Building Breakthroughs* (Wiley)

T. Kelley and J. Littman (2001) *The Art of Innovation* (HarperCollins Business)

T. Kelley, with J. Littman (2008) *The Ten Faces of Innovation: Strategies for Heightened Creativity* (Profile Books)

W.C. Kim and R. Mauborgne (2005) *Blue Ocean Strategy: How to Create Uncontested Market Space and Make the Competition Irrelevant* (Harvard Business Review Press)

F.H. Knight (1921) *Risk, Uncertainty, and Profit* (Hart, Schaffner & Marx)

J.P. Kotter (1996) *Leading Change* (Harvard Business Review Press)

J.P. Kotter (2008) *A Sense of Urgency* (Harvard Business Review Press)

J. Krakauer (1966) *Into the Wild* (Random House)

C. Leadbeater and R. Staropoli (2012) *Innovation in Education: Lessons from Pioneers Around the World* (Bloomsbury)

F. Leahy (1954) quoted in the *Charleston Daily Mail* on 4 May

F. Lee (2004) *If Disney Ran Your Hospital: 9½ Things You Would Do Differently* (Second River Healthcare)

R. Levine, C. Locke, D. Searls and D. Weinberger (1999) *The Cluetrain Manifesto: The End of Business as Usual* (Perseus)

P. Lencioni (2009) *The Five Dysfunctions of a Team* (Jossey-Bass)

A.N. Link and J.R. Link (2009) *Government as Entrepreneur* (Oxford University Press)

R. Lochridge (1981) "Strategy in the 1980s", Boston Consulting Group Perspectives (accessed September 2014, www.bcgperspectives.com/content/Classics/strategy_strategy_in_the_1980s)

N. McCrae (1982) "Intrapreneurial now: big goes bust", *The Economist*, 283: 47–52

L.G. McDonald and P. Robinson (2009) *A Colossal Failure of Common Sense: The Inside Story of the Collapse of Lehman Brothers* (Crown Business)

M. McKeown (2008) *The Truth about Innovation: A Small Book about Big Ideas* (Pearson)

J. Mackey (2009) *Passion and Purpose: The Power of Conscious Capitalism* (Sounds True)

A.H. Maslow (1943) "A theory of human motivation", *Psychological Review*, 50(4): 370–96.

A.H. Maslow (1954) *Motivation and Personality* (Harper)

A.H. Maslow (1964) *Religions, Values, and Peak Experiences* (Ohio State University Press)

A.H. Maslow (1970) *Motivation and Personality* (Harper & Row)

Michelangelo (*c.* 1530) in Ken Robinson (2009) *The Element: How Finding Your Passion Changes Everything* (Viking Adult)

A. Murphy (1986) *Richard Cantillon: Entrepreneur and Economist* (Clarendon Press)

J. Nance (2008) *Why Hospitals Should Fly: The Ultimate Flight Plan to Patient Safety and Quality Care* (Second River Healthcare Press)

F. Nietzsche (*c.* 1880) cited by ThinkExist.com (accessed September 2014)

OECD (2005) *Proposed Guidelines for Collecting and Interpreting Technological Innovation Data – Oslo Manual*, 3rd edn (OECD/European Commission/Eurostat)

OECD (2014) *OECD Innovation Strategy: Defining Innovation* (accessed May 2014, oecd.org/site/innovationstrategy/defininginnovation.htm)

S. Ogawa and F.T. Piller (2006) "Reducing the risks of new product development", *MIT Sloan Management Review*, 47(2): 65–71

M. Olsen Laney (2002) *The Introvert Advantage: How to Thrive in an Extrovert World* (Workman)

L. Olson (2013) "The top 10 lies people put on their résumés: A recent study finds that more than half of all résumés contain falsehoods", US News, 3 October (accessed September 2014, http://money.usnews.com/money/blogs/outside-voices-careers/2013/10/03/the-top-10-lies-people-put-on-their-resumes)

T. Paine ([1776] 2005) *Common Sense* (Penguin)

K.J. Patel (2005) *The Master Strategist: Power, Purpose and Principle* (Hutchinson)

J. Phillips (2012) "There's no innovation without experimentation", Innovate on Purpose, OVO Innovation's blog site, 4 September (accessed September 2014, http://innovateonpurpose.blogspot.co.uk/2012/09/theres-no-innovation-without.html)

P.R. Picasso (*c.* 1920) in H. Clark (1993) *Picasso: In His Words* (Collins)

M. Porter (1980) *Competitive Strategy: Techniques for Analyzing Industries and Competitors* (Free Press)

C.K. Prahalad and M.S. Krishnan (2008) *The New Age of Innovation: Driving Co-created Value Through Global Networks* (McGraw-Hill)

B. Pritchard (2011) *Kick-ass Business and Marketing Secrets: How to Blitz Your Competition* (John Wiley & Sons)

J. Pritchard (2012) *Bill Gates: A Biography* (Hyperlink)

B. Reese (2013) "Entrepreneurship for all: a new approach to youth development", *Huffington Post*, 30 September (accessed September 2014, www.huffingtonpost.com/bill-reese/entrepreneurship-for-all-_b_4017016.html)

F. Reichheld (2006) *The Ultimate Question: Driving Good Profits and True Growth* (Harvard Business Review Press)

P. Riley (1993) *The Winner Within* (Penguin-Putnam)

E.B. Roberts (1987) "What we've learned: managing invention and innovation", *Research-Technology Management*, 31(1): 11–29

E.B. Roberts (1991) *Entrepreneurs in High Technology: Lessons from MIT and Beyond* (Oxford University Press)

E.B. Roberts (2002) *Innovation: Driving Product, Process and Market Change* (Jossey-Bass)

W. Roberts (1987) *Leadership Secrets of Attila the Hun* (Peregrine)

J. Rosenthal (2009) "A terrible thing to waste", *The New York Times*, 31 July (accessed September 2014, www.nytimes.com/2009/08/02/magazine/02FOB-onlanguage-t.html?_r=0)

R. Rumelt (2011) *Good Strategy Bad Strategy: The Difference and Why It Matters* (Crown Business)

B. Russell ([*c.* 1915] 1985) *The Philosophy of Logical Atomism*, ed. D. Pears (Open Court)

J. Sale (2014) "Why motivation is NOT often in the work place" (accessed September 2014, www.motivationalmaps.com/Resources/Blog%20125%20Why%20motivation%20is%20NOT%20in%20the%20work%20place%200811.pdf)

E. St. Vincent Millay (*c.* 1940) quoted by K. Miles (2013) *Remarks to the 2007 Spring Convocation, Vassar College* (accessed May 2014, http://campusactivities.vassar.edu/news/announcements/2012-2013/130501-convocation-remarks-miles.html)

J.B. Say (1802) *A Treatise on Political Economy* (McMaster University Archive for the History of Economic Thought)

A.M. Schneiderman (2006) "The balanced scorecard" (accessed September 2014, schneiderman.com)

A. Schopenhauer ([1851] 2007) *Parerga and Paralipomena*, trans. E.F. Payne (Cosimo)

J. Schumpeter (1934) *The Theory of Economic Development* (Harvard University Press)

P.M. Senge (1990) *The Fifth Discipline: The Art and Practice of the Learning Organization* (Doubleday Business)

G.B. Shaw (1912) quoted by M. Caroselli (2000) *Leadership Skills for Managers* (McGraw-Hill)

R.E. Staub (1996) *The Heart of Leadership* (Executive Excellence)

R.E. Staub (2002) *The 7 Acts of Courage: Bold Leadership for a Wholehearted Life* (Book Baby)

R.L. Stevenson ([*c.* 1880] 1927) *Collected Works of Robert Louis Stevenson* (Walter J. Black)
M. Stone, B. Foss and A. Bond (2004) *Consumer Insight: How to Use Data and Market Research to Get Closer to Your Customer* (Kogan Page)
M. Strong (2009) *Be the Solution: How Entrepreneurs and Conscious Capitalists Can Solve All the World's Problems* (John Wiley & Sons)
Sun Tzu ([6th century BC] 1963) *The Art of War*, trans. S.B. Griffith (Oxford University Press)
D. Tapscott (2013) "The spirit of collaboration is touching all of our lives", *The Globe and Mail*, 7 June (accessed May 2014, www.theglobeandmail.com/globe-debate/the-spirit-of-collaboration-is-touching-all-of-our-lives/article12409331)
THECIS (The Centre for Innovation Studies) (2005) Definition (accessed September 2014, thecis.ca/index.php?catID=32&itemID=43)
B. Trilling and C. Fadel (2009) *21st Century Skills: Learning for Life in Our Times* (Jossey-Bass)
TRIZ Journal (2014) *Famous Innovation Quotations* (accessed September 2014, www.triz-journal.com/content/c090119a.asp)
J. Tyson (2014) *Adventures in Innovation: Inside the Rise and Fall of Nortel* (Library and Archives Canada)
V. Vaitheeswaran (2007) "Something new under the sun", *the Economist Special report: Innovation* (accessed September 2014, economist.com/node/9928154)
S.C. Voelpel, M. Leibold and R.A. Eckhoff (2006) "The tyranny of the balanced scorecard in the innovation economy", *Journal of Intellectual Capital*, 7(1): 43–60
Voltaire ([1764] 1984) *Philosophical Dictionary*, trans. T. Besterman (Penguin Classics)
E. von Hippel (1988) *The Sources of Innovation* (Oxford University Press)
E. von Hippel (2005) *Democratizing Innovation* (MIT Press)
E. von Hippel, J. de Jong and S. Flowers (2010) "Comparing business and household sector innovation in consumer products: Findings from a representative study in the UK", *MIT Sloan School of Management Working Paper* (accessed September 2014, ssrn.com/abstract = 1683503)
R. von Oech (1983) *A Whack on the Side of the Head: How You Can Be More Creative* (Warner Books)
E.T. Wagner (2013) "Five reasons 8 out of 10 businesses fail", *Forbes* (accessed September 2014, forbes.com)
M.A. Wahba and L.G. Bridwell (1976) "Maslow reconsidered: a review of research on the need hierarchy theory", *Organizational Behavior and Human Performance*, 15(2): 212–40.
M. Waschke (2011) "Innovation and collaboration: don't let your idea die of loneliness", 12 September, *CA Technologies Blog* (accessed September 2014, http://blogs.ca.com/2011/09/12/innovation-and-collaboration-don-t-let-your-idea-die-of-loneliness/)
M. Weber ([1922] 1978) *Economy and Society: An Outline of Interpretive Sociology* (U. California Press)
J. Welch, with S. Welch (2005) *Winning* (HarperCollins)
M. Wheatley (1992) *Leadership and the New Science: Discovering Order in a Chaotic World* (Berrett-Koehler)
O. Wilde (1892) *Lady Windermere's Fan, A Play About a Good Woman*
O. Wilde (1895) *An Ideal Husband*
S. Wojcicki (2011) "The eight pillars of innovation", *Think Quarterly: The Innovation Issue* (think with Google, accessed September 2014, www.thinkwithgoogle.com/articles/8-pillars-of-innovation.html)
F.E. Zimring (2012) *The City That Became Safe: New York's Lessons for Urban Crime and Its Control*, Studies in Crime and Public Policy (Oxford University Press)

Index

Printed and bound by CPI Group (UK) Ltd, Croydon, CR0 4YY